BLACK SPACE

RENEWALS 458-4574

DATE DUE

GAYLORD			PRINTED IN U.S.A.

BLACK SPACE

Imagining Race in Science Fiction Film

ADILIFU NAMA

UNIVERSITY OF TEXAS PRESS, AUSTIN

Requests for permission to reproduce material from this work
should be sent to:
    Permissions
    University of Texas Press
    P.O. Box 7819
    Austin, TX 78713-7819
    www.utexas.edu/utpress/about/bpermission.html

⊗ The paper used in this book meets the minimum requirements
of ANSI/NISO Z39.48-1992 (R1997) (Permanence of Paper).

Library of Congress Cataloging-in-Publication Data
Nama, Adilifu, 1969–
Black space : imagining race in science fiction film / Adilifu Nama. — 1st ed.
p. cm.
Includes bibliographical references and index.
ISBN 978-0-292-71697-1 (cloth : alk. paper) —
ISBN 978-0-292-71745-9 (pbk. : alk. paper)
1. Science fiction films—History and criticism. 2. Blacks in motion pictures.
3. African Americans in motion pictures. I. Title.
PN1995.9.S26N36 2008
791.43'615—dc22   2007033323

FOR NIA, NIZAM, AND TAMU

CONTENTS

ACKNOWLEDGMENTS

Although this project is my brainchild, the completion of it has come about only because of the talents, insights, patience, and support of colleagues, friends, and family. I must thank Sohail Daulatzai, who reviewed early drafts of the manuscript and shared critical advice concerning the direction and approach of the project. His suggestions proved invaluable, and I have truly benefited from his intellectual sincerity, keen ability for political analysis, and willingness to be a sounding board for my impromptu brainstorming sessions. He is a great academic colleague but an even better friend. I also want to thank Christine Acham for her generosity. She is an unselfish scholar who gave of her time, expertise, and experience whenever I needed advice about navigating the world of academic publishing. Freelance copy editor Rosemary Wetherold and the professional and insightful editorial staff of the University of Texas Press were extremely helpful in improving and clarifying the expression of my ideas in this project.

I would like to express eternal gratitude to Cynthia Usher, my mother-in-law, for caring for my children, which allowed me to finish this book. In addition, I must recognize the generosity of Pauline Goodin, who also helped take up the slack when my professional commitments created scheduling conflicts.

A special note of thanks goes out to Bill Germano and Megan Giller, who were way ahead of the curve in recognizing what I was doing. I am also grateful to Anthony Turner, Yusef Doulatzai, Tiffany B., Wesam, and Maurice (Mo) for their enthusiasm and encouragement.

To my mom, Marquetta Rodgers, and dad, Art Nixon, thank you for letting me be me. Most importantly, to my wife, Tamu, thank you. You kept the faith, repeatedly brought sunshine to my cloudy interludes, and made time disappear.

BLACK SPACE

INTRODUCTION

"There is nothing wrong with your television set. Do not attempt to adjust the picture. We are controlling transmission . . ." The first time I remember hearing this eerie command was as a child, sitting home one weekday afternoon while nursing a sore throat and a light case of the sniffles. Usually, when I was too sick to go to school for more than one day, I always looked forward to thumbing through a variety of comic books my mother would buy me to quell my complaints of being bored while she was gone. As a rule, I would read and reread them in bed. But this time I schlepped my blanket and pillow out to the living room to look at television and settled down to view an afternoon barrage of corny game shows and melodramatic soap operas. To my joyful surprise, I stumbled upon *The Outer Limits*, a science fiction series in which each show began with a disembodied voice commanding viewers to stay still and keep watching the TV screen. Admittedly, reruns of the black-and-white series, with its tacky special effects and overdone monster makeup, seldom lived up to the compelling introduction. Nonetheless, for me the series did serve as a significant bridge from a leisurely enjoyment of superhero comic books to a keen interest in science fiction television and films.

I moved on from reruns of The *Outer Limits* to the short-lived series *Space: 1999* and eventually found my sci-fi glee in reruns of the original *Star Trek* television series of the late 1960s. My immediate interest in the show, however, was driven not exclusively by my preference for all things science fiction but also by a fondness for Lieutenant Uhura (Nichelle Nichols), the African American female communication specialist of the *Star Trek* crew and my first television crush. Her presence on the bridge of the *Enterprise* made the absence of black people in other science fiction television shows and films all the more conspicuous. I wanted to see more black people, not only on *Star Trek* (if I'd had my wish, Uhura would have had her own science fiction show) but across the genre. To the contrary, I found that in the vast majority of science fiction television shows and films, black people were, until quite recently, absent or extremely marginal to the narratives. This observation followed me well into adulthood and, to a great extent, came to define how black representation in American science fiction cinema is commonly perceived despite a growing presence of black representation in the genre. For example, when friends or family members would ask what I was working on and I would tell them I was writing a book examining the intersection of black representation and science fiction (SF) cinema, the most common response was that it was going to be a short book. They would promptly inform me that black folk are not present in the genre or are certain to die prematurely in the second act. Admittedly, in a multitude of SF films, black people are just plain absent, which understandably leaves the impression there is very little to write about when it comes to black representation in the genre.

Yet, in spite of the overt omission of black representation and racial issues in SF cinema, I have found that both are present in numerous SF films. Albeit implicit—as structured absence, repressed or symbolic—blackness and race are often present in SF films as narrative subtext or implicit allegorical subject. Most important, for this book, is the cultural politics of race that such representations suggest not only in SF cinema but alongside the sociohistorical place that blackness has occupied in American society. As a result, the SF film genre is not merely an imaginative medium primarily focused on the future. SF film is also a powerful lens by which to observe the collective racial desires, constructs, fantasies, and fears circulating throughout American society.

APPROACH

The fantastical plots, far-off worlds, special effects, and striking portrayals of the future in SF cinema have achieved a great deal of box office success and popularity as a film genre, as well as receiving extensive critical analysis. In addition, SF cinema is recognized and, for some enthusiasts, even revered as the most imaginative genre because within its confines there are no confines. Arguably, SF films have a creative mandate to present any kind of character or imagine any type of social system within their narratives. In spite of this creative latitude, SF films have repeatedly engaged contemporary social issues. By doing so, however, the genre offers the audience the opportunity to vicariously experience a world without many of the challenges a society presently faces and, in doing so, to contemplate ramifications of and potential responses to an urgent social problem and present a hypothesized outcome or solution. In fact, numerous SF films have, quite convincingly, engaged America's cultural urges, political yearnings, and ideological dispositions around communism and postwar anxiety, along with gender and class issues.[1] Despite the numerous scholarly articles and critical cultural essays that squarely recognize that the genre is an ideological kaleidoscope, producing hegemonic and counterhegemonic social parables, ethical paradoxes, and trenchant allegories, there have been only a minute number of attempts at placing race at the center of SF film analysis.

For the most part, race as a salient topic of examination in SF film has either been discussed piecemeal within a larger edited body of work like *Aliens R Us: The Other in Science Fiction Cinema* (2002) or placed in a single chapter of a book, as in *Science Fiction: The New Critical Idiom* (2000). Certainly, seminal works such as Sierra S. Adare's *"Indian" Stereotypes in TV Science Fiction: First Nations Voices Speak Out* (2005), Daniel Bernardi's *Star Trek and History: Race-ing toward a White Future* (1998), and Michael Pounds's *Race in Space: The Representation of Ethnicity in "Star Trek" and "Star Trek: The Next Generation"* (1999) stand out as more comprehensive examinations of the intersection of race and SF representation. Yet these works explore race almost exclusively within the realm of television and are heavily focused on the *Star Trek* television franchise. Other than Charles Ramirez Berg's *Latino Images in Film: Stereotypes, Subversions, and Resistance* (2002), which contains an insightful chapter that examines how aliens in American SF films symbolize real Latin American immigrants and a host of immigration anxieties, and Eric Greene's *"Planet of the Apes" as American Myth: Race, Politics, and Popular Culture* (1996), the scope and depth of analysis of race in SF cinema have remained severely limited. Ed Guerrero's *Framing Blackness: The African American Image in Film* (1993), however, comes closest to fleshing out the cultural meaning and broader racial implications of race in SF cinema. Guerrero incisively notes:

[T]he social construction and representation of race, otherness, and non-whiteness is an ongoing process, working itself out in many symbolic, cinematic forms of expression, but particularly in the abundant racialized metaphors and allegories of the fantasy, sci-fi, and horror genres. This practice can be explained by several mutually reinforcing factors including these genres' dependence on *difference* or *otherness* in the form of the monster in order to drive or energize their narratives; the now vast technological possibilities of imagining and rendering of all

kinds of simulacra for aliens, monsters, mutant outcasts, and the like;
and the infinite, fantastic narrative horizons and story worlds possible
in these productions. (56, 57)

Because Guerrero's work spans several film genres and decades of film history, his analysis of sf film and race, through the prism of black representation, is unavoidably cursory. As a result, the full depth and range of the
cultural politics of black racial formation at work in sf film, as a genre, have
remained fundamentally untouched. Although, on a whole, the scholarship
on sf film and race is scant, bordering on obscure, the work in the field
is nevertheless, at the least, methodologically significant. The cumulative
impact of the work analyzing race and sf television and, to a lesser extent,
sf film has demonstrated that the most fruitful examination of racial representation in sf cinema is not simple content analysis, image analysis, or
highly interpretive reasoning.[2] Rather, the examination of sf film and black
racial representation is best served by sociohistorical grounding and contextualization. Consequently, I have taken my methodological cues from these
previous works, and they have informed the approach of this book.

I have purposefully avoided making connections between the sf film and
black racial representation in terms of black stereotypes as either "negative"
or "positive," which I view as too reductive in the type of conclusions offered
and shortsighted in the ideological implications one can assert. The present
work examines the symbolic discourse and ideological messages encoded
into black representation, including its structured absence, across a multitude of sf films as a symbolic dialogue with the multiple racial discourses
and ideas surrounding black racial formation, past and present, that are circulating in American culture. Moreover, sf films of the 1950s to the current
moment are discussed in this book with an eye toward drawing connections
between sf cinema, black racial formation, and shifting race relations in
America over the past fifty years. Too often the sf film genre is regarded as
addressing only signature divisions in the genre: humans versus machines,
old versus new, individual versus society, and nature versus the artificial.
In this book, however, I place black racial formation at the center of these
common dichotomies. As a result, a more complex and provocative picture
emerges of how sf cinema, in imagining new worlds and addressing a broad
range of social topics, has confronted and retreated from the color line,
one of the most troubling and turbulent social issues present in American
society.

In advancing past the dull critiques of black representation as either
"negative" or "positive" as well as stereotypical racial imagery, I have con-

centrated my analysis on the broader symbolic function and ideological message that black representation in sf cinema is presenting. Certainly, reflective theory, semiotics, structuralism, Marxism, and psychoanalytic critiques have each shared a substantial role in interrogating sf cinema and revealing what the genre articulates about women, sexuality, sexual difference, class, and social hierarchy. Likewise, interrogating blackness in sf cinema also requires a theoretical scaffolding to support an analysis of how certain sf films imagine blackness and what black characters signify and symbolize, along with the ideas, beliefs, fantasies, and fears communicated about race. On one hand, a strictly post-structuralist approach would stress the open-endedness of meaning as virtually negating the reflective approach I privilege. On the other hand, a purely reflective approach suffers from too literal and strict a correspondence between the Real, the Symbolic, and the Imaginary. Although there are connections between the three, serious slippages of meaning are also in play. In my textual analysis, however, I have attempted to walk the fine theoretical line between post-structural analysis and a reflective approach. As a result, this book incorporates the post-structural contention that, regardless of authorial intent, meaning is not fixed, and therefore unstated regimes of racial discourse circulate in sf cinema, waiting to be discovered. Yet my textual analysis rests on the firm contention that no form of cultural production stands outside the culture, the ideas, the values, the beliefs, the desires, and the fears that generate that production in the first instance. Although this book is theoretically eclectic, it is quite straightforward in one way. No matter where the film is set—in a futuristic or otherworldly backdrop—the "cultural work" that the film is performing is not divorced from the real state of American race relations.

Finally, where others have chosen to privilege the social relations of class or gender in their textual reading of sf cinema, I have purposefully privileged black racial formation. In doing so, black representation and the cultural politics of blackness in sf cinema take center stage in this book. Undoubtedly, race relations have changed. Latino and Asian immigration have spearheaded racial demographic shifts that make discussions of race relations in exclusively black-and-white terms appear obsolete in what has come to be referred to as the post–civil rights era. I recognize the contours of these changes and the type of popular discussions of race relations they engender. Nevertheless, as contentious and theoretically dense as this discourse has become, black racial formation still remains a central point of historical fact and contemporary consequences in America's ongoing racial debate.

Although the focus of my work examines the way black representation and black racial formation are operating in discrete SF films, it does not mean to diminish, nor should it be interpreted as diminishing, the place and substance of other racial and ethnic group representation, literal or symbolic, in relationship to SF film. Moreover, the examination and status of blackness in SF film are not a conceptual catchall for all other minority groups. Instead, by examining black representation and the cultural framing of "blackness" in SF film, I clearly adopt the category of race, as a social construction and, by extension, the social history attached to the category that is part and parcel of American race relations and the cultural politics of race in U.S. society. In other words, my critical reading of SF cinema examines the way black representation and black racial formation are imagined in discrete SF films. But the sum of these critical readings is greater than its parts, and the whole underscores the cultural work and sociological significance of race, not merely blackness, in SF cinema and American society. Consequently, black racial representation is the focal point of the SF films I examine, but not the end point, and my discussion includes positioning various SF films in relationship to concurrent social trends and racial discourses circulating in American society that are also germane to other ethnic and racial minority groups.

LAYOUT

From the iconic black-and-white image of a bulletlike rocket ship lodged in the eye of the moon in Georges Méliès's *A Voyage to the Moon* (1902), the lure of startling special effects has captivated audiences across decades. Below the surface special effects, however, the substantive thrust of SF cinema often projects pressing social, environmental, and moral issues into the future or sets them in alternative worlds. For me and many others this is the most significant aspect of SF film. More than the imaginative manner in which alternative worlds are presented and the eye-catching use of special effects, the best the genre has offered is found in the temporal displacement of contemporary social issues into the far future or distant past. For example, *Silent Running* (1972) and *Soylent Green* (1973) exemplify the SF film as cautionary tales that speak to the impact of environmental degradation and overpopulation. Yet, for as much as SF film is an imaginative site that, at its best, invites the audience to engage familiar yet troubling ideas and social practices in an unfamiliar setting, thereby creating the possibility of examining long-standing problems in a new light, a contravening impulse has been the predominant trend when race is a point of futuristic speculation. Indeed, this is the focus of chapter 1, "Structured Absence and Token

Presence." The chapter lays out the way in which race is represented and visually coded in SF cinema, primarily through the structured absence of blackness in the genre. Films such as *When Worlds Collide* (1951), *The Time Machine* (1960), *Robinson Crusoe on Mars* (1964), and *Logan's Run* (1976) are discussed in relationship to changing attitudes about racial segregation. Later in the chapter, *Star Wars* (1977) is brought into the discussion to map out how blackness moves from structured absence to black tokenism. *The Empire Strikes Back* (1980) and *Back to the Future* (1985) are interrogated to answer the question, What political and cultural work is black tokenism in the SF cinema performing?

Chapter 2, "Bad Blood: Fear of Racial Contamination," examines the theme of racial contamination in SF cinema and, by extension, America's fixation with racial boundary maintenance. The chapter draws on the dubious racial classificatory system colloquially referred to as the "one-drop rule" and the network of racial taboos associated with it—interracial sex, racial eugenics, black blood contamination, racial assimilation, and racial paranoia—that are present in several SF films. Moreover, whether by coded implication or overt symbolism, the association of the implosion of racial boundaries with dystopian and apocalyptic visions of the future in several SF films is discussed. To this point, films such as *The World, the Flesh, and the Devil* (1959), *The Omega Man* (1971), *Blade Runner* (1982), *The Thing* (1982), *Gattaca* (1997), and *28 Days Later* (2003) are films that tap into the symbolic fear of racial assimilation into the American body politic.

Whether marked with some type of physical deformation in *Total Recall* (1990), physical stigma in *Star Trek: Generations* (1994), or sadistic victimization in *Predator* (1987) or *Demolition Man* (1993), the black body is often a site of representational trauma, the ultimate signifier of difference, alienness, and "otherness" in SF cinema. Chapter 3, "The Black Body: Figures of Distortion," examines how the black body is often depicted in SF film not merely in ways that connect it with a sense of the grotesque or a source and site of phantasmagoric spectacle but also as a cultural and political metaphor for racial difference. The graphic distortion and stigmatization of blackness in SF films such as *Enemy Mine* (1985), *The Fifth Element* (1997), and *Mission to Mars* (2000) are examined in relationship to notions of racial difference, sexual deviance, and social stigma.

Whether it is working-class unity in *They Live* (1988), military unity in *Aliens* (1986), or religious unity cultivated in *Alien³* (1992), all of these films, for the most part, use an alien enemy to make racial strife obsolete. The film *Independence Day* (1996) is emblematic of this approach to smoothing over racial fissures in SF cinema, while *Rollerball* (1975), *RoboCop* (1987), and *Predator 2* (1990) merge with the dominant American sensibility that economic oppression, not racial oppression between blacks and whites, lies at the core of current social division and those anticipated in the future. The fourth chapter, "Humans Unite!: Race, Class, and Postindustrial Aliens," details how race has taken a backseat to the recurring theme of the corporation as the ultimate hegemony in SF film and the otherworldly alien as the ultimate enemy. In this chapter, the depictions of class fault lines in SF film are deconstructed with a critical acknowledgment of the racial dynamics operating in a postindustrial American economy.

Because SF cinema reflects the values of a society and often presents cautionary tales and social parables, many of its narratives are fertile sites of ideological meaning as they relate to popular discourses surrounding race. Chapter 5, "White Narratives, Black Allegories," examines the allegorical import of SF film not only in breaching and buttressing the ideological constructs of America's racial hierarchy but also as sources of subversive pleasure, meaning, and play that often contest the "preferred" meaning of several SF films. While the film *Escape from New York* (1981) plays to the most strident anxieties of race and class fueled by postindustrial decline, *Planet of the Apes* (1968), *Alien Nation* (1988), *Strange Days* (1995), *The Matrix* series (1999, 2003), and *Minority Report* (2002) are SF films that in various ways are open to racial readings that engage the legacy of American slavery, the racial injustice of the American legal system, black crime, police brutality, black liberation, and "race" riots, as well as racial profiling. These points are fleshed out in this chapter and illustrate how SF cinema is an inherently political genre that produces hegemonic and, periodically, counterhegemonic discourses on race that are outside the intended meaning of each respective film.

Chapter 6, "Subverting the Genre: The Mothership Connection," shifts focus from Hollywood representations of science fiction blackness to those independent and extrafilmic productions that stand not only outside the mainstream apparatus of cinematic production but in some cases outside the cultural conventions of mainstream notions of blackness. This chapter includes an examination of several SF films that were consciously produced and committed to directly confronting racism and exploring the interior dynamics of the black community. In many ways, the chapter examines the avant-garde impulse and import of combining a science fiction aesthetic with blackness, a contemporary trend called Afrofuturism. In this chapter Afrofuturism, an intergalactic vision of blackness, is explored in the independently made film *Space Is the Place* (1974), the SF liner notes of albums by George Clinton's music group Funkadelic, and a burgeoning Afrofuturist aesthetic in hip-hop music videos and SF film. All of these independent expressions of science fiction blackness become increasingly important as alternative sites of resistant black culture, which, given the cost-prohibitive nature of Hollywood studio–backed filmmaking, become viable sources for the creation of counternarratives that challenge not only the conventions of SF cinema but various racial discourses as well.

Science fiction films, with their fantastical plots and far-off worlds, have the luxury to create any kind of character, social system, and world within the confines of their narratives. We all know that time travel and a transporter that can dematerialize and rematerialize human beings do not exist. Yet, as an audience, we welcomingly suspend our disbelief for the purpose of entertainment and lightweight escapism. Similarly, common sense tells us that biological traits such as eye color, pigmentation, or hair texture does not entitle one group of people to rule over the other on the false pretense of racial superiority. Nevertheless, history has proven this fantastical proposition not only plausible but convincing enough to base entire societies around it. Thus there is an unstated hegemonic affinity between the genre of SF film and the science fiction of race in America. Perhaps this is the most compelling reason to write a book examining the representation of blackness in SF cinema. Both SF cinema and the social construction of race rely on the acceptance of fictions of the highest order to work, and the following chapters reveal the connections between the two.

CHAPTER 1

STRUCTURED ABSENCE AND TOKEN PRESENCE

It is sometimes advantageous to be unseen, although it is most often wearing on the nerves. RALPH ELLISON, *Invisible Man*

They had a movie of the future called *Logan's Run*. Ain't no niggers in it. I said, "Well, white folks ain't planning for us to be here."

RICHARD PRYOR, *Bicentennial Nigger*

American science fiction (SF) cinema has had a history of providing striking portrayals of the future, alternative worlds, sleek rocket ships, cyborgs, deadly ray guns, time machines, and wormholes through hyperspace, but, until quite recently, no black people. For decades it appeared as if science fiction cinema was the symbolic wish fulfillment of America's staunchest advocates of white supremacy. Admittedly, such a strident characterization is informed by some degree of hyperbole. Nonetheless, the structured absence of blackness has historically been a signature feature of the genre. In numerous SF films, black people are missing, or if they are present, they are so extremely marginalized and irrelevant to the narrative that they are, for all intents and purposes, invisible. The exclusion, however, of black representation in SF cinema is not unique to the genre. The Hollywood film industry, from its inception, has been extremely exclusionary and at times even hostile toward black representation. The seminal film *Birth of a Nation* (1915) exemplifies the type of antagonistic film representations of blackness in early American cinema, with its blackface stereotypes and unabashed veneration of the Ku Klux Klan.[1]

Early Hollywood cinema chronically deployed black characters in films set in the antebellum South and the jungle forests of Africa or as seemingly permanent members of the American service-class economy (i.e., the maids, chauffeurs, train porters, and butlers). Accordingly, for much of the classic Hollywood era, cinematic blackness was overdetermined by historical events or a particular geographical setting or social class status, resulting in what James Snead characterizes as a state of perpetual historical stasis for black representation in film.[2] The historical stasis of black representation and the necessary "suspension of disbelief" by the audience in sf film mixed as well as oil and water, since a fundamental pillar of the sf cinema aesthetic is temporal speculation.[3] For decades, black representation was too concentrated, too weighted down by history, geography, and social location, to aesthetically transcend and diffuse into the ethereal imaginative space envisioned in the postwar sf films of the 1950s. The presence of black people on alternative worlds, in space, on the moon, or exploring Mars was the ultimate impossibility, the ultimate aesthetic subterfuge of the genre's central requirement for viewers to suspend disbelief. With this type of representational logic saddled to black representation, it is not difficult to deduce that black characters would be absent across a vast majority of American sf cinema or that, when they were present, their representation was overdetermined, as in *Flash Gordon* (1980), where black characters appear as futuristic African tribesmen who wear metallic loincloths. For the most part, black characters are absent from sf cinema, yet their omission does not eliminate blackness as a source of anxiety. Churning just below the narrative surface of many sf films, blackness is symbolically present.

Edward Said's seminal work *Orientalism* provides a conceptual framework to account for the symbolic presence of blackness in sf films where it is not readily apparent. Said analyzed how English literature constructed not only the Orient as a geographical source of difference but also its populace as an alien "other" in the Western popular imagination. From this platform of socially constructed dissimilarity a wellspring of representations of the East emerged that relied on binary representations of culture, taste, and appearance to create essential qualities of difference.[4] Said's observation has multiple areas of application, but for this book the oppositional dichotomy that attributes immutable traits to the East in comparison with the West is similar to how the nonwhite person represents an alien "other" to the white protagonist(s) in sf film and plays a significant role in revealing the representational tropes used in sf film to signify blackness.

White Man's Burden (1995) is an sf film that dramatically demonstrates the taken-for-granted notions of immutable racial traits that define the oppositional terrain of racial meaning in American society. Although the qualitative signifiers of racial difference are purposefully employed to play against the grain of the assumptions and stigmas commonly associated with black racial identity, the film is an excellent example of how an oppositional dichotomy defines the difference between blacks and whites in culture, taste, and appearance. In this film, the coded, often stereotypical qualities associated with black people, in society as well as on celluloid, are turned on their head. In the alternative world of *White Man's Burden*, African Americans are the dominant race/class. In this hierarchically organized society, whites are depicted as poor, uneducated, inner-city ghetto residents with affected speech patterns and prone to violent behavior. Although the image of whites as an oppressed minority is visually arresting within the film, the ideological work and meaning of the film are effective only as a mirror image of the real stereotypes and preconceived notions of racial difference operating outside the film. A similar type of binary racial coding is found in M. Night Shyamalan's enigmatic superhero film *Unbreakable* (2000), except that whiteness occupies the traditional superordinate status as the opposite of blackness. *White Man's Burden* is notable, however, for demonstrating that assorted signifiers of blackness are such a powerful source of racial meaning that, despite an inverse representation of traditional racial polarities, the attributes ascribed to the white actors in the film create characters that effortlessly proxy for blacks within U.S. society.

Of course, not all SF films are as deliberate as *White Man's Burden* in symbolizing blacks and their unequal social status relative to whites. Nonetheless, many SF films are just as blatant in how they bring into bold relief the symbolic landscape of binary racial oppositions, the perception of blacks as "other," and the racial wish fulfillment encoded into the symbolic representation of blackness. For example, in a surface analysis, the films *One Million Years B.C.* (1966) and *2001: A Space Odyssey* (1968) appear devoid of any articulation of race. A closer reading of both films, however, in relationship to the structured absence of blackness presents a clear binary coding of race and suggests that nonwhites are primitive simian predecessors of modern humanity.[5]

The prehistoric dinosaur world of *One Million Years B.C.* depicts humanity as comprising two tribes, the dark-haired cruel Rock People and the pleasant blond-haired Shell People. In this film, a homogenous physical characteristic, hair color, performs robust semiotic work as a visual cue signifying essentialized states of emotional and mental development for each respective group. The omission of black people, along with the presence of the all-white blond and brunet tribes, further amplifies the symbolic significance of the brown-skinned, subhuman, apelike creatures shown later in the film. As the only other rival clan to the two white prehistoric groups, their symbolic presence suggests a racial pecking order that places nonwhites at the bottom of evolutionary development. The structured absence of black people in *2001: A Space Odyssey* is also suggestive of the same type of racial coding. The celebrated depiction of Darwinian evolution—illustrated in a single transition shot from primates using a bone as a tool to a similarly shaped white space station, its technological analogue—also conveys a visual code whereby racial difference divides the uncivilized from the civilized. In the futuristic world of *2001: A Space Odyssey* humankind is technologically advanced, civilized, socially composed, and exclusively white. The film's white world of the future, however, stands in sharp contrast to the colored primates of the past. In this case, the dark brown progenitors of humankind are primitive, violent, and wild apelike creatures.

Admittedly, *One Million Years B.C.* and *2001: A Space Odyssey* are, for all intents and purposes, two SF films respectively interested in showing individuals struggling to assert their humanity in the face of monstrous primitivism and alienating technological achievement. Given, however, the structured absence of black representation in the ancient past of *One Million Years B.C.* and the far future of *2001: A Space Odyssey*—the image of violence-prone dark brown primates being the only nonwhite presence in these films—the symbolic staging of both films suggests a racial code whereby white individuals are paradigmatically representative of humanity and nonwhiteness is animalized.[6] Yet this type of racial coding is not merely about omission and the symbolic representation of blackness as subhuman primates. The structured absence in SF film also communicates a host of racial fears and fantasies circulating in American society. A more prolonged and deeper analysis of the SF film classics *When Worlds Collide* (1951), *The Time Machine* (1960), *Robinson Crusoe on Mars* (1964), *Logan's Run* (1976), and *Star Wars* (1977) brings into sharper focus the ideological ramifications and the cultural politics of race that the structured absence and token presence of blackness in SF cinema often mirror.

POSTWAR SCIENCE FICTION CINEMA AND RACE

Georges Méliès's *A Voyage to the Moon* (1902) and Fritz Lang's iconic *Metropolis* (1927) are rightfully recognized as early SF films that imprint the form and contour of the genre. As a genre, however, SF cinema truly began to take shape in the nuclear age of post–World War II America. With the splitting of the atom, the atomic age was born, and with it, the world and particularly America had become fraught with an acute fear of instant annihilation that no other generation before had to confront and contain in the back of their collective imagination. Science fiction cinema of the 1950s became the primary vehicle for American film audiences to attempt to confront feelings of dread and despair associated with the threat of cold war annihilation. The zeitgeist of 1950s America was dominated by a collective fear of the political "other" commonly referred to as the "red scare," geopolitically framed as the "communist threat," and militarily formulated as the "domino theory." All of these incarnations drew much of their emotional alarm from the nuclear threat attached to the political gamesmanship of the cold war and is virtually palpable in *The Day the Earth Stood Still* (1951), *The War of the Worlds* (1953), *Them!* (1954), and *Invasion of the Body Snatchers* (1956).

Cold war anxiety cast a long and broad shadow across the intellectual spectrum, so much so that the SF films of the 1950s have by and large been defined as exclusively reflecting cold war jitters.[7] Against this backdrop, it might appear even logical that the overwhelming majority of SF films of the 1950s omitted black people or almost any topic having to do with race. Yet cold war anxiety was not the only issue challenging America's social and political order. On the domestic front, American race relations were a political tinderbox about to explode. Although the structured absence of black people in the SF films of the period is the dominant representational trend, their absence is nevertheless quite revealing, given the backdrop of domestic race relations at the time. In fact, in several classic films of the period, the omission of black people functions to deliver some of the most telling ideological messages and wish fulfillment associated with American race relations to date.

Take, for example, the SF classic *When Worlds Collide* (1951). The film depicts an impending collision between Earth and another planet. To avoid extinction, an elite cadre of American scientists constructs a spaceship that will ferry a small number of humans to another inhabitable planet. On the surface, *When Worlds Collide* offers a straightforward end-of-the-world scenario punctuated by a series of clumsy special effects. Below the surface, however, rests a powerful anxiety over the erosion of white imperialistic hegemony. In this case, the collision of two worlds is a veiled metaphor for the period's shifting, and frequently confrontational, geopolitical relationship between developed countries and anticolonialist developing nations. Despite the metaphorical link between an encroaching Third World anticolonialist movement and the planet's impending collision with Earth in the film, ultimately *When Worlds Collide* endorses the most strident form of American racial provincialism: "whites only" racial segregation.

By having the sole survivors of Earth consist only of white Americans,

When Worlds Collide overtly advocates white racial homogeneity as a requirement for the preservation of the American way of life and the rebuilding of a "perfect" world. As a result, a significant portion of the possible gratification derived from the film depends not only on the relief or satisfaction of seeing a deserving group of humans escape the annihilation of Earth but also on the visual absence of blackness on the new planet once they arrive. In this sense, *When Worlds Collide* revels in racial fantasy by presenting a world where only white people survive a planetary disaster. Yet, at the same time, the film is rooted in the real racial politics of segregation and rigid racial hierarchies of 1950s America. Consequently, the film does dual ideological work as a racial fantasy and as an extension and reaffirmation of the real-world practice of "whites only" public segregation near the end of the Jim Crow segregationist era. A critical reading of the ideological message present in *When Worlds Collide* suggests that the film signals a subtle awareness of an eroding European colonialism abroad and possibly an increasing awareness and anxiety that institutional segregation on the domestic front was doomed.

With the end of institutional racial segregation looming on the political horizon, *When Worlds Collide* is a naked expression of racial wish fulfillment rooted and fueled by the real politics and mounting challenges to the segregation of 1950s America. The impact of the racial struggle on the ground would have further ideological reverberations for the imaginative presence of black representation in SF film, along with the meaning of black racial formation in the genre.

SCI-FI CINEMA IN THE CIVIL RIGHTS ERA

The 1960 screen adaptation of H. G. Wells's novel *The Time Machine*, even more than *When Worlds Collide*, articulates multiple anxieties surrounding the redistribution of power and privilege that the civil rights movement represented, the demise of the separate and unequal world of Jim Crow racial segregation. In the film, George (Rod Taylor), a scientist who longs to satisfy his wanderlust, creates a time machine that will transport him from 1899 to the year 802701, where he discovers a world of two races, the Eloi and the Morlocks. The two races are the result of an earlier atomic war, which inadvertently creates an evolutionary fork in the road for those who survived the bombing and subsequent nuclear fallout. One group decides to live above ground, and the other below ground. George leaves his time machine in front of a massive stone structure (with what appears to be a gigantic statue of an African mask perched on top) and roams about before discover-

The image of a white utopia in the distant future of *The Time Machine* (1960).

ing the aboveground inhabitants, the Eloi. They are fit, youthful, vegetarian, blond-haired white men and women who passively wander the idyllic shores of a nearby river. In direct contrast, the Morlocks, who live underground, are a race of stout, cannibalistic, blue-skinned, facially deformed, troll-like creatures with oversized lips and piglike noses. At the conclusion of the film, the Morlocks are destroyed, leaving an exclusively white racial utopia, which George and his female companion, Weena (Yvette Mimieux), can blissfully enjoy.

The Time Machine is commonly regarded as a reflection of cold war fears of nuclear annihilation or a metaphor for class conflict.[8] But a closer reading reveals that *The Time Machine* also performs interesting cultural work around race. The film employs various visual codes to mark the Morlocks as symbolically black. The massive black statue of an African-like mask atop the foreboding stone entrance to the Morlocks underground quarters and the stark visual coding of the Morlocks as bright blue creatures—in contrast to the all-blond, exclusively white inhabitants of the surface—easily mark them as a "colored" race. Furthermore, the spatial division between the different "races," one above and the other below, indicates a racial dichotomy similar to the separate and unequal racial segregation of post–World War II America. Finally, *The Time Machine* intertextually draws on the history of American slavery and, by extension, America's practice of segregationist racial politics when George comments that somehow the human race had divided itself and "by some awful quirk of fate the Morlocks have become the masters and the Eloi their servants."

By characterizing the relationship between the Eloi and the Morlocks as servants and masters, the narration clearly draws on America's legacy of African enslavement. Moreover, the combination of the visual and narrative elements of *The Time Machine* functions as a symbolic metaphor for post-WWII American racial apartheid and the intense white anxiety surrounding the system's demise as the civil rights movement gained momentum. In particular, the cannibalistic relationship between the two races—the Morlocks eat Eloi—suggests broader racial concerns, the fear that whites will become victims of an unequal social system that previously privileged them. From the perspective of the segregationist advocate and passive sympathizer of the period, *The Time Machine* predicts the ultimate racial apocalypse, a reversal of fortune in which a race of "coloreds" eats white people for food. The end of the film, however, resolves the threat posed to passive whites and their idyllic paradise by these creatures-of-color—the entire nonwhite race is eliminated. What is left is a world no longer segregated into two races; instead there is only one race, a white one. In *The Time Machine* the symbolic resolution to the protest marches—acts of civil disobedience and increasing violence associated with the civil rights movement—is signaled by the elimination of all the people of color in the future. In this sense, *The Time Machine* is a notable example of how an SF film can perform ideological work as pure racial fantasy. Certainly, *The Time Machine* is a critique of the grave social impact of war, but the racial coding in the film also illustrates, on a grand scale, an acute uneasiness with the real perseverance of the organized struggle for racial justice along with the erosion of racial segregation in America.

The face of the unknown appears remarkably familiar in the form of a generic African-like mask in *The Time Machine*.

The blue-skinned creatures of the future that devour white people for food in *The Time Machine.*

Whereas the wholesale destruction of people of color in *When Worlds Collide* or the elimination of a race of colored beings in *The Time Machine* reflected the symbolic support of racial segregation, *Robinson Crusoe on Mars* (1964) reflected a shift away from such blatantly oppressive racial fantasies in the face of the civil rights movement. The tagline for *Robinson Crusoe on Mars* stated that the film "is only one step ahead of present reality." Although the tagline was meant to highlight the scientific authenticity of the depiction of an interplanetary space voyage for a generation that was fast approaching real space travel to the moon and back, the film also addressed the urgent and shifting cultural politics of American race relations in the mid-1960s.

Robinson Crusoe on Mars takes Daniel Defoe's classic novel *Robinson Crusoe,* about a man stranded on a virtually deserted island, and gives it a sci-fi twist. The film begins with two white American astronauts, Christopher "Kit" Draper (Paul Mantee) and Dan "Mac" MacReady (Adam West), strapped into their spacecraft orbiting the red planet. Their orbital research, however, is interrupted by a meteor on a collision course with their spacecraft. Consequently, both men jettison from the craft in escape ships, intending to land on Mars. Copilot Kit Draper and Mona, the pet monkey, however, are the only survivors of the emergency landing. Through a series of miraculous discoveries, Draper is able to coax oxygen out of special yellow rocks littered across the surface of the planet and to locate a source of underground water. Draper becomes so adept at adjusting to the hostile environment of Mars that he secures an American flag to the outside of the entrance to his cave residence, signifying not only a home away from home but also the intrepid spirit of American frontierism. Later, Draper discovers an alien presence visiting Mars that uses slave labor to extract precious materials from the planet. When one of the slaves escapes, Draper helps him evade capture and later gives him the name "Friday."

The racial coding of this film is rather straightforward. Although the alien character is white, his status as an escaped slave is a clear signifier of American slavery and the racial segregation born from that system of oppression. Even before Draper encounters the fugitive slave, American race relations are symbolically foreshadowed early in the film. Draper's rendition of the Confederate Civil War song "Dixie (I Wish I Was in Dixie)" (1859) as he traverses the Martian landscape signals a longing not only to return to Earth but also to return to the Jim Crow racial politics associated with the mythologized genteel racism of the South. Initially Draper is granted his Dixieland wish, a mute and submissive alien willing to submit to his commands. In no uncertain terms, Draper tells Friday that he is the boss and Friday must follow his rules in his makeshift home. By doing so, Draper symbolically becomes the "master" of an extremely perplexed and uncommunicative "house slave." But as Friday begins to help Draper shoulder the burden of survival on Mars, Draper abandons this draconian and unequal relationship with Friday for one that promises more reciprocity and equality between the two. Eventually, an American rescue ship makes contact with them. The film ends with the upbeat and optimistic impression that Draper and Friday are on their way back to Earth, having discovered they share similar beliefs and are more alike than different.

Robinson Crusoe on Mars illustrates the obsolete functionality of Southern-bred racial segregation stemming from slavery. Moreover, Draper's is the symbolic embodiment of white liberalism as a solution to America's legacy of black enslavement. The ideological message of the film suggests that, in facing the racial conflict of the early 1960s, whites and blacks would have to adopt a racial sensibility similar to that of Draper's and Friday's in *Robinson Crusoe on Mars*. On one hand, white Americans, like Draper, would have to abandon a racial agenda born of Southern plantation politics, be willing to increase their social contact with blacks, and open their homes and hearts to the racial "other." On the other hand, blacks, similar to Friday, would have to prove they could productively contribute to building American society and increase their trustworthiness in order to diminish the fears and doubts whites had of African Americans. The end result would be similar to that in the film. Like Draper and Friday's relationship of growing mutual respect, cooperation, and shared values, American race relations

would have to stand on the same social platform as the civil rights movement—racial integration.

Robinson Crusoe on Mars is a tacit advocate of the integrationist agenda
for the descendents of American slavery, except that the social integration
into American society signaled in *Robinson Crusoe on Mars* exacts a price.
Change is required primarily by blacks, even though they are the victims of
limited institutional access and obstruction of efforts to reform these institutions. By depicting a series of encounters in which Friday adapts to Draper's
rules, speaks English, and eventually becomes a self-sacrificing alien on be-
half of his benevolent benefactor, the film falls short of its promise of equality between the two. Rather the relationship is quite lopsided, almost paternalistic. As a result, the film ends up suggesting that individual reform, by
the minority, is the gateway to acceptance by the racial majority. Symbolically, the interspecies camaraderie in *Robinson Crusoe on Mars* clearly indicates that African Americans, like Friday, would need to absorb the cultural
lessons of white America to prove they were culturally fit and individually
deserving if American race relations were to be truly mended. Despite the
shortcomings of the film's narrative of acceptance for an alien "other," *Robinson Crusoe on Mars* marks a counterimpulse away from the segregationist racial fantasies of SF film's past. The decline of the civil rights movement
and the rise of Black Power would trigger a maelstrom of controversy for the
future of American race relations, not the least of which was the increasing
presence of blackness in a genre that had previously demonstrated a willingness to accept only symbolic black representation.

BLACK POWER, BLAXPLOITATION, AND THE SF FILM APPARATUS

As the decade of the 1960s was coming to a close, nearly every quarter of the
American social order was marked by political turmoil and racial unrest.
Interestingly, science fiction cinema would experience something of a renaissance during this period. A string of SF films would capture the imagination of a politically cynical, if not ideologically weary, moviegoing audience.
Emblematic of this renaissance in SF film were the visually arresting *2001: A
Space Odyssey* (1968), the psychedelic cult classic *Barbarella* (1968), and the
socially ironic *Planet of the Apes* (1968). The success of these films worked to
establish the genre as a legitimate commercial art form playing to the rising
tide of a youth counterculture. No longer was SF film merely a novelty genre
strictly appealing to the narrow taste of the post–World War II science nerd
or a leftover genre for the drive-in teenybopper crowd of the 1950s. By the

Paula Kelly played a supporting role in the SF bio-disaster film *The Andromeda Strain* (1971). She also appeared in *Soylent Green* (1973).

early 1970s the shift in SF cinema from cold war paranoia to futuristic tableaus of alienation was complete, and films like *A Clockwork Orange* (1971) and *Silent Running* (1972) tapped into a deep cultural well of social anxiety that resonated across a wide swath of the baby boomer generation. On the surface, the SF film renaissance of the time ostensibly ignored race, yet the acute racial turmoil of the late 1960s Black Power movement was having an impact on the genre. In the wake of insurgent black nationalism and race riots, black characters were beginning to creep into the previously all-white worlds of the future.

With the vociferous emergence of Black Power nationalism in the late 1960s, not only was the visibility of blacks heightened in the public and political sphere, but a newfound visibility in Hollywood cinema soon followed as well. The petition and protest of the Black Power movement, in turn, fueled the emergence of blaxploitation cinema: a genre whose raison d'être was based on the desire, if not collective need, of black audiences to have the "black experience" represented and validated. Despite the rise in black nationalism, which was ideologically fueling the justification of blaxploitation cinema, it was the profitability of blaxploitation, at a time when the film industry was experiencing a severe financial crisis, that made blaxploitation viable and valuable.[9] The dramatic increase and profitability of black films resulting from the Black Power movement's popularity had a spillover effect, sweeping black actors into predominantly white films. Films such as *Live and Let Die* (1973), *Blazing Saddles* (1974), and *Silver Streak* (1976) demonstrated that placing black actors as costars in white film narratives could attract both white and black audiences. Most importantly, this representational trend also appeared in American science fiction cinema, a genre primarily known for its structured absence of blackness. For example, *Planet*

Robert Gunner as Landon, a black astronaut of the future, in a virtually speechless part in the SF film classic *Planet of the Apes* (1968).

of the Apes (1968), *Beneath the Planet of the Apes* (1970), *Conquest of the Planet of the Apes* (1972), *Battle for the Planet of the Apes* (1973), *The Andromeda Strain* (1971), *The Omega Man* (1971), *THX 1138* (1971), and *Soylent Green* (1973) stand out as SF films that wove black characters into their brave new worlds of the future.

Yet, by the mid- to late 1970s, Black Power politics was almost completely extinguished, the blaxploitation film craze was in a precipitous decline, and a white cultural backlash against the perceived excesses of the struggle for racial justice was gathering a full head of steam. Amid this shifting racial landscape, whites who befriended the racial struggle were forced to reevaluate many of their ideological allegiances, countercultural beliefs, and social practices, not the least of which was the cultural politics of race. After eliminating legalized racial segregation a decade earlier, America in the waning years of the 1970s would witness the reestablishment of racial segregation vis-à-vis white flight to the suburbs, along with a return of the structured absence of blackness in SF cinema. For example, *Logan's Run* (1976) reflects a cultural longing to return to an America prior to the civil rights movement by imagining a future world devoid of black people and advocating a host of ideological concessions related to the 1960s revolution, race relations, and America's political future.

In the twenty-third century setting of *Logan's Run*, the world has achieved a state of perfect social harmony under several giant ecodomes perched on the edge of an ocean. In this society one's thirtieth birthday is a death sentence that only "renewal" or escape to a place called Sanctuary can circumvent. Men and women are assumed to be reborn in a ritual where they are spun into the air, as if on a carousel, and explode in a spectacle of light and fire before an auditorium filled with cheering spectators. This is the accepted reality for everyone except a small band of people who instead opt to run when the imbedded crystal in their right hand changes its color to red and begins to blink on and off. The population is replete with throngs of young, fit, eye-catching citizens, all of whom are white.

In the midst of this utopia, Logan 5 (Michael York) and his friend and co-worker Francis 7 (Richard Jordan) are police officers. They are called Sandmen, and their job is to catch and kill "Runners." Logan dutifully does his job of exterminating until he turns in an exterminated Runner's personal items. As a result, Logan is assigned the covert mission of infiltrating a clandestine network of people aiding Runners in their quest to find the secret location called Sanctuary. Logan must find Sanctuary and destroy it. Along the way, he is befriended by an unsuspecting young woman, Jessica 6 (Jenny Agutter). She unwittingly introduces him to a host of people and places, leading them on a series of events that conclude with the shattering of everything Logan's society is socialized to believe is true. As Logan and Jessica make their way to Sanctuary, they are closely followed by Francis, who is unaware of Logan's covert mission and unnerved by the dramatic change in his former partner. Determined to find out what has happened to his friend, Francis doggedly chases Logan and Jessica as they travel through a mazelike series of dead ends and unforeseen obstacles. The direst of these is their encounter with a creation called Box, part man and part machine.

Barely discernible below the metallic silver-plated mask and metal box is the black character actor Roscoe Lee Brown. Despite the bizarre silver mask used to disguise him, his distinctive baritone voice immediately identifies him. As if giving an operatic performance, he virtually sings his spoken lines, "Fish, plankton, sea greens, and protein from the sea, fresh as harvest day. . . . It's my job to freeze you." The ice cave inhabited by Box is not Sanctuary, as Logan and Jessica first assumed. Rather it has been the last

The absence of blackness is a stark visual statement in *Logan's Run* (1976).

stop for scores of Runners on the quest for Sanctuary. They are shown frozen and stored in ice compartments along opposite rows that stretch far into the distance. Before Box can freeze Logan and Jessica, however, Logan destroys him and the ice cavern, and he and Jessica wander outside the confines of the ecodome. They journey through the wilderness until coming upon the ivy-covered remnants of U.S. society. Among these ruins they meet the quirky and disheveled Old Man (Peter Ustinov), who recounts to them what society was like before their domed world. Later, Logan and Jessica surreptitiously return to the city and inadvertently trigger a destructive chain reaction that ends with the implosion of the city as the population flees outside.

On the surface, *Logan's Run* is clearly a critique of a popular edict of the leftist baby boomer generation: "Never trust anyone over thirty." The idea that anyone over thirty is socially expendable is totally skewered by the film's conclusion, and by extension so are the cultural politics and adolescent ideology that produced it. *Logan's Run* unmistakably signals that the time to experiment and explore alternative lifestyles is culturally and ideologically over. This is most readily witnessed by the way in which the idea of "free love" and orgiastic sex practices—which were a part of America's sexual revolution—are shown in the film. These sexual unions are depicted as drug-induced behavior that leaves its practitioners in a haze of hedonistic illusion. This point is emphasized later in the film when Logan and Jessica become disoriented and are nearly unable to escape the clutches of a desirous horde of naked men and women.

Outside the hedonistic ecodome, the film works to reaffirm the idea and practice of traditional pair bonding and the nuclear family. This is first communicated by the Old Man's reflections on marriage and children and later when Logan and Jessica proclaim themselves husband and wife. In this manner, *Logan's Run* is a film intent on reconciling the cultural politics of a maturing generation that had proclaimed to forsake the socially conservative, sexually frigid, and neurotically bourgeois lifestyle of their parents' generation. Ultimately, the relationship between Logan and Jessica stresses the importance of conventional domestic gender roles and reflects a maturing counterculture as it begrudgingly begins to embrace the traditions it once denounced. Again, on the surface, the film appears to stake out its ideological confrontation with the brash idealism of 1960s radicalism primarily around sexual politics. Below the surface, however, *Logan's Run* also works to reconcile the cultural antagonisms of the period along the axis of race.

Except for the distinctive disembodied baritone voice of blackness emanating from Roscoe Lee Brown as Box, blackness is absent inside the eco-

Roscoe Lee Brown as Box, the literal and symbolic impediment to true independence for numerous whites on a quest for freedom in *Logan's Run*.

dome of the future, as well as outside the dilapidated world of the past. Interestingly, the only sign of blackness in the entire film is responsible for creating a static condition for thousands of whites on a quest for freedom. At first, Box is presumed to be a facilitator of freedom, in this case Sanctuary. But his name foreshadows his purpose. Box, a signifier of restriction, will place all those who seek freedom into icebox-like coffins. Furthermore, Sanctuary is an imaginary refuge where a multitude of Runners, all of whom are white, become trapped by a captivating "black" robot with a gift for grandiose oration. This setup is quite telling, given that a fundamental feature of the counterculture movement to radically change American society was bolstered by charismatic black speechmakers.[10] With the rise of Black Power, however, and the fervent cultural nationalism that grew out of it, white participation on issues of racial empowerment became untenable on both sides of the racial divide.[11] White participation in the black freedom movement was effectively stalled, and *Logan's Run* symbolically reimagines the sociopolitical disillusionment and dead-end status of white activism in the movement for racial justice as a masked black man, Box, and his freezing of scores of white Runners. Once Logan and Jessica are able to escape the symbolic confines of race and racial rhetoric that Box suggests, they are able to discover the wellspring of American political democracy. This point is visually underscored when the two wander through the ivy-covered remnants of America's political capital, Washington, D.C.

The return to the symbolic source of American democracy is most pronounced when the pair stop to ponder the significance of the Lincoln Memorial. The mise-en-scène functions on two levels. First, it signifies past racial strife, the Civil War. Second, the scene works to transcode the past civil cleavages around race with the current sociocultural cleavages of the

Logan (Michael York) and Jessica (Jenny Agutter) stare at what has become of Runners who followed Box's directives in *Logan's Run*.

period that had America, after the radicalism and racial unrest of the 1960s, yearning for cultural unification. The final confrontation between Logan and Francis clearly illustrates this point. Francis tracks Logan and Jessica outside of the ecodome in order to convince Logan to come back with him. Instead, both men engage in hand-to-hand combat inside what looks like the remnants of the Senate floor. As they struggle, Francis breaks away and grabs a pole with a tattered American flag attached to it. Both men grapple with the flagpole, shifting leverage between them until Francis loses his grip and Logan proceeds to beat him into submission with it. As Francis lies dying in Logan's arms, he touches Logan's open palm and utters the words, "You renewed." The cultural meaning of this comment is quite striking. Logan, a symbol of wayward Americanism, after destroying a black man-machine, returns back to the symbolic cradle of American democracy, the nation's capital, and becomes reborn. Francis, a symbol of American cultural excess, fights Logan for his life on the Senate floor and eventually dies. This climatic confrontation between both men easily symbolizes an ideological civil war between the New Right and New Left. With Francis's defeat and acknowledgment of Logan's "renewal," the symbolic collapse of America's excess and the generation that came to define it, the countercultural Left, is presented as a necessary step for the renewal and triumph of traditional American values. Accordingly, *Logan's Run* ends with the destruction of the hedonistic domed city with its all-white population spilling outside, directing their sense of awe and wonder to the Old Man and, by implication, to all of the past cultural traditions he embodies.

Logan's Run blatantly trumpets a longing for America to reconcile contemporary cultural cleavages around family, sexuality, and democracy that are symbolized in the future as taking an excessive toll on the collective moral and geopolitical wherewithal of the nation. Despite the structured absence of black people in *Logan's Run*, race is a significant source of meaning because the omission of blacks and the return to traditional values of family and democracy are conflated with one another in the resolution of the film. *Logan's Run* provides the ideological out for adopting a more conservative racial assessment and outlook for the political economic possibilities in the white Left's collective future. For whites who had previously decided to "drop out" and needed to "renew" their ideological positions in the face of choices they had previously sworn to reject, the film makes sure to communicate that there is no utopia at the end of the radical rainbow and promotes the message that it is time to look back and reclaim from the dustbin of history those beliefs, values, and traditions that made America great.

Ultimately, *Logan's Run* marked the beginning of an ideological convergence between left and right cultural quarters in the realization that cultural transgression came with a cost. Drug experimentation became addiction and criminalization, free love became alienated and mechanical sex, and the utopia of color-blind race relations became a political quagmire of affirmative action, quotas, and claims of reverse discrimination. Four scant years after the release of *Logan's Run* a "silent majority" emerged in which numerous Democrats joined Republicans to vote into office a Republican presidential ticket, politically marking the type of cultural reconciliation projected in *Logan's Run*. Arguably, if ever there was a science fiction film that predicted the future, this was one that succeeded. It foreshadowed the conservative shift in the American sociopolitical landscape and the "renewal" of American conservatism that emerged in the 1980s.

A year later, *Star Wars* (1977) was released and pushed *Logan's Run* out of the American popular consciousness. Although the difference in the look,

Logan and Francis (Richard Jordan) face one another in *Logan's Run*. Their struggle symbolizes a broader cultural clash in American society as the 1970s came to a close.

feel, and popularity of the two movies was like night and day, the racial message was similar: the collective attention and public concern directed toward fighting racial discrimination by white America was over. The cultural task at hand was fixated on reclaiming the national honor and racial unity that had been severely diminished over nearly twenty years of cultural chaos wrought by racial protest and riots, the assassination of one president and the resignation of another, an undeclared military defeat in Vietnam, and an emergent women's movement. Following these multiple points of crisis in American society, George Lucas's science fiction space opera, *Star Wars* (1977), would significantly contribute to ideologically restoring America's bruised and battered white nationalistic hegemony to its post-WWII glory.

SCI-FI CINEMA AS RACIAL RECUPERATION

No other film in the history of science fiction cinema has had an impact on the collective popular consciousness of American society to the degree that *Star Wars* has. The film (and franchise) has galvanized a multitude of fans, followers, and detractors who, even decades after the film's release, champion the greatness, profundity, and even banality of its form as well as substance. Nonetheless, *Star Wars* is, next to *The Wizard of Oz* (1939), America's greatest cinematic fairytale as much as it is science fiction. The film is laden with American folklore and starkly drawn figures representing good and evil, all of which are in line with Vladimir Propp's seminal work on the typology of the magic folk story.[12] The narrative terrain of *Star Wars* also draws on the mythical ethos of frontierism popularized in classic Hollywood westerns such as *Shane* (1953). *Star Wars* maps out similar ideological territory, except territory in the infinite frontier of space replaces the vast frontier of the American West. The film, also like the classic westerns of the past, draws a stark coded color line between the good guys and the bad guys, who are literally coded in white and black. Although the film periodically inverts these simple color associations of white with goodness and black with evil—the body armor worn by nearly all of the Empire's storm troopers is entirely white—the racial "others" that populate the film are all bizarre aliens of color. The cumulative impact of the omission of black people—along with the binary visual coding employed in *Star Wars*, which is similar to that found in *The Time Machine*—produces a perfect polarization between the homogeneity of white humans against their diverse alien-of-color counterparts.[13] Undeniably, the blatant omission of black people in *Star Wars* heightens the symbolic value of the various aliens and space creatures found in the film.

The space cantina scene best exemplifies the racially coded significance of the alien "other" in the film. The scene begins when Luke Skywalker (Mark Hamill) and his newly adopted mentor, Obi-Wan Kenobi (Alec Guinness), travel to an intergalactic transportation hangout where they intend to find a pilot to secure their flight from the planet. The cantina is a sci-fi version of a western saloon where pilots, criminals, and all-around bad aliens hang out and swap insults. As Luke and Obi-Wan enter the bar, the audience is provided with a point-of-view shot that scans the interior and permits us to gaze at a fantastic display of difference. Insectlike creatures with humanoid bodies converse in a language of clicks and beeps while drinking at tables and smoking cigarette-like objects at the counter. Serenading this motley crew are several creatures with oversized eyes and bulbous heads, dressed in tuxedos and playing musical instruments. At first glance the internal reality of the bar scene appears as an imaginative alien wonderland, even though the scene blatantly draws on clichés from western saloons and film noir speakeasies. Nevertheless, the scene has become an iconic visual reference point in the American popular imagination for displaying a unique, alien, and strange universe. Most importantly, the coded racial sensibility woven into this scene, and present throughout *Star Wars*, is shrouded by the overwhelming and, as a result, overpowering display of nonhuman difference as spectacle. Outside of the diegetic reality constructed in *Star Wars*, however, the sublimated racial representation present in the scene is clearly revealed.

In the same year that *Star Wars* was released, the short-lived *Richard Pryor Show* presented a spoof of the film's famous space cantina scene. Much like the film, the comedic sketch uses an establishing shot that surveys the inside of the bar. It mimics the film by showing various alien creatures—that look surprisingly similar to the aliens in the film—drinking and conversing at tables. The only human is Richard Pryor, as the bartender in the aptly named "Star Wars Bar." He hand-delivers drinks to his alien patrons while dispensing a mix of snide remarks and observations along the way. After coming across an alien with a grotesquely large head and protruding flat nose, he pauses for a moment, then delivers this observation: "You look just like a nigger from Detroit I know." The studio audience erupts into boisterous laughter. What Pryor is able to exploit for comedic effect outside of *Star Wars* is ultimately informed by the structured absence of blackness within *Star Wars*. In other words, even though there are no black people in the film, the punch line of Pryor's comedic exchange explicitly relies on the transparent racial statement the film is ostensibly trying to hide but the audience clearly recognizes: the aliens of the film signify black people.

Darth Vader, the black figure of intergalactic doom in *Star Wars* (1977), whose mask eerily resembles the statue in *The Time Machine* (1960).

Ed Guerrero gives credence to Pryor's punch line with his succinct observation that despite the structured absence of people of color, the alien life-forms of *Star Wars* are reminiscent of the "colored sidekicks, Tontos, Birmingham Browns and Nigger Jims of the action-adventure thrillers and novels of America's filmic and literary past."[14] The result is a fiercely Manichean visual field of human whites and nonwhite aliens that invites the audience to experience the coded racial "other" as unequivocally abnormal and threatening. Moreover, the robots and nonhuman aliens of *Star Wars* are similar to the type of racial impersonation found in early Hollywood cinema. Racial and ethnic impersonation was a signature feature of early Hollywood films, and African Americans, Native Americans, Asians, and Latinos have all had the dubious honor of having white actors use makeup and adopt exaggerated mannerisms to achieve their racial identities for particular narratives.[15] In this sense, *Star Wars* carries on the tradition by using masks and exaggerated physical mannerisms to create the illusion of alien life-forms that signify people of color. This type of racial "othering" on display in the cantina scene reaches its hyperbolic zenith in the figure of Darth Vader, the villain fully clad in black, with an obtrusive and foreboding wraparound black head mask.

As with the character Box in *Logan's Run*, a black actor's distinctive vocal delivery is used for the *Star Wars* bad guy. In this case, Darth Vader is an aural cipher for the black actor James Earl Jones, who uses his distinctive baritone voice, vocal delivery, and timbre to infuse emotion into the film's charismatic villain. The offscreen voice of Jones plays a significant part in inviting the viewing audience to experience blackness aurally, as the intergalactic voice of doom, while disavowing the presence of blackness except as visual symbol. In this innovative fashion, *Star Wars* recuperates the early SF film tradition of structured black absence; blackness is absent but simultaneously present as a signifier of danger. *Star Wars*, however, is more ideologically complex than its symbolic coding of blacks and other people of color as exotic beings, its Manichean facade, and its innovative structured absence suggest. The racial themes, often only semiotically referenced, make *Star Wars* a more complex film than the domestic military fantasy, spelled out in the title, that it clearly represents. *Star Wars* also racialized American militarism, through its racially coded symbolism. In doing so, the film performed critical cultural work at a time when, following military defeat in Vietnam, America was culturally ill at ease and militaristically insecure. *Star Wars* succeeded in elevating white nationalism to the level of a cathartic morality tale of good versus evil. By cobbling together the least ambiguous and most victorious wars of the nation—the American Revolution and World War II— these dual narratives of wartime nationalism and American military success fueled the look and nostalgic buzz of the film. American nationalism is embodied by the Rebel Alliance, a crew of all-white space fighters, and the film's triumphant pageantry at the end symbolically represented the public acceptance, medals of honor, and accolades of moral courage that America was denied at the close of the Vietnam War.[16] *Star Wars* stood in victorious contrast to the ambiguous nature and anticlimactic end of the Vietnam War. And to the film's credit, it became one of the most entertaining and vicariously recuperative presentations of an all-white, all-American military nationalism to enter the collective popular conscious.

AFFIRMATIVE ACTION SCI-FI

Ironically, the blatant omission of black people in *Star Wars* served to heighten the symbolic value of blackness in the sequels (and prequels) to the original film, along with altering the representational landscape of blackness in subsequent SF films. The introduction of the on-screen black character Lando Calrissian (Billy Dee Williams), the duplicitous leader of a sky-based mining operation, in *The Empire Strikes Back* (1980) offered a new benchmark in the status of black representation in SF cinema. For the most part, Lando Calrissian's appearance in the sequels has been discussed as a sidekick or token position.[17] The importance of Lando Calrissian should not be underestimated by such a one-dimensional typology, however. His duplicity in the film—first extending refuge to Han Solo (Harrison Ford) and Princess Leia (Carrie Fisher), only to be discovered later as having made a deal with Darth Vader for their captivity—makes his character more complex and intriguing than that of a simple sidekick. Admittedly, Lando's role in *Return of the Jedi* (1983), in which he fully redeems himself by leading the search for Han Solo's frozen body and joining the Rebellion attack against a partially completed Death Star, is dreadfully static. But his role in *The Empire Strikes Back* is not only more dynamic within the film but also suggestive of broader racial themes being debated in American society.

Certainly, Lando Calrissian's roles in *The Empire Strikes Back* and *Return of the Jedi* subverted the historical structured absence of black people in American SF cinema. But even more dramatically, in *The Empire Strikes Back* the role mirrored the shifting and uncertain status of African Americans in the early 1980s. The purposeful inclusion of a black character in *Empire* occurs at a time when affirmative action as a racial remedy is fueling a national debate about American meritocracy and the idea of a color-blind society. The debate stoked a racial paranoia on the part of whites and blacks. Working- and middle-class whites perceived that their economic well-being was threatened by black workers potentially being hired or promoted over them because of affirmative action, and black workers perceived themselves as being unjustly stigmatized and virtually always having to "prove" themselves to whites as qualified and worthy of inclusion.[18] These tensions over cooperation, trust, and merit are signaled with Lando Calrissian, as a successful, upwardly mobile black character (clearly signified by his position as the head of a city in the sky) who has to balance competing loyalties to the thousands of citizens under his governance, his personal relationship with his longtime white friend Han Solo, and his tenuous alliance with Darth Vader, the other "black" character. Lando's predicament of competing loyalties was not that unlike the social dilemma many successful African Americans faced as they began to achieve upper middle-class stability in the early 1980s. Black upwardly mobile professionals (buppies) in this stratum often found themselves engaging in an internal debate over whether they were sellouts. They faced conflicting racial alliances with whites in their same class, yet, in terms of race, they grappled with guilt around their "duty" to give back to the black community.[19] Although in *Return of the Jedi* Lando is clearly situated on the side of the "good guys," the broader racial message remained: whites must be guarded toward blacks, and blacks must be evaluated according to their degree of allegiance to white interests.

Lando Calrissian (Billy Dee Williams), a symbol of black upward mobility and the quandary of competing alliances that successful professional blacks face, in *The Empire Strikes Back* (1980).

While the presence of blackness in *Empire* may have smacked of representational political correctness, it was also more forward-thinking than it has been credited with being. No matter how much one speculates on the motivations that brought Lando Calrissian to the sci-fi silver screen and the symbolic meaning of the character, it was a form of tokenism that placed one of the most optimistic faces on racial inclusion in a genre that had historically excluded black representation. Lando, in *Empire Strikes Back*, may have marked the pragmatic use of a black character to dampen criticism of the *Star Wars* saga, up to that point, as racist, or the role may have been merely a case of cinematic tokenism. But any analysis that labels Lando as simply a sidekick or a cardboard character is overlooking the significance of the role to the SF film genre. Lando was not the type of black character that usually occupied SF cinema. Up to that point, black characters in SF cinema were habitually destined to die off quickly, as in *Planet of the Apes* (1968), *THX 1138* (1971), and *Soylent Green* (1973), or to perish, valiantly sacrificing their life for their white counterparts, as in *Star Trek: The Motion Picture* (1979), *Alien* (1979), *Flash Gordon* (1980), and *The Terminator* (1984). Lando Calrissian was unique in that he got to live, not only till the end of *Empire* but all the way to and through the third installment of the series. Here was a black science fiction character who lived to fight another day, though re-

An assembly of spaceship personnel in *Star Trek—The Motion Picture* (1979) exhibits the multiracial and multispecies character of the world in the future.

deeming himself by leading the search for Han Solo's frozen body, and who got promoted, in the later installment, to commander of the Rebellion Alliance's attack on the Empire's Death Star. As a result, the inclusion of Lando in the subsequent *Star Wars* installment, at this point in SF cinema's popularity, was markedly different from the status of previous black characters in the genre.

Yet the *Star Wars* franchise also expressed a "dark side" when it came to meaningful versus symbolic racial inclusion. In the *Star Wars* prequels, George Lucas reopened a semiotic tinderbox of racial stereotypes by reanimating some of the worse examples of racial caricatures in American cinema. In the first prequel, *Star Wars: Episode I—The Phantom Menace* (1999), a sci-fi version of Zip Coon (a black comic stereotype embodied by the Jar Jar Binks character) appears, as well as caricatures of the Japanese as underhanded plotters (an image reminiscent of American WWII propaganda).[20]

Even though *Empire* and *Return of the Jedi* suggested a form of racial tokenism when it came to blackness, the role of Lando marked a trend toward increased racial inclusion in the SF film genre. The increase in black representation in SF films was nominal, however, and often one-dimensional. On one hand, at its most dystopian, black representation in the film *Escape from New York* (1981) articulated a growing anxiety with urban America (coded language for black America) as a degenerating area characterized by excessive criminality and social pathology. On the other hand, *Star Trek—The Motion Picture* (1979) brought a utopian model of racial diversity and cooperation from the television *Star Trek* series onto the silver screen.[21] That is not to say, however, that racial tokenism, exclusion, and even blatant hostility directed toward black characters were no longer present in the genre. For example, in the popular sci-fi comedy *Back to the Future* (1985), a black character is used to deliver a trenchant and cynical critique of the type of black tokenism and upward social mobility signaled by the presence of Lando Calrissian in *The Empire Strikes Back* and *Return of the Jedi.*

REPRODUCING A WHITE UTOPIA

In *Back to the Future,* Marty McFly (Michael J. Fox) is a quirky teenager who accidentally goes back in time thirty years, to 1955. His journey inadvertently starts a chain reaction of events that could cause him, as well as his siblings, not to exist in the future. His task is to redirect the affection his now teenage mother mistakenly has for him and to return to 1985. The narrative centerpiece of *Back to the Future* is an oedipal complex between son and mother. Yet the film performs robust semiotic work around race by symbolically associating the degraded cityscape of Hill Valley with inept black leadership. Marty's personal family crisis, marked by a socially impotent father and an alcoholic mother, is mirrored in the condition of Hill Valley. Boarded-up businesses, schoolyard graffiti, and an adult video-bookstore placed in the center of town indicate that the Hill Valley of 1985 is suffering from severe economic and moral decline. Alongside these visual signifiers of

In *Back to the Future* (1985), a twenty-four-hour pornographic movie house in the center of Hill Valley, the hometown of Marty McFly (Michael J. Fox), indicates the moral state of the town and, by extension, American society.

socioeconomic crisis are posters of the black mayor, Goldie Wilson (Donald Fullilove), scattered throughout downtown Hill Valley.

When Marty arrives in the Hill Valley of 1955, he experiences an acute case of culture shock. He mills around in a daze, taking in the Norman Rockwellesque sights and sounds of a pristine downtown Hill Valley with perfectly manicured parks, prosperous stores, and clean streets. Down the street, a car with a speaker mounted on top cruises by, bearing a poster of an older white man with the words "Re-elect Red Thomas." A voice states that "progress" is Mayor Thomas's middle name and that his progress platform "means more jobs, better education, bigger civic improvements and lower taxes." The voice continues: "On election day cast your vote for a proven leader." This is virtually the same motto as Goldie, the black mayor of Hill Valley in 1985, uses, except that, given the appearance of Hill Valley in 1955 in comparison to 1985, the white mayor of the past achieved significant success in improving the quality of life for Hill Valley residents. Later, Marty meets Goldie in the neighborhood soda shop. Although Goldie is employed as a busboy, Marty inadvertently spurs him to declare that one day he's going to become mayor and clean up Hill Valley. With deft comic timing, he is handed a broom by the shop proprietor and told to start with the floor.

The above visual and narrative elements are the temporal signposts that facilitate the ability of the film to juxtapose the prosperity of 1950s America, symbolized by the virtually all-white Hill Valley, against the urban decay and economic blight of Hill Valley in 1985, literally represented by the black face of the city's mayor. Although this powerful semiotic comparison appears at the margins of the narrative, it is the ideological center of the film. For example, when Marty returns to 1985, the dysfunctional family, the weak father, and the overweight alcoholic mother that he left are no longer present. Instead he discovers an economically successful and fully masculine father, a thinner and happy nonalcoholic mother, and well-adjusted siblings. But unlike the recuperative resolution bestowed on Marty's family and, to a lesser extent, Marty Junior by his return to the present, the town's economic and cultural crisis remains unchanged. Indeed, the audience is reminded of the diminished state of Hill Valley when Marty first materializes back to 1985 and causes a flurry of paper trash to float in the air while simultaneously awakening a homeless white man sleeping on a park bench. The message is unambiguous; the Hill Valley of 1985 remains as economically ailing and dirty as the day Marty left. Moreover, against this backdrop, Goldie's pledge to clean up Hill Valley once he becomes mayor is bizarrely contradictory, given that the Hill Valley of 1955 was pristine and Hill Valley in 1985 is a dirty shell of its former economic grandeur. Racially speaking, Goldie is the face most associated with the ineffective political custodian-

George McFly (Crispin Glover) appears to break out of character as a goofy adolescent upon hearing Goldie (Donald Fullilove) declare that he will become the mayor of Hill Valley in *Back to the Future.*

ship of the city's future and its contemporary decay. As a result, *Back to the Future* clearly signals that the individual success story of black upward social mobility, symbolized by a black soda shop custodian who rises to city mayor, has been at the expense and well-being of white civic society as a whole.

Yet the film also suggests that whites are, in part, responsible for the sociopolitical shortcomings of the type of ineffectual black upward social mobility that Goldie symbolizes. This point is first illustrated in a scene inside the soda shop when Goldie overhears Marty exclaim, "The mayor!" at the sight of the young Goldie ranting that one day he's going to be someone important. After hearing Marty's exclamation, Goldie decides uncritically, on the spot, that he will indeed become the future mayor of Hill Valley. The role of whites as catalysts for black success is reiterated when Marty performs his version of the classic Chuck Berry rock song "Johnny Be Good" at the high school dance of his parents-to-be. As Marty gives an inspired rockabilly guitar performance, a black band member steps offstage, calls an offscreen Chuck Berry, holds the phone up, and allows him to hear the new sound he's been looking for. Again, whiteness becomes the catalyst to explain black achievement, in this case the musical innovation attributed to black Rock and Roll Hall of Fame inductee Chuck Berry. Casting Marty as the source of Chuck Berry's success is mildly amusing. But making Goldie's political success the result of Marty's shocked recognition of him as a young man is crudely cynical. In the latter case, white incredulity has fathered the failed black leadership of 1985 in contrast to the successful stewardship of the 1955 Hill Valley under the "proven leadership" of a white mayor.

The coded critique of black success and upward mobility in *Back to the Future* perfectly dovetailed with conservative political debates and the perception of affirmative action as a policy damaging to American civic society and culture.[22] With his glaring gold-toothed smile, emotional rants, and unproven leadership, the figure of Goldie Wilson in *Back to the Future* is a vulgar signifier of the contemporary consequence of black demands for equal opportunity that are rooted in past racial protest and petition. In this case, the film registers a palpable anger toward black upward social mobility as detrimental to white America and suggests a desire to return to America's past as a blueprint to correct the mistakes of today. The use of the past as the temporal terrain for confronting and correcting contemporary problems is not unique to *Back to the Future*. This film reflected and, in many ways, epitomized a broader cultural impulse to return to a "golden age" of American domestic prosperity. After almost thirty years of social upheaval marked by the loss of the Vietnam War, the black freedom movement, the erosion of male patriarchy with the women's movement, and economic stagflation, America faced a crisis of confidence at the end of the 1970s. In response to the declining stature of the United States on the world stage, along with a battered domestic self-image, Ronald Reagan's presidency conjured up an image of 1950s Americana as a pastime paradise where the nuclear family was intact and white masculinity rode tall in the saddle. The Reagan era anointed the 1980s as the beginning of a decade in which America would return to its traditional greatness. Moreover, a number of science fiction and quasi–science fiction films of the 1980s drew on the political chimera of Ronald Reagan's presidency and his administration's populist message that America would go forward by returning to its former historical greatness. Films such as *Altered States* (1980), *Somewhere in Time* (1980), *The Terminator* (1984), and *Peggy Sue Got Married* (1986) reflected a collective yearning for a simpler time in order to escape present social anxieties. Ultimately, at its most strident, *Back to the Future* reflected this cultural nostalgia, including the regressive racial implications encoded into any political edicts advocating a return to the "good ole days."

SCI-FI CINEMA POST-9/11 AND BEYOND

Black racial representation in American SF cinema in the 1990s demonstrated a shift away from the type of simple tokenism found in the staunchly conservative 1980s. In SF films such as *Predator 2* (1990), *Demolition Man* (1993), *Strange Days* (1995), *The Fifth Element* (1997), and *The Matrix* (1999), the presence of black characters was significant. Most notably, *The Matrix* franchise set a new high-water mark of black representation in SF film far surpassing the spillover effect associated with the rise of blaxploitation cinema during the early to mid-1970s. What can explain the centrality of black representation in a genre known for leaving black people out? Will Smith.

In the same way that Sidney Poitier and Eddie Murphy were pivotal figures who secured a cinematic space for blackness during the 1960s and 1980s, respectively, Will Smith is a seminal figure in American SF cinema. His blend of the racially nonthreatening posture of Sidney Poitier with the charismatic bravado of Eddie Murphy, first placed into service as Captain Steven Hiller in *Independence Day* (1996) and later as Agent Jay in the blockbuster *Men in Black* (1997), proved quite a successful formula. As a result, Will Smith became part film trailblazer, part comic relief, and pure pop sci-fi cool. He laid the groundwork in the 1990s for a more central, defiant, and charismatic version of black cool to enter the SF film genre, even more so than Billy Dee Williams as Lando Calrissian in the 1980s *Star Wars* sequels. Although Denzel Washington starred in a mostly forgotten SF film, *Virtuosity* (1995), it is Will Smith who reinvigorated the status of blackness in SF cinema. Primarily because of his popularity, much of which traded off of his hip-hop persona, his successful television show *(The Fresh Prince of Bel-Air)*, and the mainstream popularity of rap music, he opened the door for black characters to become at least central figures, if not headliners, in a small but growing canon of SF films. In fact, Will Smith's cool-guy persona enabled him to explore strange new worlds and to go places few black actors have ever gone before, such as being the headline star of a major SF motion picture—*I, Robot* (2004).

In the science fiction cinema of the past, it was a host of white protagonists who confronted the science fiction metaphors of American cultural crisis. Now Will Smith as the ultracool black character Del Spooner in *I, Robot* spearheads the charge to confront the SF film metaphors for the troubling social and material conditions of contemporary American life. Despite the obvious racial coding at play in *I, Robot*, with a black man fighting a hoard of white renegade robots, the film is significant in ways that have very little, if anything, to do with racial antagonisms between blacks and whites. First, *I, Robot* is an important cinematic signpost for the changing status of blackness in the genre—the lead character is black. Second, and most importantly, it suggests that, in a post-9/11 America, blackness in SF cinema functions similarly to the way in which black jazz musicians were used by the State Department to stoke the fires of international solidarity with jazz

Will Smith, as Del Spooner, exuding cool when he faces off with an android in *I, Robot* (2004).

tours outside the United States during the cold war. As Penny Von Eschen elegantly underscores in her book *Satchmo Blows Up the World* (2004), the black musicians who participated in the State Department–sponsored international jazz tours were meant to promote an image of a racially integrated America for the international audience to accept. Black representation in this context was thought to be of vital importance in the ideological fight to win the hearts and minds of the populations of Africa, Asia, and the Middle East, whose nations were viewed as potential satellites for communist Russia. In the cold war context of the past, black representation was used to advance an international political agenda. In the wake of September 11, black representation in the SF films of today may function to assuage an acute case of domestic paranoia.

A collective dread and paranoia have settled across much of America, whether fueled by real or imagined details of another terrorist attack, helping to create the general impression that American society and social institutions are, at the least, threatened and will presumably be attacked in the near future. *I, Robot* symbolically expresses this paranoia by depicting an American society with a crippling dependence on robotic energy—a metaphor for America's oil energy dependency—that serves as the catalyst for society's violent downfall. Given that America is now constantly looking over its collective shoulder for the enemy at home, it is culturally comforting in the nervous America of today for black people—who have a very vocal and at times militant history of chastising and challenging white America—to lead the charge to defend America from attack in a sci-fi future. In a context of fears of terrorism, the leading-man heroism of a black character like Del Spooner functions on a grander ideological scale in relationship to the cultural politics of race in post-9/11 America. Lots of larger-than-life heroes, even black science fiction ones, are needed to assure a nation grappling with post-9/11 paranoia that voices of racial dissent, historical or contemporary, are not a threat to domestic security and to affirm the belief that patriotic solidarity transcends racial loyalty, even if only in American pop culture.

Unlike nearly all of the cold war science fiction films of the previous decades, which depict exclusively white worlds, science fiction films of today are making room for black representation to inhabit the center of the formerly racially rarefied space of American SF cinema. Whether the presence of black representation in science fiction film is a symbol of sociopolitical solidarity that serves the cultural needs of a society in crisis or an indicator of the meaningful inclusion of African Americans in all areas of American life—both the real and the imaginary—the future worlds of SF film will point the way. At its best, science fiction cinema challenges the audience to envision a world beyond our current conditions, for better or for worse. Whether or not the genre openly confronts the issue of black racial formation, American SF cinema still reflects the nation's struggle to confront and resolve the nagging problem of race, if for no other reason than that the ideological impulses, premises, possibilities, and limitations of black representation in American SF cinema have been and will continue to be a function of the oscillating state of race relations in American society.

CHAPTER 2

BAD BLOOD

Fear of Racial Contamination

> The end of the world lay in their eyes, and the beginning, and all the waste in between.
> TONI MORRISON, *The Bluest Eye*

After America's use of not one but two atomic bombs in World War II, the fear of nuclear annihilation became a common element in scores of science fiction films of the 1950s. Here was a doomsday weapon that was no mere deterrent but a military option America had proven it was not afraid to exercise. Consequently, such fears were not unreasonable. A social by-product of America's nuclear assertiveness was an increasing hysteria concerning the fate of the world, which was confirmed by everyday U.S. citizens who felt compelled to purchase bomb shelters as protection from the proverbial "beginning of the end." Even more, however, were motivated to purchase movie tickets to films that delivered the dreaded nuclear doomsday or offered unsightly images of giant insects, monsters, and human mutation, born of atomic energy, at which they could gawk in slack-jawed surprise.[1] Yet, in many ways, it was the iconic image of a mushroom cloud that scared American audiences into awareness of the negative consequences of atomic militarism that were portrayed in SF film. Radioactive contamination was the frequent trope used to underscore the destruction of the world and stir acute feelings of nuclear dread. Post-WWII SF films habitually confronted the negative consequences of nuclear warfare in the form of radioactive contamination. The genre, however, also grappled with another form of contamination—racial.

Race is the ultimate science fiction, and America has a lengthy history of promulgating how biological features such as skin pigmentation, hair texture, eye color, and facial features are used not just to classify people into different racial groups but also, unfortunately, to justify preconceived notions of each race's behavioral characteristics and mental abilities. The culmination of these superficial biological differences is the idea of and belief in superior and inferior races.[2] At its most strident, the social construction of race expresses the concept of racial purity and, through a mishmash of scientific jargon and rudimentary elements of Darwinism, legitimizes and justifies social and sexual boundaries and compels races to maintain and enforce them. Nowhere is this concept clearer in practice than in the colloquially defined "one-drop rule," which asserts that "one drop" of "black blood" compromises white racial purity.[3] Despite the spurious and pseudoscientific nature of the "rule," blood is not categorized by race but by types: A+, A–, AB+, O+, and so on. Nevertheless, this racial convention is an integral part of the cultural politics of race in American society in which "black blood" is viewed as not only a potent pollutant but also a fundamental element in assembling an essentialized racial identity for both whites and blacks. Furthermore, the fear of black racial contamination, along with the "scientific" racism that informs it, is blatantly found in American cinema.

One of the crudest representations of the fear of racial miscegenation is found in D. W. Griffith's epic film, *The Birth of a Nation* (1915). The film depicted black men in savage pursuit of white women to rape and impregnate. Such incendiary imagery provided the more-than-three-hour film with such an emotional wallop it served not only to affirm the idea that interracial sexual unions were an abomination but to justify the Ku Klux Klan as a constructive civic organization committed to protecting the rights, privileges, and integrity of white American citizenship. Although the racial extremism found in *The Birth of a Nation* drew on the post-Reconstruction racial anxiety of the era, the anxiety over racial purity, racial classification, and how "black blood" might compromise the status of whiteness in America is not anachronistic. Racial anxiety still persists around the collapse of rigid racial boundaries and is found across a range of popular media, including the SF film genre. An anxiety surrounding interracial sexuality rests at the center of several SF films, along with draconian notions of racial purity and genetic contamination. In a variety of ways, films such as *The World, the Flesh, and the Devil* (1959), *The Omega Man* (1971), *The Thing* (1982), *Blade Runner* (1982), *Gattaca* (1997), *Star Wars: Episode I — The Phantom Menace* (1999), and *28 Days Later* (2002) draw on racial eugenics and reflect America's history of hypersurveillance of racial boundaries. On a broader ideological level these narratives suggest — despite African Americans holding unprecedented, respected, and even admired social positions in U.S. society as government leaders and celebrated athletes and pop stars—a palpable uneasiness with the struggle for and consequences of full social integration of blacks (and other nonwhites) into the American body politic.

INTERRACIAL SEX IN THE CITY

The World, the Flesh, and the Devil (1959) tackles two of America's most visceral social fears in one film. The cold war paranoia about radioactive contamination is combined with the fear of racial contamination. Two men and one woman, by varying circumstances not fully explained, survive the effects of a global-wide occurrence of radioactive fallout. The three survivors—Ralph Burton (Harry Belafonte), a handsome black man; Sarah Crandall (Inger Stevens), a nubile white woman; and Benson Thacker (Mel Ferrer), a slightly older white male—eventually find one another in a deserted New York City, where they seek to rebuild a life out of the elegant ruins of the deserted metropolis. Montages of deserted buildings and streets are used to reinforce the appearance that Ralph is the only human alive as he makes his way through the center of the city. When he decides to take up residence in an apartment building with a vacancy sign advertising a two-bedroom apartment for rent, he is unaware that Sarah has been secretively studying his actions. As he scans the horizon before going into the high-rise apartment building, an empty baby carriage begins rolling down the street. The scene is flagrantly encoded with sexual innuendo. Will Sarah take up residence with him in the apartment? Will these interracial symbols of Adam and Eve have a child to fill the empty baby carriage? Despite the visual spectacle of a postapocalyptic New York City full of deserted streets and vacant skyscrapers, these are the questions driving the plot.

The sexual politics of race become even more amplified in the film when Sarah and Ralph finally meet. A strange relationship ensues in which, through stilted dialogue and crude polemics, Ralph continually rebuffs Sarah's subtle and not-so-subtle invitations to have an intimate relationship. As if Ralph's increasingly shrill protest to maintain strict racial boundaries in a world populated only by the two of them was not enough, Ralph and Sarah live in crosstown apartment residences to ensure that they do not have sex. Despite both characters expressing attraction to one another and having the entire city, if not the world, to themselves, Ralph vehemently objects to Sarah's sexual advances. This stalemate is broken, however, with the arrival of the third character, Benson, who aggressively pursues Sarah. He introduces the "world" back into the interracial equation formulated in his absence. Benson is the viable racial alternative for Sarah's affections, as well as a sym-

Ralph (Harry Belafonte) and Sarah (Inger Stevens) pensively stare into the distance in
The World, the Flesh, and the Devil (1959).

bolic wedge between the white "flesh" and the black "devil." A love trian-
gle develops between the survivors, with the two men jockeying for front-
runner position to win the affection of the only woman left alive in this
brave new world. The stakes are high—the repopulation of the planet—and
the "winner" will pair up with the last woman on Earth to repopulate it.

Benson and Sarah do pair up, but Sarah is unable to consummate the
relationship because of her residual and confused feelings for Ralph. This
spurs Benson to take matters into his own hands. The phallocentric symbolism encoded in Benson's solution to his sexual frustration with Sarah is
blatantly apparent when he acquires a rifle but gives Ralph a small pistol to
defend himself. With the entire city of New York as an urban jungle, Ralph
becomes the hunted, with both men ducking around corners, running atop
roofs, and shooting and being shot at in a two-man race war. Soon after,
Ralph arrives outside the United Nations, decides to throw away his firearm, and marches back weaponless to confront Benson. Ralph's nonviolent
gambit is rewarded, with Benson throwing aside his rifle and admitting that
Ralph is the better man.

In the aftermath of the confrontation between the two men, Sarah and
Ralph clasp hands. This is the real source of tension in the film, the possibility that Ralph and Sarah will repopulate Earth with racially mixed children. But what is Benson's future, the symbolic representative of the white
"world" of racism, now that he has been defeated and proven unworthy of
Sarah's body? He is redeemed. As the camera follows a dejected and "beaten"
Benson walking off in the distance, Sarah calls out for him to come back.
The film ends with Sarah between the men as they all hold hands and walk
down the middle of a deserted street, with the words "The Beginning" super-
imposed across the screen before it fades to black.

Certainly, the film's finale draws on the civil rights movement's integrationist ethos by symbolically affirming that the nonviolent fight for racial justice holds the moral high ground and recodes Ralph as a chaste angel and not the "devil" of the film's title. Benson's armed opposition to Ralph and Sarah's "relationship" symbolizes virulent white racism. In comparison, Ralph's nonviolent tactic mirrors the burgeoning civil rights movement's approach to dismantling the system of racial segregation. Moreover, by having Benson throw down his rifle and abandon his hatred of Ralph, the film unambiguously reveals its ideological support and embrace of the nonviolent civil rights movement of the time. But the film still struggles to reconcile the sexual politics of racial miscegenation, so discordantly developed in the film's narrative, with the sociopolitics of integration. The result is one of the oddest resolutions in SF film history: black integration is equated with sexual penetration. But instead of the overtly frightening picture of rape that D. W. Griffith provided in *The Birth of a Nation*, the film imagines the fight for racial integration in an extremely literal fashion, as indicated by the conclusion's suggestion that racial equality and the beginning of a racial utopia are to be found in a bizarre triad of a black man and a white man "sharing" a white woman between them.

On one hand, the film labors to recast interracial relationships as an archaic social taboo and get beyond the constraints of race. On the other hand, the film only partially manages to do so by having Ralph and Sarah, ostensibly the last two human beings alive, choosing to live as far apart as possible, deny their sexual attraction to one another, and, in the end, invite Benson to tag along with them. Despite the attempt to pose racial miscegenation as an arcane taboo, the sexual tension generated by the unconventional pairing of a black man with a white woman is constantly constrained by the draconian demands of the prevailing racial etiquette operating outside the film. In 1950s America, black men and white woman were, at the least, expected to stay at a distance from one another. In fact, for black men even to look at or talk to a white woman could be fatal, a reality of life that gained national attention in 1955 with the brazen murder of Emmett Till, a fourteen-year-old black boy, by white men for allegedly making a suggestive remark toward a white woman. The Mississippi murder exemplified the suffocating racism of the South, where "reckless eyeballing" of a white woman could even cost a black child his life. Given this sociopolitical backdrop, it is easy to see why an SF film that has a black character as the protagonist and a white woman as the love interest, in the final analysis, is anchored in the extremely strident racial attitudes of the time and hamstrung by the racial temperament of 1950s America.

In the final analysis, *The World, the Flesh, and the Devil* illustrates the broader cultural uneasiness with the push for black integration rising to the surface and the latent desire to make sure that racial integration, if it was going to occur, must at least be monitored if it could no longer be contained. The sexual setup the audience is left with supports this conclusion. Although the film's ending has orgiastic implications for the three characters and Benson's status as an alternative suitor is significantly diminished, the film firmly suggests that his presence is required, at least as an observer of the interracial romance that Ralph and Sarah appear to embrace. Either way, orgiastic or voyeuristic, the film symbolically associates and affirms black-white integration with not only the end of civilization as we know it but also the beginning of an unusual set of sexual mores.[4] Without a doubt this film demonstrates how SF film, although considered an imaginative canvas, not only is constrained by the racial logic operating outside the film but also is understandable only in relationship to that logic. In *The World, the Flesh, and the Devil*, the sexual politics of race is clearly overdetermined by societal racial prejudice of the period and ends up rearticulating racial taboos in a postapocalyptic setting where race supposedly no longer matters. In the decades that followed, science fiction cinema would present even more overt depictions of the strange and dangerous world of postapocalyptic racial integration.

The Omega Man (1971)—in comparison with the box office success of *Planet of the Apes* (1968), and the multitude of sequels, television shows, and toys it generated, or *Soylent Green* (1973), a cult film and subject of parody on *Saturday Night Live*—is the most obscure of the trinity of SF films starring Charlton Heston. Yet, in this writer's mind, *The Omega Man* is just as prominent because of how clearly it imagines and associates race mixing with dire postapocalyptic consequences. In the film, biological warfare has caused the release of a deadly airborne microbe, and Robert Neville (Charlton Heston), a former army doctor, was able to administer an experimental vaccine only to himself. As a result, he becomes the last man on Earth, the omega man. During the day, Neville roams the abandoned city streets of Los Angeles with an automatic machine gun, attempting to track down a "nest" of mutated survivors of the toxic microbe. During the evening, he holes up in his apartment, ignoring the droning chants and speeches by the mutant survivors who denounce him and periodically fending off their attempts to storm his fourth-floor penthouse. The small band of mutated humans has acquired an extreme form of albinism, marked by peculiar grayish white face paint similar to Japanese Kabuki makeup. The albino mutants refer to themselves as "the Family" and consider themselves a new race of men and

The ghoulish members of "the Family" in *The Omega Man* (1971).

women. Furthermore, Matthias (Anthony Zerbe), the leader of the albino mutants, sees it as their duty to destroy all those who do not bear the physical marks of the Family. Consequently, for them, Neville must be eliminated as the last remaining symbol of evil from the old world.

Interestingly, the representation and rhetoric of the albino mutants provide startling similarities to the Black Power radicals and movement of the late 1960s to early 1970s. First, like the Black Power activists of the era, the mutants wear dark sunglasses as they provide soapbox speeches to their followers regarding the evil of "the Man" (Neville). Second, the mutants wear only black robes and hoods, which work to code the colorless mutants as "black."[5] Third, the mutants use Molotov cocktails to attack Neville at night, clearly signifying the racial unrest of the late sixties that erupted across the nation with a spate of urban cities in flames. Finally, in their condemnation of Neville, the mutants' rhetoric mirrors the Nation of Islam's extremist articulation of black nationalism. The Nation of Islam, a black nationalistic quasi-cult organization, advocated the idea that whites were "devils" united in systematically oppressing black people.[6] Similarly, the albino mutants of *The Omega Man* rail against Neville, ostensibly the last remaining white man on Earth, by depicting him as the personification of evil and referring to him as a "devil." Although the text vigorously signifies the Black Power politics of the period, the focal emphasis of the narrative revolves around racial eugenics.

The eugenic aspect of the narrative emerges shortly after Neville is rescued from his mutant captors by Lisa (Rosalind Cash), a black woman, and Dutch (Paul Koslo), a young white male. The trio escapes on motorcycles to a countryside sanctuary, where Neville is introduced to a small band of children protected by Lisa and Dutch. They inform him that his expertise as a doctor is needed, in the hope that he can help Richie (Eric Laneuville), Lisa's younger brother, from transforming into a mutant, a process they call "going over." After examining Richie, Neville reveals that his own blood is the serum that can cure the adolescent black male and all the others who have not yet "gone over." Later, Richie is set up for a blood transfusion from a bottle of Neville's blood. Concerned about the effectiveness of the treatment, Lisa asks Neville, "Will one bottle be enough?" Neville lightheartedly assures her that one bottle is more than enough by telling her it is "genuine 160-proof old Anglo-Saxon, baby." Jokes aside, this statement has serious racial implications for the meaning and message of the film. The ability of Neville's white blood to reverse the symptoms of a black teenager about to "go over" is a powerful racial metaphor, with white blood presented as a means to cure and repopulate a diseased and dying world. Moreover, the use of Neville's blood as the cure-all draws on the dual racial eugenic propositions that not only is black blood a contaminant to white bloodlines but white blood is also considered a neutralizing agent for biologically dictated mental deficiencies in blacks.[7] While such propositions are shrouded in questionable "scientific" evidence and methods,[8] it is interesting to see how diligently *The Omega Man* works to construct an aura of scientific authority around the curative properties of white Anglo-Saxon blood. Indeed, Neville is shown evoking virtually all the signifiers of objective science in his drive to cure Ritchie: a laboratory, a white lab coat, tourniquets, bandages, gauze, test tubes, microscopes, beakers, and vials of blood. Eventually, Neville's scientific expertise pays off. With his Anglo-Saxon blood coursing through his black patient, the virus is neutralized and Richie is undeniably cured.

As in *The World, the Flesh, and the Devil*, the possibility of interracial sexual coupling in *The Omega Man* and repopulation of the planet is a source of dramatic tension. In *The Omega Man*, however, unlike in the former film,

The pseudoscience of racial eugenics is prominently coded as legitimate scientific research in *The Omega Man*.

Unlike the interracial couple in *The World, the Flesh, and the Devil*, Neville (Charlton Heston) and Lisa (Rosalind Cash) in *The Omega Man* (1971) consummate their mutual attraction to one another.

the sexual desires between the interracial couple are not repressed but de- monstratively confirmed. Neville and Lisa are shown basking in postcoital bliss and later visiting a dilapidated drugstore where Lisa glibly tosses a box of birth control pills over her shoulder as the two look at one another and engage in a hearty laugh. But the levity expressed toward Neville and Lisa as an interracial postapocalyptic Adam and Eve repopulating Earth soon gives way to grave consequences. The theme of racial allegiance is signaled by the competing loyalties involving Neville's family and "the Family." Neville and Lisa are certainly a couple, and with Neville's blood flowing through the black teenager, Richie symbolically represents the couple's racially mixed child. Moreover, Neville, Lisa, and Richie are a symbolic family that stands in contrast to the mutant "Family" in the film. However, Richie, as the symbolic son, runs away from "home" to tell the mutant "Family" of a possible cure, and Lisa "goes over" to the other side, allowing the mutants into Neville's apartment. The ensuing destruction of Neville's home and eventually his death show that the consequences of race mixing, both sci- entific and sexual, have volatile and unstable results, despite any auspicious beginnings. The symbolic betrayal of Neville by the black members of his family, demonstrated by their "going over" to the other side, lends support to the racial message delivered by the film's dramatic conclusion.

Although Neville, with Lisa in tow, is able to escape past Mathias's mu- tant goons and find cover outside in a brightly lit water fountain below his apartment, Mathias is able to throw a spear from the balcony that strikes Neville in the chest. Blood gushes out so profusely from the wound that it creates a pool. As dawn breaks, Dutch, driving a van full of children, arrives to see the bloody consequence of the previous night's events—Lisa sprawled at the foot of the fountain, and Neville propped up against the fountainhead, soaking in a pool of blood and barely alive. Before dying, Neville hands a bottle of his blood over to Dutch. The concluding image is a freeze-frame of Neville's dead body with his arms outstretched, as if crucified, lying across the fountain. Besides clearly signaling Neville's Christ-like status and sacrifice, the end of this film is important because of the way the color red is used not just in the gory and exaggerated loss of blood depicted in the conclusion of the film but also with semiotic significance throughout the film. Whether it is the all-red convertible Neville confidently drives at the beginning of the film, the red pieces he plays with in his solitary chess game, the red turtleneck shirt he wears under his white lab coat when working to cure Richie, or the red middle finger ("fuck you") painted on the back of the jean jacket worn by Neville's symbolic successor, Dutch, the color is associated with white male self-assurance. Red is virtually a character, a presence that is reinforced at every visual opportunity to signal a connection between the color, blood, and white male virility.

The symbolic significance of red in *The Omega Man* works as a dual source of semiotic meaning; it both signifies the diminishing stature of mature institutional white masculinity and affirms a promise of revitalized white male strength. The discovery of such signification in *The Omega Man* is not surprising, given that the film was released in the wake of race riots, Black Power, Vietnam War protests, and the growing women's movement. All of these social movements contributed to a collective perception that white masculinity and the institutions it was associated with were under attack and in decline. Politically, institutions that symbolized white masculinity were under attack at the time, but naked aggression against white men as individual citizens was a far cry from protests and petitions directed at discriminatory laws and the questionable foreign policy of the time. *The Omega Man*, however, brings the most fearful of these racial and gender anxieties to a culmination with the figure of Neville, a white military male, under siege by a horde of black-robed zealots. With its visual coding of blackness, *The Omega Man* was a thinly veiled attack against the black nationalist stage of the black freedom movement. Whereas *The World, the Flesh, and the Devil* ideologically endorsed the nonviolent integration philosophy of the civil rights movement, *The Omega Man* reflected the real-world racial paranoia over black militancy's spread to urban centers across America.[9] The film communicates the message that traditional white males are under attack. The bleak image of Neville, the failed military officer, as crucified victim foreshadows the fatalistic impulse of white masculinity and the narcissistic self-pity of white male martyrdom—represented here by Neville's wallowing in a pool of his own blood—that became a signature feature of Hollywood's post-Vietnam films. The SF film image of white male martyr-

Neville as a symbol of white male martyrdom in *The Omega Man*.

dom cropped up in films like *Coming Home* (1978), *The Deer Hunter* (1978), and *Midnight Express* (1978), films that repackaged white masculinity in tragic or flawed, yet extremely empathetic, figures.

Despite the downbeat end of *The Omega Man* signaled by Neville's death, all is not lost. Neville lives long enough to make sure that the last bottle of pure Anglo-Saxon blood is handed over to Dutch, for prudent distribution, as he heads out of the city. Ideologically, *The Omega Man* offered a strident message for curing the American body politic of its race relations problem. The end of the film suggested that the next generation of white males reassert their biological birthright in the American countryside, away from the urban cityscape haunted by "black" mutants. Indeed, in subsequent years America would experience the proliferation of a survivalist movement in which small cadres of white men and their families, similar to the group at the ending of *The Omega Man*, began fleeing to the American hinterland for peace and security. In some instances the survivalist movement advocated a back-to-nature racism, where the city was viewed as a place of moral and social decay dominated by racial minorities. This sentiment would even spawn its own racist SF survivalist literature in which white Aryan guerrilla armies would complete the mission that *The Omega Man* suggests—racial "purification."[10] For these white-power survivalists, the only effective cure to America's race problem was similar to the one stated in *The Omega Man*: a "genuine 160-proof old Anglo-Saxon" one.

CONTAINING THE RACIAL OTHER

Like *The Omega Man*, *The Thing* (1982) uses blood to explore themes of contamination and the need for "scientific" testing to ensure normality, except that the transparent allusion to the power and promise of white racial purity found in *The Omega Man* takes on a more opaque presence in *The Thing*. Nevertheless, *The Thing* is deeply inscribed with the paranoid logic of racial eugenics—that just below the surface of white racial appearance may lurk the "impure" and dangerous black racial "other" and, as a result, "experts" are required to test and measure "bad" black blood and to locate its carriers. In John Carpenter's *The Thing*, a remake of Howard Hawks's *The Thing from Another World* (1951), the hidden alien "other" must be found and destroyed by a group of racially heterogeneous scientists and support technicians (seven white men and two black men) conducting research in the Antarctic. They come into contact with an alien creature that can replicate any nearby organism. By the time the men figure out that replication is a survival technique of the alien organism, there are several Things lurking around the base camp, waiting to eliminate the remaining humans. This scenario sets into motion a series of events that play to the paranoia of the men in the film, as well as the audience's suspicions as to who is human and who only appears human. The result is a film that symbolically calls most into question the black characters' human authenticity and indulges in the notion that blacks cannot be trusted.

Yet, on an even sharper ideological note, the film draws on the eugenics movement's paranoia of racial "passing." Because the alien's survival technique of surreptitious replication enables it to pass for human, the Things have an undeniable affinity with the cultural politics of racial assimilation and black racial identity. Like the Things in the film, some African Americans have also constructed a false but convincing exterior identity as members of the dominant racial group. Moreover, in a world where racial appearances can be deceiving, the promise of eugenics—a scientific means to discern racial genealogy—offered hope for ensuring that white bloodlines would not be surreptitiously contaminated.[11] In this sense, the ability of the Thing to pass as a human is similar to the ability of blacks with exceedingly light complexions to pass as white for the purpose of infiltration and enjoyment of the power and privileges that white racial identity carries. The anxiety over "passing" and the promise of eugenic testing are symbolically underscored in one of the most humorous yet horrifyingly tension-filled scenes in American SF cinema.

R. J. MacReady (Kurt Russell), the main protagonist, creates a crude blood experiment to determine which of the remaining five men suspected of being a Thing is indeed one. The rationale informing this makeshift blood test is that the alien has an extreme drive for survival, and MacReady theorizes that placing the heated tip of a metal wire into each man's blood sample will cause a visible reaction if one of them is a Thing. After MacReady presses a heated wire inside a petri dish containing blood, a glob of it leaps out of the container and onto the floor. Almost immediately, one of the tied men begins to mutate but is burned to death by MacReady's flame thrower. Unable to trust those still alive, MacReady keeps the men tied to the charred remains of the alien while he tests each man's blood to delineate the good from the bad, the "pure" from the "contaminated," and the inferior from the superior.

On the surface, the monstrous spectacle of difference in this scene is a signature feature of the film. Self-revelation is visually emphasized throughout *The Thing* in various displays of phantasmagoric metamorphosis. A decapitated head that grows spider legs, a chest cavity that opens up to reveal sharklike teeth, and dogs that convulse and crack open to spew ropelike tendrils across the length of a room are just a few of the startling visual effects of self-revelation peppered throughout the film, underscoring how, beneath a normal appearance, these beings are monstrously deformed, defective, and, above all, mongrelized. The outrageous permutations that the Thing exhibits are both disturbing and impressive in their shocking verisimilitude, but the special effects that are a centerpiece of this particular film also intersect with a broader discourse of biological racism. Given that two of the remaining subjects who are suspected of being a Thing are black, the scene is highly charged with racial symbolism concerning the eugenics movement, which has a long record of couching nonwhite races as physically abnormal, mongrel, and alien.[12] Consequently, the phantasmagoric imagery of discovery of a Thing, a signature aesthetic of the film, also functions as a visual analogue to the hyperbolic rhetoric of racial difference associated with the eugenics movement.

The narrative lends support to the film's symbolic affinity with biological racism by depicting white and black race relations as extremely antagonistic. Of the nine men stationed at the isolated research base, the two black characters, Nauls (T. K. Carter) and Childs (Keith David), have been the most at odds with the white protagonist, MacReady. Childs has expressed open hostility toward MacReady's leadership by constantly bickering with him, and late in the film Nauls abandons MacReady in the blinding snow under the assumption that he's a Thing. When MacReady is forced to break into the camp after being purposefully locked out, Childs and Nauls are shown backing MacReady into a corner, where he delivers the racially inflected indictment, "You little sweethearts were about to have yourselves a little lynching party." MacReady characterizes the intended attack on him as a "lynching party," an extralegal practice historically used by whites against blacks. By having the principal white male character invoke lynching to underscore his

MacReady (Kurt Russell) prepares to use a flamethrower and dynamite to fend off an attack in *The Thing* (1982).

victimization, the film alludes to race relations between blacks and whites as life-threateningly antagonistic, a point clearly indicated in the film's ending.

Successful at blowing up the research camp in hope of killing the alien, but unsuccessful in determining if the alien has replicated again, MacReady can only speculate as to the human status of the only remaining person left, Childs. As if on opposite sides of a chess board contemplating the other's next move, they stare at one another from across a dwindling fire, coolly discussing which one of them could be the alien, along with their likelihood of freezing to death. They decide that their only choice is to wait and see what happens later. The film slowly fades to black. This unresolved conclusion ostensibly leaves the audience questioning who the alien is.[13] Because the narrative has followed the actions of the MacReady character as he succeeded in blowing up the base camp and has left the Childs character offscreen until this last scene, the narrative clues appear to suggest that Childs is the alien. Even if neither is in fact a Thing, the subtext of racial antagonism present throughout the film fully erupts in the unresolved ending, which points to the idea that the black character who has been the most vocal in challenging white authority is a monster in disguise. In doing so, the final scene reads as a racial standoff between the two and dredges up acute racial antagonisms fueled by rivalry in the American economic order during the 1980s. The final scene reflects the economic paranoia of the period, when, much like the characters in the ending of *The Thing*, whites and blacks viewed themselves as pitted against one another while trying to survive in the "cold" of a deepening recession. Beginning in the early 1980s, many working- and middle-class whites believed that their economic well-being was threatened by underqualified and unqualified black workers because of affirmative action.[14]

The threat was more perception than reality. Even though a waning American manufacturing economy was to blame, nevertheless a structural economic problem was interpreted as a racial one.

Because of rapidly shrinking job opportunities in traditional American manufacturing sectors, like the automobile industry, the early 1980s was economically depressing for many working-class Americans. For science fiction film fans, however, it was a boom time. The release of SF films such as *Flash Gordon* (1980), *Outland* (1981), *The Road Warrior* (1981), *E.T. the Extra-Terrestrial* (1982), *The Thing* (1982), *Tron* (1982), *Dune* (1984), and *The Terminator* (1984) and the rerelease of Fritz Lang's *Metropolis* (1927/1984) with a pop/rock-and-roll sound track marked a productive period in which many SF films attained classic or at the least cult film status. Of all the SF films released in the early 1980s, *Blade Runner* (1982), the film adaptation of the novel *Do Androids Dream of Electric Sheep?* by avant-garde SF writer Philip K. Dick, stood out as a great SF classic. Unlike SF films of the 1970s such as THX 1138, *Logan's Run*, and *Star Wars*, which presented a unified ultramodern and technological aesthetic and depicted a bright, almost antiseptically clean future world, *Blade Runner* reversed the commonly pristine image of the future. In the film, the Los Angeles of 2019 is a dark, dystopian, overpopulated, rain-drenched, and decaying metropolis. These aesthetic elements effectively combined to create a form of science fiction noir[15] in which multiple anxieties of American race relations unfold against a moody futurescape.

Ostensibly, *Blade Runner* is about Rick Deckard (Harrison Ford), a futuristic bounty hunter who is forced out of retirement in order to exterminate four Replicants—genetically engineered lifelike androids that escaped to Earth from an Off-world colony and killed several humans in the process. The Replicants are slaves on other colonized planets and are not allowed on Earth. These Replicants, however, are more than just synthetic life-forms on the run; they function as compelling symbols of black racial formation in America. First, the narrative backstory of the Replicants codes them as black. As escaped slaves from an Off-world site, Replicants share the same socioeconomic status as that of enslaved Africans during America's period of legalized slavery—their presence and existence are predicated on their exclusive use as exploited labor. Second, the site of exploitative labor and living relations for Replicants, Off-world, has the historical analogue of the southern plantation. Third, the link between Replicant slavery and African American slavery is clearly signified when Rachael (Sean Young), after being revealed to be a Replicant, openly contemplates the possibility of fleeing for freedom and asks Deckard, "What if I go north? Disappear? Would you come after me?" The reference to the "north" as a site of freedom and economic promise has long been associated with the aspirations of blacks during enslavement and the Jim Crow segregationist era.[16] Finally, as if this blatant coding of the Replicants as black was not enough, there is the use of the word "skin-jobs" by Deckard's superior, Captain Bryant (M. Emmet Walsh), when referring to Replicants. In the theatrically released version of *Blade Runner*, the word "skin-jobs" is signaled as racially derogatory when Deckard narrates that "in history books he's [Captain Bryant] the kind of cop that used to call black men niggers." With that statement, Bryant's use of "skin-job" is equivalent to the racial epithet "nigger."[17] Consequently, although there is an absence of any black people in the film, the Replicants of 2019 are coded as the "niggers" of this future world. This places *Blade Runner*, as a film, in a broader web of racial meaning than the narrow and primarily postmodern readings the film has generated.[18]

Blade Runner blatantly references America's racially exploitative past and imagines a return of the repressed. By having several symbolically black Replicants come back to kill their white creators, the film also expresses America's fear of racial contamination vis-à-vis genetic manipulation and infiltration. The biological testing and scientific inspection of blood that are central to *The Omega Man* and *The Thing* are replaced in *Blade Runner* by an emotional test akin to a "psychological" IQ exam, but nevertheless, as in the two previous films, the testing of the racial or racially coded "other" is presented as "scientific" spectacle. Early in *Blade Runner* a Replicant is shown sitting across from a well-dressed man who asks several questions. When the interrogator asks about his mother, the Replicant responds by firing a concealed weapon that literally blows the interrogator across the room. Later, Rachael, a Replicant unaware of her nonhuman status, is tested in a cavernous, ultrastylized Egyptian art deco corporate office. These two scenes respectively revel in the hyperbole of violence and extreme wealth to communicate the explosive and sublime wonder of discovering the disturbing information that those who claim to be like "us" are in reality the racialized "other." Blackness, however, in *Blade Runner* is purely symbolic. The presence of black people in *Blade Runner* is squarely located in the past—that is, the "history books" that Deckard's narration suggests—and the visual absence of black people in *Blade Runner* further reinforces the idea that "blackness" itself is historical and no longer exists or at least exerts no visible influence on the Los Angeles cityscape of the future.

The only visible overt racial imprint of significance is the hypersaturation of Asian cultural signs throughout the city in the form of language, people, and advertisements. The structured absence of black people in this

The cityscape of Los Angeles in the future is overshadowed by Asian iconography in *Blade Runner.*

context is primarily constructed as a historical foil to juxtapose the old race-relations problem of the past with the impending race-relations problem of the future. This contradistinction between old and the new is an aesthetic staple of the film. *Blade Runner* creatively juxtaposes urban decay and dilapidation against the technological wonder of flying cars that seamlessly escape the pull of gravity. Likewise, the encoded racial discourse of the film is about juxtaposition. In this case, the historical model of black-white binary race relations symbolized by the Replicant "other" is juxtaposed against the impending multicultural future signaled by the Asian iconography that has displaced all that is "American" in the Los Angeles of the future. In this sense, although "blackness" figures as a substantial part of the racial coding presented in *Blade Runner*, it is by no means the defining aspect of this hyper-racialized text. Rather, "Asian-ness" operates as a powerful oxymoronic aesthetic in *Blade Runner*, in which the *background* use of Asian iconography *foregrounds* Asian-ness in the film.

Emblematic of the background/foregrounding of the Asianization of Los Angeles is a giant television-billboard that alternates between a Coca-Cola logo and an Asian woman, in traditional attire, pantomiming the consumption of a small pill. Along with this striking imagery, traditional Japanese music, which periodically plays as an ambient diegetic melody, and the language spoken on the street—"city-speech," an amalgamation of Japanese, Spanish, and German, as defined by Deckard's narration—both cumulatively underscore the displacement of American hegemony in the film. It is against this backdrop of Asian "otherness" that Rick Deckard's whiteness starkly reflects multiple points of crisis in American hegemony and cultural self-perception. This identity crisis is illustrated in the narrative eulogy Deckard gives, toward the end of the film, to explain why Roy (Rutger

Hauer), the remaining Replicant, decides to let Deckard remain alive after hunting him down in a lengthy and violent pursuit through an abandoned building.

The chase concludes on a rooftop, where Deckard is bloody, beaten, and trembling at the feet of his enemy. As Roy kneels and quietly dies, Deckard narrates over this surprising turn of events, "All he'd wanted were the same answers the rest of us want: Where do I come from? Where am I going? How long have I got?" These reflective ruminations on the meaning of existence are more than just a narrative shortcut for explaining a set of motivations that appear out of character, given the series of murders Roy has previously committed without any remorse. The questions—above all, the last two— that Deckard, as narrator, raises speak to the existential crisis of American identity in the early 1980s. Where was America headed after almost thirty years of social upheaval marked by the militant Black Power movement, erosion of male patriarchy with the women's movement, the undeclared defeat suffered in the Vietnam War, the resignation of a president, economic stagflation, and a deep sense of cultural malaise? Given the scope and depth of such societal maladies, the longevity of America's stature as the moral and economic compass of the world appeared, as Roy eloquently expressed before his demise, "lost . . . in time . . . like tears in the rain."

Fundamentally, the rain-drenched dystopia of Los Angeles in *Blade Runner* reflected a growing uneasiness with American postindustrial decline in the face of Asian technological and economic ascendancy of the early 1980s. The beginning of the decade witnessed the rise of the Pacific Rim as an economic juggernaut, particularly in relation to Japan's burgeoning automobile industry. The phenomenal success of imported Japanese cars prodded many American consumers and producers to reconsider the socioeconomic pride and power signified by the slogan "Made in America." In some, America's diminishing manufacturing status even fanned the flames of racial prejudice. The savage murder in 1982 of Vincent Chin, a Chinese American, with a baseball bat—by two white males who blamed Japan, and by extension anyone who looked Japanese to them, for undermining the American automobile industry—epitomized how America's declining global economic stature could bring out the worst in domestic race relations. In the popular consciousness of white America, the ethnoeconomic writing was on the wall. It appeared that Japan was on the verge of accomplishing economically what it could not accomplish militarily—the defeat of America—and *Blade Runner* was the projection of that future defeat, represented as cultural subordination to the Pacific Rim vis-à-vis the film's Asian cityscape.

In terms of the cultural politics of race, what is unique about *Blade Run-*

ner is that it demonstrates a shift away from a black-white binary-coded paranoia about American race relations found in most American SF films. Instead, a growing anxiety with the Asian "other" is present in the film, despite Asian Americans often being singled out as the perfect embodiment of successful assimilation, America's "model minority."[19] Although the narrative of the film alludes to racial eugenics, racial containment, and a crisis of contamination vis-à-vis the racially coded Replicants as dangerous, genetically manufactured beings that "pass" as humans and must be discovered and destroyed, the arresting vision of a future Los Angeles cityscape transformed to look like downtown Tokyo overshadows the biological racial anxiety represented by the Replicants. The visual hyperbole of Asian iconography in *Blade Runner* culminates in signifying America's fear of economic subordination to the Pacific Rim by using the trope of cultural contamination and projecting it on a grand scale. In the end, the film ideologically functioned as a cautionary tale, warning America to keep a vigilant eye toward the Pacific Rim, as well as toward the Asian American at home.

DISCOURSES OF BIOLOGICAL DETERMINISM

In the genetically perfected future of *Gattaca* (1997), humans are no longer tied to the wheel of genetic chance or to commonsense notions of racial inferiority. Instead humans are engineered. In the film, scientists have created a society where parents pick the attributes of their children in order to provide the best opportunities for advancement in a highly competitive world. In *Gattaca*, genetic engineering has made notions of racial superiority a moot issue. All races are genetically perfectible; therefore racial difference matters only in terms of the parental choice of pigmentation. In the context of the film, race is not a social or political issue but merely a matter of personal choice. Ironically, the genetic perfection of humans has eliminated the type of racial logic commonly associated with eugenics and its theories of superior and inferior races. Instead, sexual couplings that naturally produce a child are a significant source of stigma in this society and assure the product of such unions a social death certificate. The children of such couplings are unable to compete with the genetically manipulated men and women who populate this society. Those who are not members of the ranks of the genetically engineered are labeled "In-valids" and assigned the society's most menial work as unskilled manual labor. At the pinnacle of this social order is the astronaut, a position that requires the highest degree of perfection in human specimens. Despite the subtle attempt to remove the racial significance of the film by showing occasional black characters as members of the genetic elite, the salience of race symbolically remains in a narrative that worships American-style, "bootstrap" upward social mobility, as the panacea for confronting and overcoming the most blatant forms of institutional discrimination.

The main character in *Gattaca*'s genetically fascist society is Vincent (Ethan Hawke), a white male not conceived under the genetic control of scientific engineering. Since everyone in this future world is tested and achieves a place in it according to genetic merit, Vincent is deemed inadequate for a position as an astronaut because he has a heart condition. Yet Vincent still dreams of traveling to the stars. He takes on the Herculean task of becoming an astronaut by implementing excruciatingly tedious rituals of deception and working extremely hard to overcome his scientifically assessed inferiority. He deceives everyone around him by engaging in an elaborate series of body-transfiguring surgeries, meticulous hygienic procedures, and enlisting the help of a paraplegic, whom he pays to be his genetic donor. As Jerome Morrow, the paraplegic's identity, Vincent is able to enter the world of the genetically privileged. Although Vincent successfully infiltrates the Gattaca Institute, the company responsible for daily moon launches from Earth, his genetic ruse is made even more difficult because of the constant blood testing and samples of bodily matter the company requires. At every turn Vincent is tested (blood tests are a daily event) to ensure that he is a member of the genetically elite. Nonetheless, aided by empathetic individuals who look the other way, Vincent is successful in proving he is just as good as, if not better than, his genetically superior colleagues. As a result, he gains a girlfriend, career advancement, and eventually the trip to the moon he always dreamed about.

The astronauts in the concluding scene of *Gattaca* overcome the power of Earth's gravity to reach the limitlessness of outer space, and space travel becomes a metaphor for the personal commitment of individuals to transcend institutional discrimination. The message of the film is clear. A person's inferiority, genetic or otherwise, can be overcome not through sweeping institutional change but by individual chutzpah on a case-by-case basis. Like Vincent, who was scientifically evaluated as genetically inferior, racial minorities and other socially disadvantaged groups can—by dint of hard work, dogged determinism, and an iron will—overcome their social and even their genetic inferiority to earn a privileged place in American society. This point is further ideologically underscored in the film when Vincent, after beating his genetically engineered and physically superior brother at long-distance swimming, shares his secret of success. After his brother inquires as to how Vincent, the genetically weaker specimen, could have prevailed over him,

Vincent informs him that he never tried to conserve energy for the swim back to land. Thus the drive to win, even if it means being impractically committed to going so far as to die in the process, is the ideological gold standard and motivational message of the film. That message dovetailed perfectly with the neoconservative configuration of race relations in the 1990s, a decade that saw the reassertion of the idea that institutional discrimination, such as that which Vincent faced in *Gattaca*, was no longer an accurate explanation for the failure of blacks to achieve economic success. Instead, culture and personal responsibility had to be taken into account.[20] In *Gattaca*, genetic discrimination, like the neoconservative take on racial discrimination, is a personal issue that is solved by a personal response. From the neoconservative perspective, the pernicious impact of liberal governmental programs like welfare and affirmative action institutionalized black inferiority.[21] For this political faction, the time had come for blacks to begin to compete with their white counterparts with the tools of delayed gratification and hard work rather than handouts.

As a whole, *Gattaca* is a film filled with contradictions. On one hand, it stresses conformity, a tireless work ethic, and hypercompetitiveness. On the other hand, the film indicts institutional discrimination for its proclivity to stifle the dreams of the individual based on preconceived notions, whether scientifically derived or socially constructed. Accordingly, *Gattaca* works to affirm the position that discrimination is not a social ill while simultaneously promoting the idea that personal responsibility is the panacea for institutional wrongs. In the end, Vincent and his collaborators edify rather than destroy the source of their inequity. In this way, the film vigorously absolves institutional discrimination of its pernicious and stifling impact on those who are clustered at the socioeconomic bottom of society. The result is a film that affirms an American ethos of "bootstrap" upward social mobility as the most effective means to confront social inequity, whatever its source. And blacks, other ethnic minorities, women, and the poor alike can—like Vincent, the first corporate Horatio Alger of science fiction film—achieve success if they really and truly commit to do all they can to overcome their underprivileged social position.

Star Wars: Episode I—The Phantom Menace (1999), the prequel to the original *Star Wars* trilogy, is another SF film that links genetic makeup to physical abilities and potential social accomplishments. Ostensibly, *The Phantom Menace* charts the seminal events that contribute to the creation of the iconic villain of the *Star Wars* franchise, Lord Darth Vader, the disfigured henchman clad in all black and master of the "dark side of the Force." But below the surface lurks a powerful discourse around race, biological determinism, and social outcomes. Despite casting a cherubic white child actor, Jake Lloyd, as Anakin Skywalker, the character is cloaked in familiar signifiers of black racial identity. First, he and his mother are narratively constructed as slaves. Second, a pivotal discussion between a slave merchant, Watto, and his future Jedi sponsor, Qui-Gon Jinn (Liam Neeson), clearly signifies Anakin as symbolically black. In the midst of bartering for the boy's freedom, Watto exclaims, "Don't get me wrong. I have great faith in the boy. He's a credit to your race." Given that the phrase "credit to your race" has been used at various periods in American history to connect the image of respectable blackness for blacks who prove exceptional—epitomized by Joe Lewis, Jackie Robinson, and Sidney Poitier—with their receiving the rights and respect of first-class American citizenship, the use of the phrase in referring to Anakin's status blatantly ensconces him in symbolic blackness.

What is most striking about the racial coding of Anakin is that many of the elements used in the film to explain his pathological outcome as the destructive Darth Vader are synonymous with the crisis of black male underachievement put forth in the controversial Moynihan Report. The historical legacy of enslavement, the increase in absentee fathers and households headed by single females, and a need for respectable male role models were theorized as significantly contributing to social maladjustment for many young black men in America.[22] Moreover, these same social factors, which supposedly contribute to black male underachievement, sound eerily familiar when examining the elements that play a part in Anakin's disappointing development. Anakin Skywalker is a descendent of slaves, is born in a single-female-headed household, has an absent father, and lacks respectable male tutelage until he is befriended by a Jedi knight. All of these factors—like those in Moynihan's assessment of why many young and gifted black men have tragic outcomes as adults—are used to signal why Anakin Skywalker becomes the evil Darth Vader as an adult. Yet all of the socially based explanations for why Anakin becomes the violently destructive Darth Vader end up taking a backseat to the biological argument in *The Phantom Menace*.

Before the prequels to the *Star Wars* trilogy, the Force was defined as an omnipresent ethereal energy for good that was particularly responsive to Jedi Knights. The caveat of being a Jedi Knight, however, was that if one was not constantly vigilant, one could go over to the dark side of the Force and become an agent of evil. In *The Phantom Menace* the Force is a condition biologically determined and is measured through one's blood. The Force is not an achieved status but a biological birthright. When the young Vader has his blood tested to measure his Jedi potential, it has an usually high reading of "midichlorians," a biological indicator that the Force is present. What is important here is that Anakin registers an abnormal biological reading. Despite the judgment that Anakin's repressed fears are the ostensible reason for his denial of Jedi training, his unusual blood analysis is the authoritative factor for defining him as abnormal and unfit for Jedi Knighthood. Of course, the audience is well aware that the decision to train him in spite of such biological and intuitive warnings occurs and will lead to dire consequences along with the dire consequences of this training. Little innocent Anakin Skywalker grows up to become the nefarious agent of evil Darth Vader, a master of the dark side of the Force, and nearly conquers the galaxy.

The ideological message is arresting. Anakin, symbolically a young black male, is given a blood test, the results of which are abnormal. Nevertheless, he is provided tutelage despite the genetic warning that such training is ill-fated, and he subsequently becomes an intergalactic sociopath, meting out violence and murder to anyone he disapproves of. The genetic message encoded into the film is strikingly evocative of the real-world racial biological determinism found in the book *The Bell Curve: Intelligence and Class Structure in American Life*, by Richard J. Hermstein and Charles Murray (1996), which uses biological determinism to explain black intellectual failure, and the book *Taboo: Why Black Athletes Dominate Sports and Why We're Afraid to Talk about It*, by John Entine (2001), which links genetics to black athletic success. Both books would ignite a firestorm of criticism for their racial reductionism, which suggests that biology rather than environment is the most definitive factor explaining differences between whites and blacks. Indeed, the racial argument of both books, that genetic qualities are predictive signposts for future outcomes, is signaled in *The Phantom Menace*. For Anakin Skywalker and young black men in America alike, their hypothesized success or failure is not based primarily on social environment but is significantly determined by their genetic makeup.

The signifiers of the interconnectedness of race, blood, and biology in *The Phantom Menace* are also stridently illustrated in *28 Days Later* (2002). Although *28 Days Later* is set in Britain, the film dramatically resonates with the cultural politics of race in America, a characteristic that arguably might have contributed to the film's successful reception by American moviegoers. The story begins in a laboratory full of caged monkeys that are later discovered to have been purposefully infected with a rage virus. Unwittingly, an animal rights organization circumvents security at the lab where the animals are kept, and before an attendant can warn one of the activists not to release a caged monkey, she does so, thereby introducing the virus into the populace of England. The disease is transmitted by bodily fluids, and even coming into contact with a speck of contaminated blood will, within minutes, turn the unfortunate victim into a pathologically crazed serial killer. Nearly a month later, England is almost entirely populated with rage-filled killer zombies. Interestingly, as in the films *The World, the Flesh, and the Devil* and *The Omega Man*, the postapocalyptic scenario of *28 Days Later* includes an interracial pairing of the film's two principal protagonists. The lead female character, Selena (Naomie Harris), is black, and the lead male character, Jim (Cillian Murphy), is white. The two of them, along with a white father-daughter duo, decide to make an intrepid journey from the heart of London to a military sanctuary in the countryside, in the hope of finding refuge from the infected zombies that roam the city.

Everyone except the father is able to make it to the sanctuary, a camp set up on an abandoned estate by a band of soldiers. While there, Jim is taken on a tour of the mansion. He is shown a black man chained like a rabid dog to a stake, with a steel leash around his neck. The lead officer and Jim stare at the black man as he wildly struggles to get loose and frothy blood gushes from his mouth. The rationale for keeping him in this captive state is the need to see the full impact of the virus. Later, Jim discovers even more shocking surprises. The soldiers have made it their imperative to repopulate the world, using the two remaining uninfected women at their disposal. In order to save the women from sexual assault, Jim frees the black zombie to distract the soldiers. As the freed black man scurries around the base camp and infects soldiers with his diseased blood, Jim rushes to save the girls and escape. In an end similar to that in both *The Omega Man* and *Blade Runner*, they flee elsewhere in the English countryside and set up residency in a tranquil cottage.[23] The film ends with military jets flying overhead and the three remaining protagonists happily anticipating their escape from a quarantined England.

Certainly, *28 Days Later* is a film critiquing Britain's political order. The quarantining of the country and the inability of British governmental institutions to stem the rage virus, along with military impotence, collusion, and criminality in the face of the disease, cumulatively signify that British society is ailing. Unfortunately, the subversive élan woven into the critique of British society and its military-industrial complex as "sick" is attained at the expense of reanimating retrograde signifiers of the black "other" as contaminated and contaminating. By presenting a black male as a diseased subject of observation, *28 Days Later* evokes the historical use of black men in America as human guinea pigs to observe the effects of syphilis. Between 1932 and 1972, white doctors allowed hundreds of poor black sharecroppers in Tuskegee, Alabama, to remain untreated for syphilis in order to document the advanced stages of the sexually transmitted disease.[24] The relationship between the military commander and the infected black man in *28 Days Later* is dramatically similar. Like the victims of the Tuskegee "experiment," the ailing black man in *28 Days Later* is an object of pathological spectacle and voyeuristic subjugation. Moreover, the depiction of a captive, diseased black man who, when freed, goes about savagely mauling his white captors is also intertextually evocative of America's cultural stereotype of the "angry black man" who indiscriminately strikes back at any and all whites, perceived as the source of his oppression.

On one hand, the representation of the infected black zombie who attacks whites in *28 Days Later* is similar to the racial conflict in *The World, the Flesh, and the Devil*, *The Omega Man*, and *The Thing*—all four films reinforce the idea that black and white race relations are violently antagonistic. On the other hand, the proclivity for black and white interracial pairings with reproductive overtones to crop up in SF films with a postapocalyptic setting or approaching an apocalyptic end—like *Daybreak* (1993), *Strange Days* (1995), and the visually arresting *Children of Men* (2006)—may possibly reflect an even deeper desire for the destruction of rigid notions of race and black and white racial antagonism. Certainly, the films *28 Days Later*, *The Omega Man*, and *The World, the Flesh, and the Devil*—and to a lesser extent, *Children of Men*—suggest that the only way the color line can be permanently erased is through interracial sexual unions. But such relationships appear viable only within an apocalyptic or postapocalyptic motif. As a result, the audience is left with the implication that only after the collapse of Western civilization, as we know it, can a more racially tolerant future rise from the ashes of a society obsessed with racial categorization and notions of racial purity. Certainly, the crude "scientific" racism of eugenics is, for the most part, no longer considered a significant or legitimate part of the mainstream discourse on race. Yet the idea of "black blood" as a destructive quality and a threat to white racial purity remains present in America's collective consciousness and crops up in an assortment of sophisticated guises across varying spheres of social and cultural activity.

THE POLITICS OF BLACK BLOOD

Although blacks have made impressive economic gains and experienced increased acceptance from white America over the last decades, whites and blacks remain segregated across the American social landscape.[25] Despite the elimination of legalized racial segregation, racial divisions in American society still exist. The persistence of these racial divisions has fostered a cultural logic that justifies America's continued racial divisions, a logic that sounds surprisingly similar to the type of racial Darwinism endorsed by eugenics. Take, for example, the harsh critiques of the impact of black popular culture on white American youth, the demands on academic standards posed by multicultural education, or the "white flight" of the American middle class from urban areas to the safety of the suburbs.[26] These issues, once distilled down to their core element, reveal that the familiar trope of racial contamination underlies the discourse. Equally important is that SF film is a part of the discourse around the increasingly porous boundaries of race in America and the anxiety they generate. Most notably, SF films are significant cultural texts because the genre—like its cinematic cousin, horror films—is a medium whose symbolic stock-in-trade is the problems and issues that a society has difficulty confronting and resolving.[27] Accordingly, the threats of contamination commonly found in SF film are ideas, images, and narratives that symbolize the unresolved cultural anxieties associated with changing race relations in America and resonate on a broader ideological scale than is usually acknowledged.

The civil rights movement of the 1960s established that blacks would no longer be socially silent or politically invisible and garnered, at the least, tacit white support. Yet, in the face of chants for "Black Power," forced school busing for racial diversity, and the aggressive political posture of black nationalism with its trenchant critique of the "white man," a white backlash emerged, rather than a reflective, albeit reluctant, acceptance of the remaking of America's racial order. *The Omega Man* is possibly the most strident example of the mounting white backlash against Black Power politics and the pressing paranoia associated with the declining status of white male patriarchy from its post–World War II position. The film suggested that traditional white male authority was under attack and that the institutions associated with that authority were being destroyed and, ultimately, negatively transformed by blacks. The kangaroo court scene in which Neville is put on public trial and given a death sentence by the Family signals the institutionalization of reverse discrimination. Moreover, the co-option of the American legal system by blacks is signified when Neville, who has searched in vain for the Family's hideout for more than two years, discovers that it is located in the basement of the city courthouse. Both uses of the courthouse by the racially coded black mutants suggest that the American legal system not only has been transformed by blacks to serve their unfair demands but also provides a political cover for blacks to hide behind. In this sense, *The Omega Man* is somewhat prophetic, given the momentum the white conservative backlash against affirmative action had gained in the 1980s.

The film symbolically foreshadows the perception by whites that America's courts had become too liberal, almost to the point of being unfair, when it came to adjudicating minority claims of racial discrimination.[28]

The racial crisis of the 1960s also created a lingering source of anxiety for white working- and middle-class Americans. In the subsequent decades an influx of Latino and Asian immigrants stoked already-existing fears of job loss during the recessionary early 1980s. Their presence generated concerns about whether these new nonwhite minority populations could ever be just like "us." This question struck a deep chord in the collective American psyche, because it is inextricably tied to issues of national identity and civic loyalty. On one hand, for minority groups, assimilation has often been posed as the most effective and logical approach to achieving success in America. On the other hand, the assimilated minority often retains a stigma of suspicion that they might be more loyal to their nation of origin than to their nation of opportunity. This type of racial mistrust found its most virulent expression in the internment of thousands of Japanese Americans during World War II, even though they were model U.S. citizens. SF films like *Invaders from Mars* (1953) and the multiple productions of *Invasion of the Body Snatchers* (1956, 1978, 1993) reflect the vestiges of the collective paranoia of WWII America that feared "the stranger among us" and "the enemy within" and justified Japanese internment. A similar undercurrent of civic paranoia lurks below the surface of both *The Thing* and *Blade Runner*. These SF films speak to past and present American anxieties over the issue of national identity and civic loyalty. Whether they portray blood testing or psychological testing, these two films illustrate that any debate involving American identity versus ethnic group identity contains an almost paranoid obsession with accurately knowing who the "other" is and, by implication, what the "other" truly wants.

The racial coding of MacReady's and Deckard's mission in their respective films—to root out a virtually imperceptible foe—reflects a broader social uneasiness not just with blacks but with any nonwhite immigrant populations in general. The theme of racial eugenics, however, has even broader implications for the real cultural politics of racial surveillance that is presently practiced. In post-9/11 America, the enforcement of the Patriot Act and the scrutiny given to Arab Americans and to people who "look" suspicious are expressions of the amplified anxieties around immigration and political loyalty that ideologically resonate with the overbearing motif of paranoia depicted in *The Thing* and *Blade Runner* and, to a lesser extent, the hypersurveillance shown in *Gattaca*. In the final analysis, all of the SF films discussed in this chapter are symbolic expressions of a nation yearning to protect racial identity. But as eerie, entertaining, frightening, intriguing, and racially disturbing as all the films discussed in this chapter are on the whole, they could provide only temporary and partial relief from the pressing anxieties born of race riots, affirmative action, globalization, and impending racial demographic shifts. Unfortunately, the majority of these sr films offered little promise for future race relations, beyond the fear of black contamination of the American body politic.

CHAPTER 3

THE BLACK BODY

Figures of Distortion

There may be a "knowledge" of the body that is not exactly the science of its functioning, and a mastery of its forces that is more than the ability to conquer them.   MICHEL FOUCAULT, *Discipline and Punish: The Birth of the Prison*

And black has become a beautiful color—not because it is loved but because it is feared.   JAMES BALDWIN, *The Fire Next Time*

Black racial representation has had a long and dubious history in American popular cinema. The thick-lipped, bug-eyed Sambo; the jovial eager-to-please servant; the obese, head-wrapped-with-a-handkerchief mammy; the noble bare-chested black savage; and the frighteningly muscular black buck— these were the crude racial representations of black people that populated the American minstrel stage of the antebellum era and American cinema well into the 1950s.[1] Films such as *The Birth of a Nation* (1915), *King Kong* (1933), and *Gone with the Wind* (1939) stand out as demonstrative examples of classic Hollywood films that overtly and symbolically presented black racial caricatures and endorsed a vision of blackness as radically different, to the point of becoming comically repulsive. Today, however, the signature, easily identifiable distortions of the lips, eyes, noses, and buttocks of blacks as lopsided and oversized have virtually disappeared from American popular culture. The acceptance of the black body—and in some cases laudatory fetishism of it, as, for example, in the field of professional sports—has contributed to its no longer being wedded exclusively to the profane and the repulsive. Yet, to imagine that the literal and symbolic distortions of black corporality for more than one hundred years—from the early years of American blackface minstrelsy circa the 1820s to subsequent minstrel-inspired imagery— has been completely eradicated is very short-sighted. Rather, the tradition and impulse to represent the black body as strange, repulsive, or reductively sexual have only been repressed. Most important, however, is what psycho-analytic film theory suggests about the response to any form of repression, be it voluntary or involuntary: that repressed conflicts, desires, wishes, and fears not allowed to operate fully in the open will return in ostensibly be-nign and acceptable characters, situations, and settings that appear unre-lated to the unsettling stimuli or issue in the first instance.[2] Accordingly, the concept of repression is of particular value for unveiling how past racist con-structions of the black body as primitive, a repository of unbridled sexuality, and a phallic danger—constructions that have been deemed overtly stereo-typical, racist caricatures and too politically taboo and incorrect to discuss openly—return camouflaged in science fiction film.

Admittedly, the psychoanalytic approach to analyzing film is a thorny topic in and of itself. Moreover, when the topic of racial representation is added to the psychoanalytical mix, the propositions as well as the conclu-sions become more complex, possibly convoluted, and certainly provocative. Despite criticisms that psychoanalytic film theory is an ahistorical metanar-rative of the unconscious, it remains useful for interrogating how repressed racial imagery, banished to the margins of America's collective conscious, returns in powerful spectacles of alien difference. Certainly, mainstream Hollywood racial melodramas like *The Legend of Bagger Vance* (2000) and *The Green Mile* (1999) are appropriate examples of how past stereotypical racial imagery return in contemporary cinematic canvases, reworked and re-presented. The first film resurrects the archetype of the faithful black ser-vant in the form of a mystical guru golf caddy, while the latter presents the audience with an infantilized pious black man wrongly accused of murder.

For my purposes, the psychoanalytic approach is similar to the digital picture enhancer in *Blade Runner*, which allowed the protagonist to exam-ine a two dimensional picture as if it were three-dimensional and to see around corners. Likewise, as a methodological tool, psychoanalytic film analysis is useful in the same manner. It provides a method for examining around and behind the surface image and symbolic spectacle of the aliens, uncanny events, strange worlds, bizarre beings, and fantasy futurescapes that are the visual and narrative stock-in-trade of SF cinema. These elements of SF film represent the displaced, externalized, and, in many instances, re-pressed cultural ideas, desires, behaviors, and beliefs circulating in the col-lective unconscious of American society.[3] Race, in general, and most spe-cifically the black body are an integral part of this generic matrix of genre conventions and expectations routinely offered for audiences to consume. Just beneath the special effects, monster makeup, and futuristic narratives churn and bubble repressed racial conflicts, mythologies, desires, sexual impulses, wishes, and fears. In many instances, however, race emerges from the murky realm of America's collective unconscious and breaks through SF film's racially detached and formal veneer to reanimate racist caricatures thought long dormant.

Certainly, the horror genre has been critiqued for reanimating racist caricatures of blackness in films such as *The Fly* (1958) and *Gremlins* (1984).[4] But American SF cinema is also culpable for associating physical spectacle with persons of color. Although SF cinema, for the most part, has been mildly interrogated for the manner in which it has chronically constructed the black body as a repository of radical *alien* difference,[5] the genre is a fertile cinematic field for observing the return of repressed racial imagery. I argue that the deformation of the black body in SF cinema is a consistent theme, but that it is not solely a function of negative stereotyping. Negative stereotyping of black characters has often involved the contention that they are habitually linked to social villainy within particular narratives.[6] They are chronically cast as villains, bumbling sidekicks, and overall "bad guys/gals." Certainly, this stereotyping is present in American SF film.

Yet, in several instances, the black body in SF film simply functions to associate physical difference with racial difference. For example, in *Star Trek: First Contact* (1996), Lieutenant Worf (Michael Dorn), an exceedingly brave Klingon crew member, has an extremely uneven and corrugated prosthetic forehead and nose placed on his face. Furthermore, although "good guy" Geordi La Forge (LeVar Burton) upgrades his protruding wraparound eyewear—which nearly obstructs his entire face on the television series—for strangely discolored ocular implants in the *Star Trek* films, he still clearly expresses a physical handicap. Both black characters are firmly established as occupying hero status or at least as being on the side of "good," but their bizarre physicality amplifies their racial difference. In the case of La Forge, his impaired vision does double semiotic duty. The reptilian-like ocular implants remind the audience of his past blindness but also signals that blackness is a social handicap that can also be overcome in the future. Here the use of "positive" and "negative" racial stereotypes as categories to evaluate black characters is too simplistic to address how the use of a significant physical disability such as blindness, along with the dramatic use of reptilian-like ocular implants to signify sight, functions to associate the black body with the strange and unknown. Films such as *Enemy Mine* (1985), *Predator* (1987), *Total Recall* (1990), *Demolition Man* (1993), *The Fifth Element* (1997), and *Mission to Mars*

(2000) make this point by portraying the black body not as a static figure but as a complex signifier of racial meaning. These are some of the most cogent examples in SF film of how the black body is a representational canvas coated with signifiers of alien unsightliness, danger, fear, social inferiority, and even transgressive sexuality that evoke a wide range of racial anxieties and cultural politics circulating in American society.

Enemy Mine is a sci-fi version of John Boorman's Hell in the Pacific (1968). Instead of two men, an American and a Japanese, stranded on a deserted island during World War II, a human and an alien are marooned on an inhospitable planet as an interplanetary war wages between the two species. In Enemy Mine, humans are pitted against Dracs, a similarly advanced species, in a deadly struggle over laying claim to various planets they want to inhabit. Two members of these sworn enemies—an Earth fighter pilot, Willis Davidge (Dennis Quaid) and his Drac counterpart, Jeriba "Jerry" Shigan (Louis Gossett Jr.)— crash-land on a strange planet after failing to destroy each other. Marooned on a hostile world, however, they are compelled to cooperate with one another in order to survive. Unlike in Robinson Crusoe on Mars, in which the human-alien relationship is unilaterally paternalistic from beginning to end, the alien counterpart in Enemy Mine fares much better. Yet the binary coding of race is much more severe in the latter film, and different phenotypes are used to signify the physical and cultural differences between whites and blacks. As a result, an extremely dichotomized visual schematic reinforces and amplifies the idea that blacks and whites are radically different. The white human is clad in an all-white jumpsuit. The alien, played by a black actor, is clad in all-black attire that covers his dark brown reptilian body, which has numerous encrustations.

The stark division between the two is affirmed not only visually but also through the dialogue as a running gag in which Davidge and the Drac periodically comment to one another about how ugly each one appears to the other. Such comments turn the film's coded representation of race on its head and invite the audience to adopt the perspective of the racial "other," and the film at times does succeed in decentering the white male as the paradigmatic reference point. Yet the declaration that Dennis Quaid is the ugly one, given his status in the Hollywood film industry as having leading-man good looks, serves more as comic fodder for the audience than as a serious opportunity to contemplate the value of cultural and aesthetic relativity. Ultimately, the "blackness" of the Drac/Louis Gossett is presented as comically unattractive and strange in comparison with Dennis Quaid's aesthetically pleasing whiteness. Later in the film the "otherness" of the "black" alien is further amplified when the male Drac becomes pregnant. Although

The crude cutout design of the mask incorporates Louis Gossett Jr.'s own mouth as a feature of repulsive alien corporeality in *Enemy Mine* (1985).

the pregnancy of the male alien character invites the audience to question accepted norms of masculinity and femininity in American society, the hermaphroditic construction of the "black" alien perpetuates a strident visual coding of racial difference that suggests that the black body is utterly alien in relation to its white counterpart.

To the film's credit, a certain degree of sincerity is present in the portrayal of each species' attempts to befriend the another. Despite all the back-and-forth bickering between the two foes, the film tries to convey a message of racial acceptance, particularly after the death of Jeriba and the birth of the alien infant. The film draws attention to this point by showing Davidge develop a true bond with the alien offspring, even risking his life and career to save the Drac child from enslavers. Here the film suggests that cultural exchange can lead to increasing degrees of shared tolerance and even mutual respect. But with Jeriba gone, the power struggle between the two characters is eliminated, and the racial message of *Enemy Mine* shifts ideological gears into paternalistic overdrive with an interspecies adoption narrative in which, by default, Davidge becomes the father and raises the "black" alien child as if it were his own. Because Davidge and the Drac child are isolated from both warring factions, Davidge is no longer burdened by the cultural baggage of hate and prejudice that has defined the relationship between the two civilizations. As a result, Davidge, as surrogate father, and the Drac, as maturing child, develop a profound respect and love for one another.

Certainly, the transformative element of the relationship between the species—from antagonistic enemies to surrogate family members—has allegorical implications for white and black race relations. The film promotes the idea that race relations between whites and blacks outside of the film could one day mirror the growing respect depicted between the opposing species in the film. Indeed, the humanist impulse reflected in Davidge's rearing of the infant Drac to late childhood is commendable, although idealistic, and evokes the idea of a "color-blind society." Unfortunately, the kind of racial acceptance and equality imagined in *Enemy Mine* is shown as being possible only at the expense of the mores, norms, and folkways of the alien child's culture and, to a lesser extent, his "racial" identity. The culmination of that idea is expressed in a scene in which the adolescent Drac laments that he wants to look like a white human.

The film ends with a closing voice-over narrative relating that Davidge successfully delivers a declaration of the Drac child's lineage, of which he is now a part, at an initiation ritual on the alien boy's home planet. This "happy ending," however, does not leave any clues as to the state of the bitter war being waged between the two groups. Is Davidge a diplomat for peace between the two groups? Have the humans and the Dracs learned to validate and respect each other's existence, as Davidge and Jerry did when they were stranded on a hostile planet surface? Can the two groups peacefully coexist without prejudice and hatred? These questions are all left lingering as the film draws to a close. Ultimately, the ending avoids all of these questions and settles for suggesting that American racial conflict and division are best resolved at the individual level and ceremonially applauded rather than collectively challenged and institutionally changed. Yet, as flawed as *Enemy Mine* is at delivering a message of racial reconciliation and acceptance—successfully attained only at a personal level and possible only outside the societal structure of each respective group—the film succeeds in demonstrating that racial differences are needlessly complicated by political interests and competition over scarce resources. *Enemy Mine* at its philosophical best offers a universalistic solution for overcoming racial and ethnic strife by showing that below the surface of physical appearance and competing, if not antagonistic, political agendas, we are more similar than different. In *Predator* (1987), however, the alien/black body as a nexus of difference and danger cannot be as easily transcended; rather it is a constant source of menace and fear that demands destruction.

Like the villains Box in *Logan's Run* and Darth Vader in *Star Wars*, the Predator in *Predator* is an African American actor, Kevin Peter Hall, hidden behind a strange and foreboding helmet-like mask. The Predator is an alien that hunts humans for sport and attacks a team of military operatives who are on a search-and-rescue mission deep in an Amazonian jungle. The intersection of alien creature and blackness, however, goes far beyond a black actor hidden behind a mask. The physical characteristics of the alien jungle stalker clearly code it as black. First, long, thick black braided coils protrude from the top of the alien's dull metallic mask like Rastafarian dreadlocks,

The face of the ultimate jungle stalker in *Predator* (1987).

streaming down nearly to his shoulders. Second, when the alien creature re-
moves his helmet, enlarged, protruding fangs jutting out of his mouth are
revealed, clearly evoking *National Geographic* pictures of tribal Africans
with white animal bones piercing their noses and other parts of their faces.[7]
Third, as if these clichéd signifiers of blackness were not enough, the blackness of the Predator is further indicated by ambient African drumming in the
background to signal the alien's presence, despite the film's setting in South
America. Fourth, although the alien uses a cloak of invisibility to stalk his
human prey, the cloak is invisible to everyone except the black characters,
a condition that intertextually invokes the social invisibility of blackness
in America, discussed in Ralph Ellison's racial tome, *Invisible Man* (1952).
Ultimately, by having the black characters in the film be the only ones able
to "see" the "invisible" alien, the film suggests a racial affinity between the
Predator and the two other black characters.

Although *Predator* is littered with semiotic clues that racialize the mur-
derous alien, the film's camera rhetoric also reductively frames the black
members of the mercenary squad, Mac (superbly played by the enigmatic
character actor Bill Duke) and Dillon (Carl Weathers), as phallic objects that
require containment. Sexual anxieties commonly associated with the black
body are rearticulated with the sequential destruction of the black officers.
The phallic objectification of Mac occurs when he encounters the alien for

the second time and chases after him. But before charging deeper into the jungle, he takes off his heavy flak jacket and snatches his cap off to reveal his bald head. Ostensibly this is done so that he will not be slowed down by the weighty material. The true significance, however, of his undressing, the symbolic nudity signaled by the removal of his hat and, most importantly, the phallic implications of Mac's bald black head are found in the graphic depiction of his death. In his attempt to kill the Predator, Mac slowly slides along the ground for a clear shot. The alien, however, turns the tables on him and is shown standing above Mac before firing a red laser beam directly at his forehead. The audience's point of view is behind Mac's shoulder, staring directly at the weapon as the Predator fires. Mac's head is shown exploding and subsequently releasing thick gooey blood that fills the entire frame. Immediately afterward, Mac's body is shown twitching as the Predator retreats to the trees.

Later, Dillon sees the site of Mac's slaughter. From his vantage point, however, Mac's head remains intact. Furthermore, Mac's body is shown lying face up, and blood is splattered across his chest, as if his throat had been severely slashed. Certainly, showing Mac's head exploding from behind and subsequently showing it as being fully intact can be chalked up to a continuity goof by the editor. Nevertheless, within the diegetic reality of the film, the image the audience is left with is that of a bald black head that "explodes," releasing a screenful of red goop, and a limp black body spastically twitching, as if in a postorgasmic convulsion. The sequence and semiotic culmination of these three images work to reductively code Mac's body as a totalizing symbol of black phallic power, which is ultimately destroyed by symbolic castration.[8] As metaphorically far-fetched as this interpretation may appear at first glance, the phallic coding of the black body in *Predator* is glaringly perceptible when the other black character, Dillon, is killed after Mac's slaughter.

Dillon's death scene begins with him spotting the Predator in a tree and firing his machine gun. In response, the alien fires a laser beam, which severs Dillon's arm almost to the shoulder. The arm is shown falling to the ground in slow motion as the finger remains tightened on the trigger, causing numerous bullets to spew from the opening even after the arm has landed on the ground. Clearly, whether it is a pistol, revolver, rifle, or ray gun, the firearm in American cinema has long been symbolically synonymous with the threat of male sexual power and domination.[9] In *Predator*, all of the usual phallic symbols are put into play: cigars, both long ones and stubby ones, along with several immense gun barrels, are purposefully propped between the legs of male soldiers. In fact, the only female character in the film is denied the opportunity to carry a firearm for most of the film, ostensibly on the grounds that the Predator will view her as a threat. But, symbolically, the denial of a machine gun to the sole woman character clearly affirms the idea that wielding a firearm is the province of men and an exclusive extension of masculine authority.

Clearly, the gun and various other phallic props used in *Predator* proxy as a symbolic penis and signal male authority. As a result, the graphic depiction of Dillon's severed black arm clinging to a machine gun that discharges bullets as the arm falls to the ground is more than visual spectacle. The scene is loaded with phallic symbolism that includes Dillon's symbolic castration, the ultimate loss of male power and promise. In *Predator* the phallic coding of the black body is a specific racial articulation of the recurring phallic motif and anxieties present throughout the film. The spectacle of the black body as a source of visual distortion and destruction in *Predator* is symptomatic of the film's overall fetishistic focus on the human body as a source of visual objectification and on the white male body, in particular, as a metaphor of militaristic power. Whether it is the bare-chested soldiers flexing their muscles as they labor to catch the Predator, the skinned bodies of several corpses hung upside down from the trees, the body parts collected by the Predator, the real-world moniker of costar Jesse "the Body" Ventura (Blain), or the principal figure, Arnold Schwarzenegger (Dutch), with his exaggerated physique and massive biceps from years of professional bodybuilding—the male body is the central focus of voyeuristic scrutiny in this film.

Yet, buried beneath the exhibitionistic display of male physicality and phallic signifiers is an anxiety over race, sexual promise, and power. For example, in an early scene a white crew member declares he is surrounded by "faggots" when the men in the helicopter refuse to sample his tobacco. A Latino character responds to this comment by placing a massive firearm between his legs with the barrel pointed up and exclaims, "Strap this on your sore ass, Blain!" This is one of several scenes that, although easily interpreted as engaging in homoerotic hyperbole, also suggest an acute sexual anxiety informed by race. The sublimated racial pathos, however, suggested by the overt dialogue and visual allusions to male sexual endowment, fully surfaces in the display of Dillon's limbless black body after his arm has been severed.

Against a backdrop of tall trees and jungle brush, the camera slowly pans around Dillon before the invisible alien impales him, then lifts him into the air. Dillon's body is suspended in air, with the stump of the severed arm occupying the center of the screen. The appearance of Dillon's black body "hanging" in the air with a missing a limb invests this image with a significant degree of racial pathos. The image is eerily evocative of a lynching, in

Firepower on display in *Predator*.

which black men were hung from trees and had their ears, tongues, knuckles, and/or penises severed from their bodies.[10] Mac's and Dillon's death scenes are excellent examples of how repressed sexual anxieties and social practices involving the black body, such as lynching, return cloaked in the contemporary camouflage of SF cinema.

The sociosexual threat associated with the black body in *Predator* is not unique but rather a part of a representational continuum seen in numerous Hollywood films. For nearly a century since D. W. Griffith's *The Birth of a Nation* (1915), American cinema has, directly or indirectly, exhibited an acute anxiety with the sexuality of the black male body and imagined it as a threatening phallic presence. *Predator* is an example of an SF film functioning as a contemporary outlet to reimagine the historical construction of past racial caricatures; it reanimates multiple retrograde expressions of black racial caricatures within its representational parameters. Phallic objectification is but one representational code projected onto the black body in *Predator*. Blackface minstrelsy and the black body as inextricably linked to dirt and dirtiness, jungle primitivism, and social invisibility are also symbolically represented in the film. In a scene prior to the climactic confrontation with the alien, Dutch is shown meticulously applying black mud to his white face. Looking almost directly into the camera, Dutch wipes mud across his face as if he were in front of a mirror.

Ostensibly, the covering of Dutch's body with black mud allows him

Dutch (Arnold Schwarzenegger) prepares for battle in *Predator*.

to escape detection from the heat-sensing vision of the Predator. Symbolically, however, the depiction of Dutch covering his face and body with black mud opens up a Pandora's box of disturbing racial semiotics. On the surface, the symbolic import of having the white protagonist slather his body with mud to, in effect, make himself symbolically black, before fighting another symbolically black character, evokes the idea of the black body as inextricably linked to dirt and dirtiness.[11] A deeper analysis, however, reveals that Dutch's actions are akin to Al Jolson's application of blackface makeup in *The Jazz Singer* (1927) and the use of burnt cork or black greasepaint by white minstrel entertainers of America's past. The image of Dutch applying mud to his entire body in order to cover his "whiteness" clearly references the historical use of blackface by white performers in order to engage in a racial masquerade.

With blackface, white performers symbolically became "black"—whiteness physically and culturally vanished, and an imagined and exaggerated black racial subjectivity took its place.[12] Likewise, in *Predator*, when Dutch's white skin is no longer visible, he is capable of performing feats of cunning similar to those of his symbolically black rival. In blackface, Dutch, the minstrel mercenary caked over in black mud, with bright, bulging white eyes and red lips, artificially achieves invisibility and is able to sneak through the jungle night on equal footing with the Predator. Dutch's racial transformation from white to "black" alien is firmly established when he climbs a tree and lets loose a banshee-like howl, signaling he is ready to battle this SF film version of the black jungle savage.[13] Ultimately the multiple psychosexual anxieties and retrograde racial tropes projected onto the black body in *Predator* demonstrate how the black body is constructed as a source of sexual threat and shocking dissimilarity that demands destruction. These themes are even more crudely reimagined in the sci-fi action thrillers *Total Recall* (1990) and *The Fifth Element* (1997).

Total Recall revels in the display of the human body in various exaggerated and disturbing forms. In the film, a segment of the human population living on Mars has mutated because of defective air generators. As a result, an orgy of deformed humanity exists on the red planet. There are humans with half of their faces melted and misshapen, a man with a head embedded in his torso, and a woman who periodically unbuttons her top to encourage passersby to fondle at least one of her three breasts. While in general such imagery is shocking, if not revoltingly comedic, *Total Recall* particularly illustrates the crude construction of the black male body as a phallic threat with the character of Benny (Mel Johnson Jr.), the gold-toothed black taxicab driver of the future.

Except for the anachronistic and irritatingly poor imitation of black urban street dialect that Benny delivers in the film, he appears "normal." Later, however, he is given the opportunity to disprove that initial impression when he unfolds a greasy, antenna-like arm hidden under his jacket in order to prove he is on the side of the mutant resistance movement. Within

Benny (Mel Johnson Jr.) revealing what is hidden underneath his clothes in *Total Recall* (1990).

A shot of a Mangalore alien before he reverts to his original form in *The Fifth Element* (1997).

the narrative his revelatory act is constructed as a necessary one. But when Benny fully extends his mutated arm for the protagonists as well as the audience to gawk at in disgust, it performs additional semiotic work.

Benny's fully "erect" arm foreshadows a comically grotesque depiction of the black male as a monstrously large phallic threat in a subsequent scene in which he attempts to kill two of the film's main characters. The scene begins with Benny sitting inside a gigantic tunneling machine shaped like oversized protruding male genitalia. What the shape of the tunneling machine suggests is made quite apparent by the dialogue. Benny yells, "I'm coming . . . I'm coming for you, baby," as he tries to impale the female protagonist against a cave wall. Certainly, this type of imagery signals a blatant visual association between the black male body and overpowering phallic prowess — namely, the sexual mythology of the oversized and punishing black male penis.[14] But as visually outrageous, grossly deformed, and sexually threatening as the construction of the black body is in *Total Recall*, this film is no match for the pure spectacle of perverse oddity attached to the black body in *The Fifth Element* (1997). In *The Fifth Element* the black body is represented as an unsightly alien, as perversely strange, and even as a cockroach.

In *The Fifth Element*, black racial identity is expressed as alien with the depiction of the Mangalores, a race of destructively violent space aliens. They are an unsightly, light brown species with rotund heads, negroid facial features, extremely thick lips, and very broad noses. As if this phenotypic link between the alien species of *The Fifth Element* and common physical traits associated with the black body were not adequate to visually establish the aliens as representative of black people, the link is explicitly made clear by a sequence of special effects. A black man is shown morphing into a Mangalore alien upon command by the human villain of the film, Zorg (Gary Oldman). The morphing special effect signals that the black body is not only clearly alien but also a site of transgressive spectacle.

The Mangalore after reverting to his original form in *The Fifth Element*.

Along with racial coding of the appearance of the aliens, the film stridently reimagines the mental/physical dichotomy imposed on the black body whereby a presumed intellectual inferiority is contrasted with the common racial trope of black hyperphysicality. A scene early in the film articulates this notion by reimagining a scene from *The Birth of a Nation* in which the newly elected black members of government are presented as bumbling self-destructive incompetents when left to their own devices. Similarly, after purchasing a cache of military weapons from Zorg, the "black" Mangalores are shown ineptly using the firearms, scratching their heads in dumbfounded confusion, and eventually blowing themselves up by pushing the wrong button. The racial rhetoric of the scene communicates that blacks are, at the least, comically inept and, at most, grossly negligent without the supervision of white superiors. On the surface the racially coded "black" Mangalores along with their dumbfounded behavior would appear to indicate what is most racially repulsive about *The Fifth Element*. But none is more shockingly abhorrent than DJ Ruby Rhod (Chris Tucker), the black rapping talk show host of the future.

Although the coded connection between blackness and alienness is a recurring feature in SF cinema in general, a rarer occurrence is the presentation of black racial identity as a spectacle of oddity in and of itself. Yet this is the case with the DJ Ruby Rhod character, the easily frightened, bumbling sidekick of Korben (Bruce Willis), the white main character of the film. Ruby Rhod is a flamboyant, effeminate, cross-dressing, heterosexual black television personality of the future. Obscene in both presentation and content, he sashays his way through the film, making loud and lewd comments. He is constantly shown prancing about with a hairstyle that has been designed with an enormous phallic appendage jutting from his forehead. Unlike in *Predator*, however, where the top of one black character's head and another's severed arm are reductively coded as penises, in *The Fifth Element*

DJ Ruby Rhod (Chris Tucker) in *The Fifth Element* (1997).

the symbolic becomes the literal. Notwithstanding the phallic interpreta-tion signaled by the last name of his moniker, Rhod, in an even cruder visual scheme, the phallic hairpiece is intimated as contributing to a flight stew-ardess's ability to achieve an ear-piercing orgasm as their spaceship blasts off.

Yet the savagely cartoonish construction of DJ Ruby Rhod—combined with the principal white protagonist's demonstrative disdain of him, ex-pressed throughout the film—performs more semiotic work than just an over-the-top form of comic relief in a "serious" SF film. The derision directed toward DJ Ruby Rhod by Korben, along with Ruby Rhod's strange appear-ance, operates on a broader social level. Arguably, DJ Ruby Rhod is a thinly veiled play on and critique of the popular presence of hip-hop in the public sphere throughout the late 1990s. Clearly the name "DJ Ruby Rhod," along with a scene showing him on television as he delivers mile-a-minute gib-berish for a sweepstakes advertisement, mockingly signifies on the various monikers that hip-hop artists adopt and the ubiquitous presence and verbal style of the rapper persona. But most importantly, DJ Ruby Rhod's black body, encased in an aesthetic of sexual hyperbole and homoeroticism—along with the constant derision directed to the black character by the white lead—signals white hostility toward the in-your-face bravado and hyperhet-erosexual masculinity of the hip-hop aesthetic.

Of all the black characters in SF film, this one epitomizes how easily ret-rograde racial representations of blackness are reanimated in the contempo-rary genre. Despite the grotesque disfiguration, deformity, and sexual anxiety associated with the black body in *The Fifth Element* or the frightening, strange, and destructive qualities the black body symbolizes in *Total Recall* and *Predator*, retrograde racial representations are not limited exclusively to black corporeality. Indications of racial stigmatization are also found in the use of one of the most iconic symbols of SF cinema—the spacesuit.

The spacesuit is literally a second skin that permits the wearer to exist in space, but in American SF film it also functions as a powerful signifier that underscores the transcendent aura of the astronaut when fully clad. More than functionality, the white spacesuit of the astronaut in American SF cinema is a powerful symbol/signifier of social purity and even sexual virginity.[15] In SF films such as *2001: A Space Odyssey* (1968) and *Marooned* (1969), as well as the true-life space dramas *The Right Stuff* (1983) and *Apollo 13* (1995), the spacesuit not only functions to enable the astronauts to exist outside Earth's atmosphere but also is a powerful signifier of intrepid exploration and moral courage associated with space travel. In *Mission to Mars* (2000), however, the antiseptic, hyperrational, and chaste morality that the spacesuit signifies across a host of SF films is ruptured by a black astronaut, Luke Graham (Don Cheadle).

Early in *Mission to Mars*, three of the principal male astronauts are shown in a tree house, talking about their upcoming mission. One of the astronauts, Woody Blake (Tim Robbins), wears a small toy rocket attached to a necklace and, in an exchange with his friend and colleague Jim McConnell (Gary Sinise), characterizes the wonder of space travel as an undertaking for guys who have read too much science fiction as kids. The tree house, the memories of science fiction books, and the toy-rocket necklace all work to signify how childhood innocence is a core qualification for attaining the status of an American astronaut and, by implication, for spearheading the first landing on Mars. Although Luke is highly qualified (at least on paper)—he is a research scientist whose PhD was on how to colonize Mars—he is not fully vested with the same reverential childhood innocence that, according to the expository dialogue, his white colleagues possess and space travel requires. In fact, his presence threatens to undermine it. Even though Luke shares a seat next to the other two astronauts in his son's tree house, the virtuousness of his character and the stature of his ability are compromised. The audience is told that Jim, the frontrunner to spearhead the mission to Mars, withdrew from the training program because of the unexpected death of his wife. Furthermore, Luke does not successfully win the command of the first manned mission to Mars but is given it. As a result, Luke does not possess the same degree of reverential capital and purity associated with being an astronaut that his white colleagues have, a point later visually underscored by the degraded and dirty condition of his spacesuit, along with the physical transformation he undergoes in the film.

Aware that Luke's exploratory team encountered some form of cataclysmic crisis but not knowing the nature of the emergency, a rescue team is dispatched to save any remaining survivors. When the team arrives on Mars several months later, they discover that the earlier team's home base has

A disheveled Luke Graham (Don Cheadle) struggles to remember past events while his friend and rescuer, Jim McConnell (Gary Sinise), stands in the background in *Mission to Mars* (2000).

been transformed into an air-producing African jungle–like greenhouse tent. Although the clichéd use of ambient African drumming to signal that danger is approaching is absent as the rescuers tiptoe their way through the faux jungle, *Mission to Mars* does provide the audience with the requisite black jungle stalker, lurking in the shadows. Luke emerges from the ersatz tropical forest a wild-eyed and bushy-bearded psychotic intent on killing his white rescuers. Even though Luke is promptly talked out of his irrational mental episode, the semiotic message sent by Luke's physical transformation from the clean, nonthreatening black friend and colleague constructed at the beginning of the film to an unruly, frightening figure with a sullied spacesuit is ideologically telling. His devolution into a jungle primitive, along with his dingy spacesuit, visually confirms the narrative setup that Luke was the wrong man for the job. Although his colleagues' spacesuits are not pristine, Luke's soiled and blood-stained spacesuit markedly stands out as extremely unclean relative to theirs. Symbolically, Luke's physical transformation and his discolored spacesuit signal that he is most dissimilar to his colleagues. Consequently, his spacesuit is a diminished signifier, not able to connote the valiant virtues associated with space exploration and the American astronaut. Instead it signifies the stigma of unmerited career promotion.

Although the sublimated racial tension between Luke and the other astronauts in *Mission to Mars* masquerades as normal male heterosexual competition, the jocular rivalry is rife with acute racial anxieties because of Luke's unmerited career promotion. Ostensibly, Jim is shown racked with sorrow by the loss of his wife and, by implication, saddened by the relinquishing of his position as the leading astronaut on the first mission to land on Mars. This sentiment is visually signaled by a garish use of black eye-liner around Jim's eyes to amplify his suffering, downtrodden emotional state with a comparable external appearance. A broader racial implication of the sullen look and feel of Jim's emotional state is that the character symbolizes the virtuous suffering and disappointment of white males in the labor market who have been denied or delayed promotions because of race-based preferential treatment of black workers. In this sense, *Mission to Mars* stridently reflects both white America's persistent uneasiness with affirmative action and the perception that qualified whites often lose out to less qualified blacks when the policy is enacted. The end of *Mission to Mars*, however, fully restores Jim and, by extension, whiteness to their proper place of power and promise in the face of unmerited promotion. With the handing over of Woody's toy-rocket necklace to Jim by his copiloting widow, Terri Fisher (Connie Nielsen), the small trinket performs big symbolic work. He is a husband again (at least symbolically), vested with patriarchal authority, and the designated custodian and true representative of idealized American innocence and heroism. With his virtuousness symbolically secured, Jim, not Luke, fully occupies the status as the chosen and most chaste representative of humanity and is able to take on the most important and courageous mission an American astronaut has ever faced, first contact with a benevolent alien civilization. As a result, Jim enters the transportation chamber and journeys to meet the alien civilization of Mars's past.

All things considered, the "friendly" competition signaled in the beginning of the film, the compromised promotion of Luke, and the eventual ascendancy of Jim past the black astronaut all work to signify an uneasiness with black upward social mobility and, by extension, a perception of affirmative action as an unfair policy of career promotion that benefits blacks. Even though affirmative action remained relatively untouched as a national policy, the idea and practice of affirmative action had taken a political beating for nearly two decades. Throughout the 1990s the notion of racial quotas and preferences helped push the issue of affirmative action into the foreground and reinvigorate the notion of American rugged individualism. Symbolically woven into the visual rhetoric and the narrative outcome of *Mission to Mars* is a narrative that ideologically represents working- and middle-class whites as competing against blacks in the labor market and for entrance into college and losing to unqualified blacks.[16] This is the racial subtext of *Mission to Mars*, even though the film works to establish a high degree of camaraderie among the crew members, irrespective of race and, to a lesser extent, gender.

Although Luke's racial identity is never addressed, discussed, or identified, the text remains a provocative site of racial meaning with the eventual success of Jim and the failures of Luke. The film affirms a sympathetic vision of white male suffering in the face of perceived racial preferences for blacks, as well as the superiority of white male leadership in the face of racial and gender diversity. In the end, the black body in *Mission to Mars* is a signifier of unmerited black upward mobility and functions as an ideological foil for the white protagonist to triumph over. But even more importantly, this film demonstrates that the black body in SF cinema is not merely constructed and coded as alien nor restricted to its corporeality to suggest particular racial conclusions. Rather the black body also functions as a political refer-ent with broader social discourses projected across it. In *Demolition Man*, this function is amplified, with the black body and its eventual destruction serving as a proxy for broader racial conflict over political power, as well as for racial geography and demographic trends.

THE BLACK BODY POLITIC

Demolition Man (1993) is billed as a science fiction film, but it has almost as much in common with the first three *Rocky* films (1976, 1979, and 1982) as it does with a vision of the technocultural landscape of the future. On the surface, *Demolition Man* is a retooled science fiction version of the *Rocky* franchise, with Sylvester Stallone once again squaring off against a physi-cally formidable black man in a spectacle of hand-to-hand combat and—like the underdog white Italian boxer, Rocky Balboa—going on to win fame, for-tune, respect, and ultimately redemption by beating black men into submis-sion. Admittedly, the antagonisms presented in *Demolition Man* are more comedic than dramatic, and the film's overall aesthetic is a hokey version of Aldous Huxley's novel *Brave New World*. Yet *Demolition Man* should not be dismissed as pop sci-fi drivel or only appreciated for its unintended camp. It is important within the canon of American SF film because it ex-emplifies the use of the black body as a symbol and source of racial anxiety associated with changing racial demographics and the predicted "browning" of America.

    Demolition Man was released on the heels of the 1992 racial unrest, and given that the opening shot is a depiction of Los Angeles ablaze, with a psychopathic black man leading the charge, the film clearly plays to the jangled nerves and fears in America's collective consciousness that blacks would create a wall of fire to demark the geographical space between them-selves and white residents. Moreover, the gladiator-style confrontations be-tween John Spartan (Sylvester Stallone) and Simon Phoenix (Wesley Snipes)

Simon Phoenix (Wesley Snipes) is interrogated by a prison official before he escapes in *Demolition Man* (1993).

are symbolic of much deeper and broader racial antagonisms than whites against blacks. The Los Angeles of the future, as presented in *Demolition Man*, draws on Southern California's racially inflected geographic tensions and uses the black body as a visual cipher to express a myriad of political desires and racial wish fulfillment that are emblematic of the politics of race, space, and locality in the region.

Demolition Man begins in the Los Angeles of 1996, with the Hollywood sign and the surrounding area on fire. Simon Phoenix, a black supercriminal, sits at the center of power in this urban inferno, having declared that no one is allowed to enter the area. Only John Spartan, a decorated but controversial police officer, dares to enter this zone to capture Phoenix and rescue the thirty hostages he has hidden in his compound. Unfortunately for Spartan, Phoenix has killed the hostages, but Spartan is made to appear responsible for their death. As punishment, both Phoenix and Spartan are sentenced to cryogenic freezing. Forty years later, Phoenix is thawed out for his parole hearing and escapes. The year is 2032, and Los Angeles is a nonviolent totalitarian utopia—signified by Nazi-like leather police uniforms—where foul language is the most egregious crime and the population is completely passive. Consequently, the police department of the future is ill-equipped to combat Phoenix's new killing spree. As a result, Spartan is awakened from his cryogenic slumber and enlisted in the police department's mission to apprehend Phoenix.

The Los Angeles of 2032 is a sociogeographically divided society. Aboveground is a bright, pristine, and orderly social world depicted as the hub of a reconfigured and overwhelmingly white idyllic Los Angeles. In the film, the predominantly white suburban middle- and upper middle-class coastline communities of Santa Barbara, Santa Monica, and San Diego are represented as one geographical region called the San Angeles Metroplex. The underground social order is depicted as a dark subterranean Third World barrio, crowded with dirt-smeared people milling back and forth. The underground inhabitants are called Scraps and are virtually starving to death while the population above enjoys material abundance. The underground space stands in sharp contrast to the reconfigured San Angeles region above, not only in visible resources but in racial demographics as well. Most importantly, the subterranean space is clearly coded as Latino.

Spartan and his two colleagues go below the city into the sewer dwelling of the Scraps and are more or less welcomed as tourists. They are greeted by a Peruvian-dressed peasant woman who speaks Spanish and happily serves Spartan a hamburger made of rodent meat. Here, through the costuming of the Latina actress and the food served, Latino-ness is linked to Third World exoticness and the political demands of a population circumscribed to the most basic expression of competition over scarce resources, a struggle for food and the ability to feed oneself. Certainly, this plays to the most reductive notions of Third World poverty and overpopulation as well as to postcolonial spectacles of televised pictures of poor children of color, malnourished and in need of food, an image commonly used by Western religious and relief organizations to induce public donations. Yet the construction of the subterranean space and the acute conflict between the two geographically divided social orders in *Demolition Man* also reflect a more localized struggle.

By juxtaposing San Angeles of the future against the underground Third World hideout of the Scraps, the film openly invites the viewer to draw direct comparisons to the present's shifting geographical fault lines of race that make up Los Angeles. In this sense, the film dovetails with actual suburban-versus-urban real estate politics in Los Angeles, where Santa Monica—colloquially referred to as the Westside—stands in stark contrast to the brown urban communities that populate East Los Angeles.[17] In this manner, the film mirrors the racial politics and tensions between the ocean-shoreline white communities of Santa Monica, Santa Barbara, and San Diego and an encroaching urban Latino population. In addition, the political ambition of the Scraps—to have access to food—appears almost benign in comparison with the black South Central Los Angeles of the past. The tripartite juxtaposition between the Anglo-dominated world above, the Latino-coded subterranean space below, and the black South Central of the past—represented by the Phoenix character—is the dramatic narrative undercurrent of the story. Moreover, this narrative subtext contributes to raising the confrontational stakes associated with Phoenix's wish to eliminate Spartan and kill Edgar

Friendly (Denis Leary), the leader of the Scraps, in order to rule both social spaces.

Phoenix is poised as the criminal ringleader, political catalyst, and racial instigator who can provoke the subterranean Latino population to overrun the suburban white paradise above. The anxiety surrounding a political alliance between blacks and Latinos is foreshadowed at Simon Phoenix's parole hearing. After Phoenix is brought out of suspended animation, he begins spontaneously parroting what the official in charge has to say about him in Spanish. Incensed, the white official emphatically commands him to stop it. It is not clear whether the official is more agitated that Phoenix is speaking or more perturbed that he is speaking in Spanish. Nevertheless, my reading of the warden's response is that Phoenix's decision to speak in Spanish is the source of his frantic demand for silence, since the official does not appear to speak or understand that language. Consequently, the scene signals an undercurrent of institutional hostility toward Spanish speakers, which contributes to the black body's taking on a more complex racial meaning than mere physiological difference. In this context, Phoenix not only signifies the unruly black body, which must be made to submit, but also is a symbolic stand-in for the Spanish-speaking Latino "other," who must be authoritatively silenced. As a result, Phoenix's black body in *Demolition Man* works to destabilize the strict black-and-white binary construction of American race relations and symbolizes the shifting racial-political demography of Los Angeles itself. While a broader racial politics is signaled by the use of language in his speech to the warden, racial duality is also inscribed onto Phoenix's body. The iris of one eye is brown, and the other is blue, along with the stark visual contrast of his dyed-blond hairstyle against his dark skin complexion. This dramatic juxtaposition of color and his spontaneous demonstration of fluid Spanish suggest that Phoenix's black body is also a cipher of racial hybridity that transgresses binary constructions of American race relations as only black and white, making Phoenix a symbol of a burgeoning realization that a more complex racial geography and political possibility looms in America's future.

Indeed, the anxiety associated with a growing Latino population and its radical potential is not surprising, given the cultural politics of the 1992 riots. Although the police brutality against black motorist Rodney King was defined exclusively in terms of black and white race relations, the urban unrest that followed the verdict showed an unprecedented participation of Latinos in the attacks on stores and property that took place in Los Angeles. *Demolition Man* rearticulates this racial dynamic with a narrative that has a law-abiding white citizenry aboveground and a criminalized Latino popula-

The leader of the Scraps, Edgar Friendly (Denis Leary), accepts heartfelt congratulations from Alfredo Garcia (Benjamin Bratt) in *Demolition Man*.

tion below ground, with blackness leading the charge to create the violent conflict between the two. The racial landscape I have mapped out for *Demolition Man* is not an imaginary construct but is rooted in the real racial and political fault lines of Los Angeles, which has historically been divided between assertive black, white liberals, and, until recently, a Latino community caught in the middle.[18] *Demolition Man*, however, provides a solution to the conundrum of Los Angeles's racial ecology in the lengthy fight scene between Spartan and Phoenix.

At the cryogenic facility, Phoenix inadvertently becomes completely frozen, and Spartan kills him by kicking his head off his shoulders. The head is subsequently shown tumbling to the ground and shattering into a thousand pieces. After this spectacle of destruction, the nonthreatening white leader, aptly named Mr. Friendly, is shown securing his leadership of the underground population. Instead of Phoenix spearheading an army of underground denizens to violently plunder and seize control of Anglo communities of wealth and privilege, a white male named Mr. Friendly marches through the city, intent on brokering the transition to a society with more freedom and equality.

The last image of a throng of dispossessed minorities in *Demolition Man* overrunning white civic society is not unique. Although the threat of racial invasion is deeply sublimated in the SF alien invasion films of the 1950s, nearly all the alien invasion SF films of the period are steeped in racial paranoia.[19] This theme crops up again, however, in *Demolition Man*, a cynical diatribe on the politics of race, place, and locality in which oppressed poor people of color threaten to overrun a peaceful, predominantly Anglo society. The symbolic message of *Demolition Man* is clear. Southern California race relations will require that black militancy be eliminated and that a moderate white alternative or certainly more "friendly" representative of the socially marginalized and economically dispossessed is put in place to negotiate the shifting racial fault lines and centers of racial politics and power in Los Angeles.

THE BLACK BODY IN SCIENCE FICTION FILM

Because the vast majority of sf films are guilty of chronically affirming white heterosexual heroism—except for, most notably, the *Alien* franchise—the "black" alien archetype, present in *Enemy Mine, Predator, Total Recall, The Fifth Element,* and to a lesser extent *Demolition Man,* raises the racial representational stakes to towering heights and with grave consequences. When a "black" alien figure is juxtaposed against a white male, it reaffirms a strident binary divide between whites and blacks that suggests that blackness is unusual in physical form, cultural content, and sexual habit. Take, for example, how the binary racial coding of white protagonist and "black" alien in sf film works as a template for coding normative conceptions of masculinity and femininity. *Enemy Mine* clearly epitomizes and delineates such a synthesis when the "black" alien is gradually recoded as feminine by adding stereotypical gender cues such as showing him wearing a long robe rather than his spacesuit and having him become physically weaker. In comparison to the static white character, the feminized "black" alien symbolically signals that the male black body is also a site of sexual transgression. This theme is repeated in *The Fifth Element* with the pairing of a flamboyantly effeminate heterosexual, dj Ruby Rhod, and Bruce Willis's hypermasculine character.

Insofar as these images of the black body are a representational foil for dominant versions of white masculinity, they also include a homoerotic impulse. In other words, a psychoanalytic interpretation of what the sublimated homoeroticism between the "black" alien and the white protagonist of sf film symbolizes includes a coupling of racial fear with sexual intimacy. For example, even the title of *Enemy Mine* signals a forceful, if not intimate, possessiveness between the white space pilot and the "black" alien. A less subtle illustration of this premise in *Enemy Mine,* however, is the symbolic sexual relationship between the white human and the "black" alien suggested by the pregnancy of the male Drac. Even though the Drac's pregnancy is accounted for in the film by the biological uniqueness of the species, the homoerotic connotation is amplified by the qualitative shift in the relationship between the two protagonists. The white male and the "black" alien take on more of the characteristics of an expectant couple than of intergalactic adversaries.

The Fifth Element stands out as a richly psychoanalytic repackaging of

America's repressed fears and fascination with black male sexuality. The hypersexual objectification of DJ Ruby Rhod in *The Fifth Element* is comparable to the phallic spectacle represented by Robert Mapplethorpe's controversial series of nude photos of black men, where special photographic attention was directed at their semierect penises. The DJ Ruby Rhod character invites viewers to experience the black body as a site of sexual revulsion, ambivalent fascination, and profound sexual spectacle and is reductively equated to a male sex organ. Yet reductive and exaggerated black sexuality is not merely symptomatic of SF film but also is a manifestation of broader anxieties and myths associated with black men and women as sexualized objects in American society.[20] The projection of the black body as a punishing figure of sexual excess and a source of white fear is a theme that periodically crops up in American politics. During George H. W. Bush's 1988 presidential campaign, the mug shot of Willie Horton, a disturbed black man who had repeatedly raped a white woman, was used in a television advertisement attacking his Democratic opponent, Michael Dukakis, to fuel the idea that Bush, if elected, would be tough on crime and criminals. A similar ploy arose in the 2006 Senate race in Tennessee between black Democratic candidate Harold Ford Jr. and white Republican Bob Corker. A TV ad contained a bare-shouldered white woman addressing the camera and saying, in a low voice, "Harold, call me." Concern was voiced that the ad was created to scare whites into supporting the Republican candidate by an implicit appeal to racial fears about black men having sex with white women.

American politics and SF cinema are too often representational sites where the black body is used as a cipher to symbolize fear and contamination. In some instances, however, the black racial imagination appropriates this image and recasts it for a subversive political statement. For instance, the title of the SF film *Predator* was appropriated by the hip-hop artist Ice Cube in his 1992 release *The Predator*. The CD contained a series of rap songs detailing the urban terrain of South Central Los Angeles in the aftermath of the Rodney King verdict. Many of the songs are dark, violent diatribes that embrace the idea of young black men, in particular, as "predators" who exist as both the victim and the embodiment of the worst form of alienated blackness in America—armed and angry black men anxious to attack and even kill anyone who crosses their path. Ice Cube effectively drew on the cultural reservoir of fear and public paranoia surrounding black men as urban "predators" and exploited it for all of its lurid potential for commercial success and social significance.

Whether it is the iconic figure of a black body suspended in midair right before dunking a basketball emblazoned on athletic apparel or the maelstrom of praise, criticism, and surprise surrounding the nudity of Halle Berry in *Monster's Ball* (2001), black corporeality remains a source of visual spectacle and cinematic titillation in American culture. Although the contemporary moment suggests that the black body is no longer a source of the kind of grossly stereotypical images of the past that imagined it as both comically and frighteningly abnormal, American sf film still provides a representational space for repressed racial anxieties associated with black physicality as a source of revulsion, fascination, phallic fear, and desire. Ultimately, black corporality in sf cinema is a reminder of the way the black body is imagined and the real sociopolitical struggles associated with it.

CHAPTER 4

HUMANS UNITE!

Race, Class, and Postindustrial Aliens

> The poor and the underclass are growing. Racial justice and human rights are
> nonexistent. They have created a repressive society, and we are their unwitting
> accomplices.
>
> *They Live*

Despite the appearance of otherworldly or distant temporal settings in American SF film, the genre is very much linked to the real political changes, dominant social discourses, and cultural practices at work in American society. Films like *The Day the Earth Stood Still* (1951), *It Came from Outer Space* (1953), and the original *War of the Worlds* (1953) are unmistakable examples of how narratives ostensibly about close encounters with aliens are in fact thinly veiled political metaphors of the pressing geopolitical concerns of the cold war era. Although the cultural fallout from the cold war paranoia of the 1950s made an indelible imprint on American SF film, it is not the definitive sociohistorical event that shaped the genre. The shock waves of postindustrial decline made a deep impact on the American economic order and cut a wide swath across the cultural landscape, which included SF film.

From the 1970s to about the early 1990s, America entered and remained in a period of precipitous erosion of the industrial and manufacturing sectors of the economy. This new stage of economic existence, called postindustrial decline, made it increasingly difficult to achieve, much less imagine, upward social mobility for working-class Americans, given the numerous factory shutdowns and massive layoffs. Moreover, the disappearance of employment opportunities in the manufacturing sector drained flourishing working- and lower middle-class communities of their economic lifeblood and left high-poverty, crime-ridden neighborhoods, often in inner cities, overwhelmingly populated by blacks and other people of color.[1] On one hand, the SF films

Soylent Green (1973) and *Escape from New York* (1981) forewarned and projected into the future the social and cultural consequences of postindustrial decline for America as imploding public institutions, moral decay, corruption, crime, and mounting antisocial behavior. On the other hand, sf films like *The Man Who Fell to Earth* (1976), a narrative ostensibly about a humanoid alien in search of water, metaphorically mirrored the increasing anxiety over the American energy crisis in the wake of the Arab oil embargo of the 1970s and the growing economic gap between the rich and the poor in U.S. society. Yet other sf films not only registered the effects of deindustrialization but also offered radical criticisms of the shifting economic landscape by signaling that a political economy of racism was also driving America's economic slide and too often worked to divide whites and blacks, creating a splintered and increasingly ineffective workforce in the face of consolidated corporate power.

In the Reagan era, white working-class Americans became increasingly hostile to helping black and brown underclass, poor, and working-poor communities either because their own economic wishes were stymied or because they perceived that America could ill afford to invest in resource-draining domestic entitlement programs, such as welfare and affirmative action, given the need for the country to reassert its economic dominance in a hypercompetitive global marketplace. As America became more mired in postindustrial decline, successive government administrations became increasingly candid about abandoning policy-driven racial reform and capitulating to corporate interests. In contrast to this patter, however, several sf films stand out as compelling texts that exhibit a counterimpulse. *Rollerball* (1975), *Alien* (1979), *RoboCop* (1987), and *They Live* (1988), along with being radically critical of the established economic order, presented racial cooperation as a necessary stage in mounting an effective challenge to economic elites and the institutions they control. These postindustrial sf films are notable because they offered models of resistance to corporate power on-screen and, in the process, signaled that the same could and needed to be done off-screen. Most of all, the strident binary coding of the heterosexual white male conquering a monstrous alien, often as the symbolic racial "other" in American sf invasion films of the cold war past, was replaced in the postindustrial future with another type of rapacious monster—the American corporation.

CORPORATE GAMES

On one hand, Fritz Lang's seminal sf masterpiece, *Metropolis* (1927), embodies the most literal indictment of the relationship between capital and labor, but it is a product of the cultural currents embedded in German expressionism and is far removed from the political economy of America. On the other hand, *The Matrix* (1999) and *The Matrix Reloaded* (2003), postmodern sequels to *Metropolis*, are the most recent SF films of significance to critique the alienating power of capitalism on human life. But the class and racial critiques of advanced capitalism presented in the *Matrix* franchise are couched in so much cryptic religious metaphor and psychobabble that the ideological edginess of the films becomes increasingly dulled and ultimately is blunted by an excessive series of kung fu–inspired fight scenes. The SF film *Rollerball*, although somewhat fragmented, presents a clearer critique of race relations under advanced capitalism along with the function of American nationalism in a global economic context.

In the post–economic apocalypse, corporate-controlled world of *Rollerball* (1975), the ultraviolent Rollerball game—a cross between baseball, football, motocross, basketball, and wrestling—is used to displace the pent-up anger and aggression of a populace dominated by various corporate cartels. In this futurescape, the nation-state exists no longer as a political entity but as various incarnations of a corporation that now control the everyday lives of their citizens. Moreover, each corporation has a team that participates in an international Rollerball derby, which provides a spectacle of violence for the laboring masses across the world to watch obsessively. Admittedly, much of the discussion of this film has revolved around the creation of the game and the violence presented in the film.[2] But *Rollerball* also calls attention to American race relations and the political economy associated with it.

The white protagonist of the film, Jonathan E. (James Caan), plays on the Houston team, which includes several black members and has a black team trainer. Initially, any form of racial dissension between white and black players appears nonexistent because of the overwhelming display of team unity and player camaraderie presented in the film. Although the black team members are not given anything substantial to say (they basically cheer for and exalt the main character), they play a central symbolic role in creating the appearance, and possibly the belief, that racial diversity and equality will exist in the America of the future. The multiracial camaraderie witnessed among the teammates and between Jonathan and his black friend and mentor, Cletus (Moses Gunn), is a striking contrast to the blaxploitation film craze of the period that habitually pitted blacks against whites as corrupt officials or a destructive presence in black communities.[3] In addition to being Jonathan's mentor, Cletus is also his personal trainer and confidant. Although Jonathan's closest white friend on the team, Moonpie (John Beck), accompanies the protagonist throughout the film, it is Cletus who is shown comfortably relaxing at Jonathan's secluded ranch. Cletus is even

The strategy trainer (Robert Ito) cautions the Houston team about the tactics of its next opponent in *Rollerball* (1975).

included in a video montage of Jonathan and his former wife, before the corporation dictated that she be assigned to another man. The three are shown lying next to one another as they lounge in a park, with Jonathan basking in the glow of love. The video is significant because the high point of their interracial friendship is firmly rooted in the past, and although the montage is presented within the framework of personal reflection, it still resonates on a broader level as social metaphor. Their relationship signals a nostalgic yearning for the integrationist sensibility of the civil rights movement, before the intense racial animus associated with the Black Power movement and the subsequent white political backlash against it fully emerged. Despite a romanticized ideological nod given to Martin Luther King's utopian dream of racial harmony, *Rollerball* illustrates how contemporary race relations, projected into the future, are in the end a product of economic manipulation and corporate fear mongering. An example of this dynamic is first depicted when the Houston team faces the prospect of competing against its Asian counterpart in an upcoming Rollerball match.

While taking a shower, Moonpie engages in casual racist banter regarding the Tokyo team. With a pronounced southern drawl, Moonpie refers to the Japanese team as "Orientals" and "tiny little men." He further states, "I can't get on a man-to-man basis with a pygmy or an Oriental. I don't know what it is." Given that he delivers these comments while showering alongside the rest of his teammates, their nudity suggests that the question is rhetorical and whatever "it" is, Moonpie's is definitely bigger. For him, size definitely does matter, and his comments are a crude articulation of male bravado meant to insinuate that white men are more physically/sexually

A belligerent Houston team rudely rejects the advice of the Asian trainer in *Rollerball*.

endowed in comparison with their Asian counterparts. But his statements are also a metaphor for an almost palpable racial anxiety associated with the growing stature of a competitive Japanese economy—coded as "tiny" and articulated as physical/sexual competition and standing—that was emerging in the 1970s. A subsequent scene in which an Asian consultant is hired to instruct the Houston team on how to avoid the "death blow" technique of the Japanese players makes the previous coded connection between American economic anxieties and racial prejudice clearly visible.

The scene is shot from the point of view of the Asian trainer, with the black players in the foreground as he tries to deliver his lecture. As he talks, Moonpie sporadically heckles him and later inspires his team members to stand and move toward the lecturer, chanting "Houston! Houston! Houston!" The team's actions eventually compel the trainer to stop talking. This scene is notable because it offers a model of how racial animus is cultivated and the purpose it serves in a context of global economic competition. The ability of Moonpie, given his prior callous articulation of racial prejudice, to motivate the black players to intimidate the Asian lecturer into abandoning his lecture is a powerful metaphor for how the economic insecurity of white *and* black working- and middle-class Americans is manipulated to stoke the fire of American nationalism. Furthermore, given the growing success of Japan's compact car industry, which directly contributed to the decline of the manufacture of gas-guzzling American automobiles, the Japanese "death blow" is an obvious metaphor for the real-world economic anxieties that gripped America in the face of global competition from Japan.

With only two "American" Rollerball teams left to compete in a championship death match, the film signals how domestic race relations are also informed by competitive capitalism. First, several visual cues in the concluding scenes indicate the racial character of the final match. For example, by the time the Houston team has reached the final match, the number of black teammates has been severely depleted, and they are no longer visually prominent, as they were in the previous competitions. In comparison, however, the New York team has several black players who are prominently shown. Third, a subtext of racial rivalry is visually accentuated by the racial composition of the opposing coaches of the Houston and New York teams, the former white and the latter black. Fourth, the camera rhetoric of the film works to establish the racial import of the match by framing the profiles of the opposing coaches facing one another with contempt while their teams inflict fatal injuries on one other. Lastly, the racial politics signaled by the face-off between the white and black coaches are further underscored when Jonathan strangles to death his racially symbolic counterpart, a black player on the New York team who has the same jersey number. The film suggests, however, that the destructive confrontation between the two men and what they symbolize—racial conflict—is manipulated by powerful economic interests outside the field of actual competition and direct confrontation. The savage killing of the black Rollerball player occurs directly in front of Bartholomew (John Houseman), the corporate director.

Yet, by the end of the film, the sharp indictment of the uses that a political economy of racism can achieve on a domestic and global scale is blunted by a message of triumphant white-male American individualism and hero worship. The point is driven home with a succession of close-up reaction

Moonpie (John Beck) is the recipient of the Japanese "death blow" in *Rollerball*.

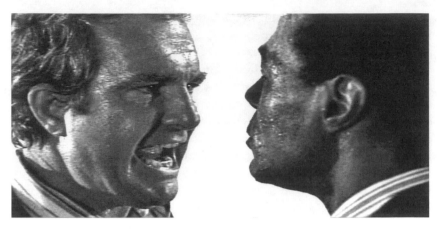

The composition of the frame symbolically underscores racial opposition between whites and blacks in American society in *Rollerball*.

shots of three different black men—the Houston trainer, the New York coach, and Cletus, shown rejoicing over Jonathan's last-man-standing victory. By foregrounding several black men who are cheering Jonathan as he makes his way around the track, the racial tension in the climactic confrontation between the two teams is resolved with a dramatic display of multiracial spectator support. As a result, Jonathan becomes fully vested as the "people's champion," regardless of race. Ultimately, the ending succumbs to the representational demands of American popular cinema, which requires its rebel-protagonists to affirm American individualism, albeit color-blind, rather than organized class revolt.

The conclusion of *Rollerball*, with its encoded racial critique of domestic and global political economy, is disappointing, given that Norman Jewison directed the film. Jewison shepherded the introduction of the groundbreaking black character Virgil Tibbs (Sidney Poitier) and the slap heard across America when Tibbs smacks a white man in the racial drama *In the Heat of the Night* (1967). The scene was a powerful political metaphor for the shifting of racial politics away from the nonviolent civil rights movement to the aggressive, confrontational stance of Black Power. *Rollerball* does not present a signature scene loaded with the same racial significance and visual shock as *In the Heat of the Night*. Nevertheless, *Rollerball* remains significant in suggesting that the fires of American nationalism are stoked for economic purposes and that corporate interests are the decisive racial broker between blacks and whites in America. The ending of *Rollerball*, however, abandons the radical class critique woven into the narrative. Instead of showing whites and blacks as unified against corporate totalitarianism, the conclusion offers an exaggerated performance of white masculinity in which the effective use of violence by an individual garners admiration for him from the masses and elevates him as a unifying symbol of individual freedom rather than collective struggle.

POSTINDUSTRIAL FUTURESCAPES

Ridley Scott's *Alien* (1979) paints a more progressive picture of labor united across race, class, and gender fault lines than *Rollerball* does. Admittedly, because the central protagonist of *Alien* is a woman, the cultural significance of the film has, for the most part, remained wedded to the deconstruction of gender.[4] At best, there has only been a passing reference to what the film has to say about race, with the most common racial analysis focused on the interracial camaraderie between the black crew member, Parker (Yaphet Kotto), and his white co-worker and friend Brett (Harry Dean Stanton).[5] Both of them are explicitly coded as blue-collar, working-class laborers in comparison with their more administrative, white-collar superiors. While the relationship between Parker and Brett in *Alien* is a central point of analysis for discussing the intersection of race, class, and gender, the interaction among the various crew members in the *Alien* sequels reveals a more complex, nuanced, and potentially radical reading of how sf film engages the multiple intersections of American race, class, and gender in a postindustrial U.S. society.

In fact, the reason the crew of the *Nostromo* space-mining vessel find themselves in a hostile setting and facing daunting circumstances metaphorically represents broader tensions present in the postindustrial labor market. The crew are contractually bound to investigate the source of a signal emanating from a nearby planet and must forfeit their pay and bonus percentages if they fail to do so. The crew's compulsion to adhere to their contract in order to keep their jobs reflects the limited options and forced concessions that many working-class laborers were beginning to make in the American manufacturing sector and foreshadows the type of draconian punishment, exemplified by Ronald Reagan's firing of thousands of striking air traffic controllers in 1981 for refusing to accept unfavorable working conditions. Forced to do the bidding of "the Company," the crew in *Alien* land on the planet and discover that a derelict spaceship is the source of the signal. While exploring the ship, one of the crew members is attacked by an alien life-form that surreptitiously completes its gestation inside him before bursting through his chest and taking refuge somewhere on the *Nostromo*.

Brett (Harry Dean Stanton) and Parker (Yaphet Kotto) rely on subversive humor to deflect their devaluation as workers in *Alien* (1979).

As a result, the remaining crew members are forced to go on a search-and-destroy mission on a spaceship that is simultaneously claustrophobic and a colossal labyrinth.

The immediate external threat posed to the crew is the violent alien life-form, which causes the crew members, many of whom are in conflict with one another, to put aside their personal differences for the goal of destroying it. But the most insidious threat to the crew is not necessarily the alien lurking in the shadows of the spaceship but the business logic of the Company, which values the alien life-form more than the human workers. Parker and Brett are the first characters in the film to signal working-class animosity toward the Company by their attitude toward its most identifiable and accessible representatives, the pilots and research staff of their space-mining mission. Like the laborers tolling beneath the city in Fritz Lang's *Metropolis*, Parker and Brett occupy the bottom rung of an exploitative and contradictory relationship in which they are the most indispensable members of the mining operation but also are the least valued and the least paid. The subterranean nature of their antagonistic relationship with the other members of the crew is underscored when Parker jokingly laments to Brett, "You ever notice how they never come down here? I mean this is where the work is. Right?" Parker's rhetorical question signals that a clear class divide is present in the film. But it is a divide that does not go unchallenged.

Parker requests that their bonus allocations be renegotiated because they are the least paid. The scene where Parker demands more pay is interesting in the way that he and Brett engage one another and confront their superior officers. As a case in point, the humor expressed by both men—in the form of jocular wisecracking about their superiors, various coded hand signals, and eye winks—not only is used to communicate with one another but also is a subversive technique for indirectly engaging in class struggle to mitigate their subordinate position. Parker, the black worker, is the most vocal and aggressive of the two men in challenging the authority of his white superiors by constantly signifying his distaste for them. When the captain, Dallas (Tom Skerritt), tells him to get a move on, Parker responds, "Can I finish my coffee? It's the only thing good on this ship." After returning to the main meeting area, Parker informs the science officer, Ash (Ian Holm), that he is in Parker's seat. After Ash moves, Parker brushes the seat with his hand before sitting down, in effect communicating that the officer is dirty. Parker's actions signify a strong distaste and dislike for his white colleagues who not only outrank him but also outearn him; such tactics are the type adopted by subordinate classes and minority groups to symbolically attack economic and racial elites.[6] Yet the camaraderie between Parker and Brett, along with Parker's constant gestures of defiance, suggests the possibility of black and white working-class solidarity and resistance that transcend racial fissures in the face of exploitative economic arrangements. Furthermore, their relationship lays the groundwork for the type of trade union humanism, articulated later in the film, when the last three remaining crew members discover the callous business logic of the Company, which has placed them in a life-threatening situation in the first place, and must combine forces to fight the alien.

Ripley (Sigourney Weaver) is the first to discover the ulterior motives of the Company when she queries the computer about their mission directive. She finds that the Company wanted the alien for its military-industrial commercial interests and deemed the crew "expendable." This message was a startling discovery for Ripley, but many American workers, particularly those in the car and other manufacturing industries of the late 1970s, were increasingly aware of the expendability of their labor in a postindustrial America. Despite having dedicated decades to their corporate employers, thousands of auto workers and manufacturing employees were underemployed or being laid off as the industrial-manufacturing boom began to grind to a slow halt in the late 1970s and early 1980s.[7] In the American economic past, workers could reasonably assume (or were socialized to believe) that loyalty and diligence to the company would be rewarded with lifetime employment, a modest but stable retirement package, and maybe even a gold watch for twenty, twenty-five, or thirty years of service. The late 1970s marked the beginning of the end of the romanticized reciprocity between employee and employer, along with the informal categories of recognition it produced—the "company man" and the corporate yes-man. The white male android science officer, Ash, symbolically brings to bear all of the anxieties associated with the demise of the corporate yes-man in postindustrial America.

"Corporate yes-man" is a derisive title that calls attention to the more unsavory aspects of corporate loyalty and the eager malleability of the worker. The yes-man agrees with everything his corporate superiors advocate as if he possesses no free will. Ash, programmed to comply with and protect the wishes of the Company, even if that means killing his crewmates, is the pure embodiment of the corporate yes-man. In *Alien*, however, the idea of a worker solely committed to the interests of his employer is eviscerated to reveal a soulless automaton, when Parker and Lambert (Veronica Cartwright) stumble upon Ash as he tries to suffocate Ripley with a rolled-up magazine forcefully pushed down her throat. Parker, Lambert, and Ripley struggle to pull Ash off of her until Parker literally knocks Ash's head off, only to witness his robotic body become seized with convulsions as it continues to attack Parker. Shortly thereafter, the decapitated head is shown sharing Ash's mission directive and informing them that he is an organic android sent by the Company to facilitate the recovery and return of the alien life-form to Earth for the Company's bio-war division. Indeed, Ash, as a decapitated talking head espousing his corporate mission, is an uncanny image, but it pales in comparison with the symbolic message of an android that signifies rational white male corporate authority, power, and knowledge having his head knocked off in a struggle against two white women and a black male. Ash's decapitation and later destruction signify both the last gasp of the "company man" and, more importantly, a simmering fear and resentment by white males toward women and racial minorities in the corporate workplace.

In the wake of the women's movement and affirmative action, the 1970s was a decade in which women and African Americans began entering, in a very short period, virtually every all-white, all-male bastion of the American corporate structure. The figure of Ash symbolically brings to bear all of the gender and racial anxieties associated with the transformation of the American workplace as postindustrial decline set in. On one hand, the phallic intrusion of a "girlie" magazine into Ripley's mouth suggests male hostility— even to the point of misogyny—directed at the idea, image, and reality of the ambitious, competent, professional, and successful career woman that Ripley symbolizes in the film and that a multitude of white men found themselves competing against and resenting in the American workplace. On the other hand, Parker symbolically proxies for a host of blacks who overwhelmingly worked in sectors of the American economy that required cheap expendable labor. Furthermore, his overt hostility toward his superiors, his destruction of Ash, and his hyperaggression toward the alien life-form (he engages in hand-to-hand combat with it) suggest that black workers—because they occupy a low status, receive low wages, and experience diminished opportunities for upward social mobility—are the most economically exploited and socially aggravated workers, spurring them to exhibit overt behavior that challenges institutional authority and legitimacy.

The fleeting pact to destroy the alien and flee the ship—a pact made between the last three remaining crew members in *Alien*, a black male and two white women—does an exceptional job of amplifying intersecting race, class, and gender tensions as well as illustrating the importance of forming a coalition among competing subjectivities to fight savage corporate capitalism. Indeed, what Ash admired the savage alien for—being "unclouded by conscience, remorse, or delusions of morality"—epitomizes the worst qualities of corporate capitalism and brings into sharp focus the corporate dominance that working-class blacks and managerial middle-class whites would face as the 1970s came to a close. The economic prosperity of post-WWII industrialism that had fueled the expansion of the American middle class for nearly forty years began to savagely consume its own as deindustrialization set in. As a metaphor, *Alien* expressed this shift with horrifying terror, but the film also suggested that race, class, and gender cooperation vis-à-vis organized labor was necessary, in the face of monstrous capitalism, to fend off the life-threatening consequences of this economic shift.

For as much as Ridley Scott's *Alien* subversively tackled racial anxieties amid a crumbling manufacturing and industrial American economy, James Cameron's sequel, *Aliens* (1986), presents a more fragmented and contradictory picture of the intersection of race and class in the far future. *Aliens* picks up fifty-seven years after Ripley destroyed the alien aboard her escape vessel. After her vessel is discovered adrift in deep space with her in a state of suspended animation, Ripley is recruited to help an advance party of Colonial Marines investigate the planet where the alien was found. The Company had authorized and funded a colony of workers on the planet, and they are no longer transmitting or acknowledging any form of communication. With the Carter Burke (Paul Reiser) character, an administrative flunky for the Company who is constantly weighing the cost to the Company when human life is at stake, the sequel is consistent with the original film's anticorporate theme. However, the antagonisms between labor and capital that were central to the first film recede to the background in the second installment. Instead, *Aliens* foregrounds military heroism and, in doing so, robs the film of the progressive racial politics suggested in the original film and makes the sequel stand primarily as a recuperative military text.

In *Aliens* the space marines of the future are a tough-as-nails outfit, ready to kill first and ask questions later. Gratuitous foul-mouthed banter and affected military bravado help create the appearance of an aggressive and mentally tough military unit ready to destroy alien intruders. Whereas in *Alien* the black character expressed a certain degree of contempt for his white commanding officers as representatives of the Company, the sequel offers a black drill sergeant, Sergeant Apone (Al Matthews), as the commanding officer of the predominantly white search-and-destroy squadron. By doing so, the sequel reverses the racial status of the black character from a subordinate in *Alien* to a figure of institutional power and authority who commands whites. The result is a text drained of the black and white class tensions that made the original so critically engaging. Although the subtext of working-class and minority conflict in a postindustrial labor market is missing in the sequel, racial conflict is not completely absent in *Aliens*. Instead, an acute racial anxiety surrounding American border politics is significantly present in *Aliens* and symbolically underscored by the character of Private Vasquez (Jenette Goldstein), the tough-talking butch Latina.

The private's last name, her affected Spanish accent and sporadic use of Spanish, the Spanish words written on her breastplate, and finally the red bandanna prominently wrapped around her head—a clichéd reference to Los Angeles Latino gang attire—are all signifiers of ethnicity that aggressively work to overdetermine her racial/ethnic "otherness" and firmly construct her as Mexican. This semiotic overkill is significant because Vasquez's racial ethnicity stands in contrast to the symbolic construction of the black sergeant and the black private, Frost (Ricco Ross). Both black characters—and particularly the black sergeant, who spearheads the mission—clearly illustrate that black racial integration is the accepted norm. In contrast, even some hundred years into the future, Latino assimilation into the American mainstream remains extremely marginalized. For example, a racist comment is directed toward Private Vasquez that highlights her status as an unassimilable racial "other." At a group military briefing, a white male marine blurts out, "Somebody said 'alien.' She thought they said 'illegal alien' and signed up." In spite of a narrative set far into the future and occurring on an entirely different world, here is a clear example of Latino subjectivity projected into the future but remaining reductively coded according to contemporary U.S. border politics. The semiotic exaggeration of ethnicity and the verbal hostility directed to the Latina character all work to accent her otherness. Such racial coding is not surprising, however, given the increasing economic and cultural anxiety surrounding the influx of Latino immigrants, particularly from Mexico and Central America, that began in the early 1980s.

Private Vasquez (Jenette Goldstein) in *Aliens* (1986).

As cinematic metaphor, *Aliens* invokes the most paranoid economic fears associated with undocumented immigration with a narrative of parasitic creatures that feed off their human hosts before becoming self-sufficient. Accordingly, it is not a large allegorical leap to connect a film titled *Aliens*—and which contains a scene defining the only Latino character in the film as an "illegal alien"—to the anti-immigration hysteria associated with the border politics of the American Southwest. Ultimately, multiple anxieties born of post-1980s Latino immigration are (re)imagined in *Aliens* as hordes of giant buglike humans sneaking past well-defended militarized blockades and fortifications. As Renato Rosaldo states:

> The US-Mexico border has become theater, and border theater has be-
> come social violence. Actual violence has become inseparable from
> symbolic ritual on the border—crossings, invasions, lines of defense,
> high-tech surveillance, and more. Social scientists often think of public
> rituals as events that resemble formal rituals separated from daily life
> in time and space and marked by repeated formal structures. In contrast
> *the violence and high tech weaponry of border theater is at once sym-
> bolic* and material. (Emphasis mine)[8]

In this sense, the symbolic work that *Aliens* performs—by referring to Vasquez as an illegal alien, in a film about alien creatures as trespassers that must be destroyed by the military—is a part of a broader sociocultural project found in a range of films to address the fears, fantasies, and reality of economic anxieties spurred by not only Latino immigration but the "browning" of America.

On one hand, films like *El Norte* (1983) and *Salvador* (1986) captured a new wave of Latino immigration and the political chaos that pushed many Latinos to gamble on America as an economic promised land. On the other hand, SF films such as *Aliens* and *Men in Black* (1997) stand out as probably some of the most vicious symbolic attacks on undocumented immigration.[9] Where the former symbolically associates Latinos with giant buglike creatures, the latter film equates a Latino person with an actual alien from another world that has illegally immigrated to the planet Earth. Early in *Men in Black*, two white middle-aged agents of a secret organization, MiB (Men in Black), are assigned to monitor space aliens disguised as humans who have immigrated to Earth, and the men confront a Latino male trying to cross the Mexico border into America. The Latino male is later revealed to be a grotesque green monster that is destroyed when it turns to attack a white border patrol officer who has stumbled into the area. Not withstanding the comedic nature of the film, the representation of a Latino as a violent alien creature being obliterated by law enforcement is a stern reflection of a desire to militarize the U.S. border and of hostility toward undocumented Latino immigrants. Although *Aliens* is not as crude as *Men in Black* in how it symbolically attacks undocumented immigrants, it still expresses significant hostility by reinforcing a link between illegality and Latino subjectivity. Consequently, although the first film's action elements are amplified to create a successful sequel, the progressive class and racial possibilities suggested in the original are disappointingly absent. By the next installment of the series, *Alien³* (1992), the progressive racial and class politics suggested in the original have been fully turned on their head.

In *Alien³* an escape pod carrying Ripley and several survivors from the previous film land on a distant planet. Ripley is the sole survivor of a crash landing and awakens to find herself an unwelcome guest in an all-male prison colony. She is not the only unwelcome guest to arrive, however. Unbeknownst to everyone, the escape pod was carrying two embryonic aliens, one on the ship and one inside Ripley. Whereas *Aliens* was a recuperative text in its affirmation of the American military-industrial complex, *Alien³* is a socially conservative text that articulates a narrative of racial self-help and Christian fundamentalism. By placing Ripley in an all-male prison, the film tries to capitalize on the gender anxieties and feminist tensions that were so deftly engaged in the original and to a lesser extent in the sequel. Yet, by this third installment, SF cinema's paradigmatic protofeminist emerges from the escape pod a considerably diminished figure. Radical only in her appearance (she has a completely shaved head), Ripley is quite satisfied in playing second fiddle to her male counterparts. The reconfiguration of Ripley as a dependent character occurs almost in direct proportion to the affirmation of male authority and general patriarchy exhibited in the film, first, in relationship to her doctor and short-lived lover, Clemons (Charles Dance), and, second, to Dillon (Charles S. Dutton), the messianic black leader of a Christian fundamentalist religious cult that has taken root in the prison population.

The men in the prison are extremely hostile to Ripley's presence because of the destabilizing threat she poses as an object of sexual desire for men, who have, as a part of their atonement for previous crimes, pledged strict vows of chastity. As a result, Ripley is inscribed with all of the historical, theological, and social paranoia associated with women as temptresses, along with introducing the profane into the realm of the sacred—Ripley is "pregnant" with a "queen" alien growing inside her. Ripley's pregnancy also registers a sublimated anti-abortion theme, mirroring similar gender anxieties that were part and parcel of the "culture wars" that heated up in the 1990s as the Christian Right mounted an aggressive campaign against contraception, feminist politics, and personal choice. *Alien³*, in keeping with its religious Right references and the vigorous pro-life stance the movement emboldened, has Dillon vehemently reject Ripley's requests to kill the alien baby she is carrying by killing her. Ostensibly, Dillon rejects killing Ripley because she is too valuable as bait for the alien that is on the loose. But by allowing Dillon, the Christian leader of the prison population, to dictate what Ripley does with her own body along with the destruction of the alien baby only after it bursts from her torso, the film ideologically dovetails with a reaffirmation of male patriarchy and religious Right arguments about the sanctity of *all* unborn life, a staple of the anti-abortion movement in America.

Alien³ delivers a kinder and gentler Ripley than the one in the previous films, while the black character represents the power of Christian theology to unify a range of men and morally inspire them to fight the alien monster. In this sense *Alien³* evokes the populist Christian men's movement that sprang up in the early to mid-1990s. Groups like the Promise Keepers spread across America, filling large stadiums with men-only gatherings in a public attempt to reassert a male moral authority and reinvigorate the power and status of traditional patriarchal relationships. Like the repositioning of Ripley in a manner that affirms female dependence, in *Alien³* the cultural politics of black economic self-help are also couched in the cresting cultural conservatism of the time.

The early 1990s witnessed a continuing critique of liberal social programs associated with race, such as affirmative action and welfare. Such programs were cast as economic handouts that pandered to blacks and cultivated a compromised sense of individual and community wherewithal for blacks who advocated, accepted, or benefited from them.[10] *Alien*[3] affirms these same principals and emphasizes a return to the cherished idea of American rugged individualism by African Americans in the figure of Dillon, the black male leader of the religious prison cult. In a rousing speech to the men, he chides them for deciding to wait for a Company supply ship to help them take on the alien creature lurking in the prison facility. Dillon rejects the idea of help from the Company, even though the men have no weapons, and he rails against the men for doing nothing except waiting for the alien to pick them off one at a time. He delivers his motivational sermon in a tone of righteous indignation, saying, "You all are going to die. . . . Do you want it on your feet or on your fucking knees, begging? I ain't much for begging. Nobody ever gave me nothing." Dillon's coarse declaration against personal complacency and his vehement rejection of institutional assistance in the face of inadequate resources and a physically superior alien creature register an ideological chord similar to that of conservative critics who assailed the American welfare state. Poor blacks, like the socially marginal and stigmatized men of the film, needed to do what Dillon railed against: stop "begging" for help, and reject government handouts.

Even the controversial leader of the Nation of Islam, Louis Farrakhan, appeared receptive to some of the chords of conservatism that echoed throughout the 1980s and into the 1990s. Farrakhan's call for a day of atonement for black men motivated nearly a million of them to go on a sojourn to Washington, D.C., in 1995 for what was titled the Million Man March. Dillon's inspirational oration and stern chastisement directed at a group of dispirited white men in *Alien*[3] is in form and spirit, if not audience, not that unlike Farrakhan's message of atonement delivered to African American males to inspire them to assume personal responsibility for themselves and their families. Both speeches promoted a neoconservative take on black social responsibility, whereby a lack of personal responsibility is viewed as contributing to cultural excesses that are detrimental to personal success and self-respect. Moreover, Dillon's stature as a self-made black man symbolically dovetails with the "pull yourself up by your bootstraps" racial rhetoric of upward mobility that neoconservatives often champion, along with American rugged individualism, as the solution for scores of African Americans trapped in a cycle of poverty. Dillon's vehement rejection of help from the Company in *Alien*[3] easily fits into a broader affirmation of black self-help success stories—such as that of Colin Powell, the first black secretary of state, and of Supreme Court justice Clarence Thomas—alongside criticism from black conservatives, like Thomas Sowell. The combination of success stories and criticisms is used to call into question the existence of virulent systemic racism in a post–civil rights America and to place the onus of black economic failure and welfare dependency on the detrimental behavior of blacks.[11]

In the end, Dillon's diatribe against "begging" motivates the remaining white men and single woman to join with him in a coalition to destroy the alien creature, similar to the coalition that formed in the first *Alien* film. Yet the embrace of multiracial (and gender) politics, as suggested by *Alien*[3], is infused with conservative undertones in which personal discipline is a panacea for racial and gender inequality in America and easily outweighs any message about progressive coalition politics and the token critique of corporate greed tacked onto the end of the film. For the most part, religious transformation is foregrounded, and the masculine morality of Dillon symbolizes the transformative power of religious faith, not institutional assistance, to deliver socially marginalized people with limited life opportunities from their deplorable socioeconomic conditions. Ultimately, *Alien*[3] signals that racial disparity between blacks and whites in America is not a function of postindustrial decline or even of the type of corporate manipulation suggested in *Rollerball* but is due to a lack of willpower and moral discipline.

BLUE-COLLAR DYSTOPIA

Not all of the SF films that emerged in the postindustrial economic quagmire of the 1980s and early 1990s took such a dramatic conservative turn as the *Alien* franchise. *Alien Resurrection* (1997), with a superficial and at times campy attempt at political correctness, casts a motley crew of victims for the alien to consume, including a wheelchair-bound mechanic and two female principals intimated to be lesbians, but the film fails to deliver any meaningful social metaphors for race and class in America with these characters and their interrelationships. In contrast, Paul Verhoeven's *Robo-Cop* (1987) and John Carpenter's *They Live* (1988) are two of the most radical SF films to emerge in the postindustrial era, explicitly critiquing America's class divisions and the way racial inequality operates to further corporate interests. *RoboCop* and *They Live* confront the increasing deregulation and privatization of public services and take them to their absurdist conclusion. *RoboCop* is a brash sociocultural satire of the implosion of Detroit, one of America's most prominent industrial cities. *They Live* is a biting critique of Reaganomics, as well as a populist proletarian call to arms.

In *RoboCop* the future Detroit is a city in crisis, where privatization and corporate control have usurped the state as the social institution of last resort. Old Detroit, as it is called in the film, is depicted as an economically and morally bankrupt city braving rampant crime and social chaos, with only a beleaguered, underfunded, and overworked police force left to combat the city's social decay. Unable to stem the tide of unbridled criminal violence, the police force comes under the stewardship of Omni Consumer Products (OCP), a corporation that plans to build a robotic police force that will be more cost-efficient than the human officers who patrol the city. Certainly, what *RoboCop* says about the man-versus-machine dichotomy, a topic frequently found in American SF studies, is a compelling area of analysis.[12] That Detroit, with its rich and contentious racial and class history and its past as a symbol of American industrial predominance, is represented as a cesspool of crime and chaos in *RoboCop* requires scrutiny in and of itself. The ideological center of the film is not the part-machine, part-human police officer of the future but the socioeconomic conditions of a city that requires such a machine. Consequently, in *RoboCop* the cityscape of Detroit is as much a central character in the narrative as the cyborg that traverses its streets on a quest to stop crime and catch criminals.

The real Detroit was an economic promised land for many whites and blacks who were drawn to employment opportunities in the Motor City's automobile industry. Although both racial groups were attracted by the same expanding industry and its demand for assembly-line labor, racial cleavages ran deep, both inside and outside the factory. Racially segregated neighborhoods sprung up as blacks made their way from the South and found themselves crowded into the city's ghettoes.[13] With the violent and costly race riot in 1967, segregation became further entrenched by wide-scale "white flight" from the city to the surrounding suburbs. In the aftermath of the racial uprisings of the late 1960s, it began to appear that the civic vitality and future of Detroit were shaped more by racial issues than by labor issues and that the crisis of color was no longer over blue-collar working conditions and pay but had to do with black and white racial tensions. Consequently, race began to define Detroit politically and socially just as much as the popularity of Motown music defined it culturally. In the end, Detroit became known as a "chocolate city" surrounded by "vanilla suburbs."[14]

By the mid-1970s, Detroit was beginning to fray along the economic edges, as layoffs and plant closings marked the beginning of an economic meltdown. The 1980s ushered in the city's transition from a symbol of economic prowess to a symbol of economic failure and urban abandonment. Detroit became a modern version of the "boom and bust" ghost towns that littered the West of the 1800s after the gold rush. By the 1980s the American "car rush" had run out of steam, and Detroit was a shadow of its former economic self. Emblematic of the dramatic decline was the startling development that one of the Big Three car companies, Chrysler, was courting bankruptcy, and even Motown had to relocate in Tinseltown (Hollywood). Skyscrapers and factories, the metal and concrete testimonies to the heyday of Detroit's car-driven industrial revolution, now stood as abandoned ruins of industrial decay for self-proclaimed urban archeologists to explore. The proverbial "rise and fall" of Detroit ushered in various accounts of how this metropolis became the site of so much social and economic trauma, inflicted not only by politicians and economists but also by Hollywood. *RoboCop* is such a Hollywood film, synthesizing contemporary events into a futuristic narrative that has a fictional Detroit being overwhelmed by violent crime, political impotency, and economic crisis.

RoboCop opens with a television news segment in which the top story is a report on Pretoria, South Africa, that mirrors the racial fault lines existing in Detroit. The newscaster relates that the "ruling white military government of the besieged city-state" has unveiled a neutron bomb and affirmed its willingness to use it as a last line of defense. The broadcast is an excellent example of intertextuality, whereby one text is marked by a sequence of images and descriptive narration that have a meaning and connection to another text. In this case, although the film is set in an indeterminate future, the racial turmoil and images of confrontation in the South Africa of the future draw on the politics of South African apartheid of the late 1980s along with signifying a link to the racial politics of Detroit. By describing Pretoria as "besieged" by racial violence and chaos and then subsequently reporting on the crime and budget problems of Old Detroit, the narrative underscores a signifying link between Pretoria's race problem and Old Detroit's economic issues. The Old Detroit of *RoboCop* is a transparent attempt at temporal displacement. Instead, the juxtaposition of the racial crisis in Pretoria and the crime in Old Detroit in an indeterminate future works as a prefiguring framework that signals to the audience that Old Detroit of the future politically parallels the Detroit of now. Unfortunately, the fictionalized movie version of a violent future Detroit is not significantly more ominous than the actual contemporary version of the city. Detroit has periodically led the nation in murders, a dubious distinction that cropped up in the tagline for the movie *Detroit 9000* (1973): "Visit the murder capital of the world—where the honkies are the minority!" In this sense, when an OCP executive refers to the first Robocop prototype as programmed for "urban pacification," the fictional world of the film overlaps with the historical reality of racial discord, de facto racial segregation, and violence that has plagued inner-city Detroit since the late 1960s. Yet *RoboCop* is not merely reflective of these impulses; it also is critical of them.

RoboCop offers a vision of racial accord vis-à-vis blue-collar working-class unity that stands in opposition to the racial discord historically associated with Detroit. In *RoboCop* the police officers of the Metro division are the proletarian labor force of beleaguered racially diverse men and women fighting to serve the public while being financially squeezed by their corporate owners. The film is significant for depicting meaningful working-class alliances as a source for transcending racial and gender cleavages. A working-class coalition between whites and blacks is signaled early in the film when Murphy (Peter Weller) first arrives at the police station. Various black and white police officers are shown preparing for duty as Murphy walks through the locker room. Both men and women are dressing in the same common area, with nude men taking showers in the background. A seminude white woman is shown placing a vest over her torso while sitting next to a black female officer who laments the adverse working conditions in the face of massive cutbacks. In *RoboCop* the use of nudity in various shots of racially diverse men and women undressing and dressing among one another—along with running dialogue detailing the massive firings, lay-offs, and transfers, punctuated by a white male police officer loudly threatening to strike—symbolizes a utopian model of blue-collar vitality and class unity that transcends race and gender differences in the face of corporate downsizing.

Yet, arguably, no other American SF film is as perversely ironic as *Robo-Cop* in quickly unraveling the politics of working-class unity. By having a cyborg—intended to replace the human police officers—as the blue-collar hero the officers rally around, the film courts being defined as cynically pessimistic if not utterly tragic. On one hand, the symbolism of a robotic police officer as the savior of Detroit is quite absurd, since it is the increasing use of robotics to assemble cars that contributed to the downsizing of automotive labor and the displacement of scores of assembly-line workers. On the other hand, however, having a beleaguered police force threatened with their own planned obsolescence as they are replaced by robotic police officers in the film perfectly parallels the demise of the automobile assembly-line worker in the face of increasing automation. This juxtaposition of social satire with symbolic realism is an awkward ideological aspect of the progressive race and class politics suggested in *RoboCop*, because the acceptance of the robotic cop by the human police officers undermines their working-class unity and siphons their potential as organized labor ready to exert leverage on their corporate bosses.

In many ways *RoboCop* symbolizes a "coming to terms" with the significant impact that automation had on assembly-line workers when American industries began downsizing as a quick fix for lowering costs to compete

with foreign manufacturers. The acceptance of the man-machine police officer as a hero in *RoboCop*, along with its sequels, marked the begrudging
acknowledgment that the handwriting was on the wall for both black and
white members of the American blue-collar workforce. The forward march
of capitalism would include a technological overhaul that, in many cases,
would make factory laborers redundant in assembly-line manufacturing
plants, regardless of their race. Ultimately, *RoboCop* satirized both the symbols of corporate power and the mass media as collaborating institutions
that would indiscriminately rubber-stamp any type of corporate privatization, no matter how bizarre it sounded or how damaging to the American
public. *RoboCop* warned of the consequences of unbridled corporate power:
the colonization of the lives of people, and the death of the American working class.

Not since the film adaptation of Paddy Chayefsky's *Network* (1976) has
there been such a scathing indictment of mainstream media as cultural propaganda than John Carpenter's *They Live* (1988). It is an SF film that places
alien creatures at the seat of corporate power through human collaboration
and media mind control. In *They Live* the television station is a medium
for the transmission of a jamming signal that makes the population unable
to see the hideous alien creatures that occupy the authoritative economic
and social positions of American society. A small underground resistance,
however, knows the truth and is trying to organize a revolt. They distribute
sunglasses to new recruits that allow the wearers to penetrate the slick facade of advertising and authoritative proclamations proffered by aliens that
only appear human. The glasses (and later contact lenses) act as a sensory fil-
ter, allowing the real images and messages bombarding the subconscious of
the population to be perceived. With these glasses in place a true picture of
the American social order comes into frightening focus. Magazine and book
pages that appeared crowded with images and dense information are in fact
blank or have simple statements such as "Consume" or "Sleep" on the cover
and inside. Furthermore, there is constant surveillance of the population
by mechanical flying sentinels and a moderate number of skinless humanoid aliens scattered among the power elite of the population. The revelation
of the true nature of the American social and political order is witnessed
through the point of view of Nada (Roddy Piper), an unemployed, homeless,
white male day laborer.

The film begins with Nada walking the streets of downtown Los Angeles
in search of employment. He eventually finds work at a construction site
and is befriended by Frank (Keith David), a black co-worker who offers him
directions to a makeshift tent commune. A volunteer church group located

across the street from a large lot provides the city's homeless with food, bathroom facilities, and tents. As both men become more familiar and comfortable with one another, they share their desperate struggle to survive in a harsh economic world. Frank tells Nada he was laid off from a Detroit steel mill and laments the closing of factories in a "dog-eat-dog" system where the opportunity to achieve upward socioeconomic mobility is dramatically shrinking. Nada, his white counterpart, expresses a diametrically opposed vision of America when he says to Frank, "I deliver a hard day's work for the money. I just want a chance. I believe in America. I follow the rules." Not only does their discussion raise important issues about social inequality, power, and the cultural politics of white working-class ideas of American meritocracy and black working-class beliefs that the "system" is inherently unfair, but it also expresses how racial subjectivity informs different perceptions of the American dream. As a result, the politics of race comes to the narrative surface along the lines of perception, as a raced way of seeing and defining social reality.[15]

The Horatio Alger myth is the backbone of the American dream, and its conventional narrative of rags-to-riches upward social mobility is tied to the belief that economic success is a function of merit and hard work. Moreover, where upward mobility is stagnant, the assumption is that failure most often reflects the shortcomings of the individual and not society. In terms of the politics of race, the increase and decrease of the black middle class are often used by social scientists, race relations scholars, and politicians to confirm or critique the degree to which America is living up to its promise of judging individuals by their merit rather than their membership in a devalued race or ethnic group.[16] The increase or decrease of black folk entering middle-class status is often used to gauge the macro effect of racial discrimination. For African Americans, the Horatio Alger myth becomes the standard for judging the effects of racism, because conventional wisdom argues that the presence of a black middle class revolves around access to opportunity, education, and capital that a system of virulent racial discrimination does not permit. Consequently, black middle-class success is, to borrow from William Wilson, "proof" that race is declining in significance in American society.[17]

Indeed, when Nada tells Frank that he believes in America to make good on compensating him for delivering "a hard day's work," he not only invokes the "by your bootstraps" mythology of Horatio Alger but also stands in stark contrast to Frank's call of institutional foul. Nada implicitly stresses the viability of meritorious entry and membership into the middle class in proportion to the meaningful participation one is willing to contribute in the form of hard work. Symbolically, Nada's position draws an ideological line between himself as a white male who believes in America, and Frank, a black male who does not believe in what America has to offer. Later, however, when Nada is able to see how human collaborators curry favor from alien colonizers for economic advantage, his belief in American meritocracy under competitive capitalism is severely eroded, a sentiment that his black counterpart had already expressed. This is a noteworthy example of how *They Live* periodically has white characters see the world as it exists, not only from the perspective of the socially and economically marginalized in general, but also from that of the black working class and underclass. For this reason, the issue of racialized perspectives, which are part and parcel of the white and black racial divide in America, is a significant subtext throughout the film.

Along with the use of glasses and contact lenses to denote an impairment and correction of one's political vision, the camera rhetoric of the film also underscores how the world appears from the perspective of the socially dispossessed and homeless underclass according to race. For example, the vantage point of a black character becomes an important device for establishing a shared perspective between him and a group of whites so that they can, in effect, see the world together as it truly exists. This point is highlighted when a white family, fleeing a violent police raid on their homeless camp, enter an abandoned building to hide from pursuing police officers. Inside the building a black man sits in a chair in the middle of the room, visibly intoxicated from the marijuana cigarette he calmly inhales. He looks out the window, which frames the mayhem outside. Police officers are brutally beating and, in some cases, shooting unarmed homeless civilians. He whispers to the family to "come on in and join the party" as they stand behind him, peering at the violent spectacle outside the window. His reaction to the outside police violence is one of emotional detachment and apathy, aided by the use of an intoxicating drug, and gives full expression to Frank's prior articulation of black disillusionment with the American dream. The shock, fear, and horror expressed by the white family (father, daughter, and surrogate son) are in stark contrast to the nonchalant demeanor of the black squatter. His lack of alarm and outrage suggests that he is accustomed to seeing such capricious state violence against his community, himself, and possibly others who look like him, a homeless black male. Consequently, the emotional urgency, generated by the social chaos outside, that the white family and Nada, as their proletarian guardian angel, bring with them into the black character's social setting grinds to a halt when they encounter the squatter. For him, there is no emotional or even political urgency, because

Nada (Roddy Piper) finally subdues Frank (Keith David) so that he can see the true source of their oppression in *They Live* (1988).

he has already been there and done that. This theme is later echoed in an extended fight sequence between Nada and Frank.

The marathon brawl has Nada attempting to make Frank wear the glasses he has found. Given Frank's disconsolate sentiments about his and, by implication, black peoples' lot in life, as victims of a system that is rigged against members of subordinate groups like him, he has no desire or need to see how the inequality of an alien-controlled America works. Indeed, he is well aware of it because he is a victim of it. Against this ideological backdrop the lengthy fight scene between Frank and Nada is not symptomatic of John Carpenter's tendency for visual hyperbole or self-indulgence. Instead the scene is a sincere attempt to convey the protracted nature of the struggle to bridge the racial gap in America and how difficult it is to bring both racial groups together to see and confront the political order of the day. Eventually, a subdued and exhausted Frank puts on the glasses and sees the unmitigated source of his disenfranchisement. As a result, both men unite and seek out the underground movement against the aliens and their human collaborators. The film clearly indicates that when black and white perceptions of American society are no longer clouded by divergent perspectives, it is possible, and in fact necessary, for these separate racial groups to unite and fight against growing corporate totalitarianism. This point is underscored by the ranks of the underground movement, which is populated primarily by poor and working-class blacks and whites (there is also a white leftist intellectual figure) who have come together to mount a resistance movement.

They Live is saturated with signifiers of racial reconciliation, social activism, and revolution needed to mount sustainable and effective working-class warfare against monstrous alien economic elites. The film references the civil rights movement by having a black church as the home base of the resistance movement and a blind black preacher (Raymond St. Jacques) as one of the principal leaders of the group. Foremost, *They Live* is a semiotic interrogation and radical critique of Reaganomics and the culture of greed that emerged with it as the 1980s came to a close. The film draws on the postindustrial cultural and economic landscape of America in the period, in which a dramatic widening of the gap between the wealthy and the poor continued unabated, mindless consumerism became fashionable, a savings-and-loan industry scandal with estimated costs to the taxpayer in the billions was ushered in and promptly out of the public consciousness, and a staggering increase in the homeless population became normalized. In *They Live* the hideousness of the economic elites, who are in reality space monsters, symbolized the horrific consequences of postindustrial decline: decreased wages, increasing unemployment, pollution, media escapism, political complacency, and violence against the poor. For American race relations the ideological implication of the film was as radical as it was economically condemning. The source of socioeconomic dispossession for African Americans and other people of color in America was not purported black pathology, black single female–headed households, or black criminality but the failures of capitalism, experienced as postindustrial decline.

THE REVOLUTION WILL BE COLOR-BLIND

A multitude of Hollywood films attest to the contradictory expressions of class and racial conflict that help define the national and global identity of American society for producers and consumers of the cinematic experience. In many ways, the SF films examined in this chapter, at their most critical, responded to the consequences of postindustrial decline and racial segmentation by confronting growing race cleavages with images of class unifica

The real world of *They Live*.

tion. SF films such as *Rollerball, Alien,* and the cult film *They Live* even go so far as to suggest that racial formation, racial conflict, and the possibility of working-class unity across racial lines not only are informed by the very economic crises that gripped America from the early 1970s to today; the ideological topography of these films is filled with symbolic expressions that economic oppression lies at the core of past, current, and future racial divisions. Even though black inner-city residents and blue-collar workers bore the brunt of American deindustrialization, the white middle class was not unaffected.

Although many white middle-class Americans were able to scramble to the safety of the suburbs, they were not able to escape the consequences of postindustrial decline. Corporate mergers resulted in managerial downsizing, and white middle-class workers also felt the shock waves of economic contraction. The ideological message in several SF films warned that corporate elites were undermining the American dream and that racial reactionaries on both sides of the political spectrum had better prepare to move beyond the cultural politics of black and white racial subjectivity in order to effectively deal with the erosion of the "good life" and any notion of early retirement for a great majority of the American workforce. Interestingly, American SF cinema became a site where these shifting economic dynamics and their cultural fallout were confronted and periodically critiqued through the presentation of a progressive image and model of American race and class relations.

In several important SF films of the postindustrial era, cooperation between blacks and whites is presented as a necessary stage for resisting corporate power. Although such themes are expressed within fantastical plots and far-off worlds, they suggest that offscreen economic oppression, not racial oppression, rests at the core of current social divisions between blacks and whites in the present and most probably those anticipated in the future. Despite the attempts in SF film to engage race and class issues, there remains, for the most part, a collusion of silence in the American body politic when the intricacy of race and class oppression is the topic. Class oppression and elite power are rarely discussed openly in the popular American press, and the shrill edicts of neoconservative political pundits and respected liberal scholars alike that proclaimed the end of racism in the post–civil rights era have marginalized and stigmatized discussions around white supremacy as outdated. As a result, class and racial hierarchies are a taboo political topic that instead finds expression in alternative cultural outlets such as the imaginative medium of SF film as entertainment, sometimes art, and on rare occasions a critical rallying cry to the dispossessed.

CHAPTER 5

WHITE NARRATIVES, BLACK ALLEGORIES

Cinema, taken generically, signifies in a de-differentiated manner. No other
form of cultural representation—not painting, nor literature nor music nor
even television—can signify quite as figurally as can cinema.

SCOTT LASH, *Sociology of Postmodernism*

Like the American western, SF film has played a significant part in affirming a myriad of myths and constructing historical relationships that are, at
the least, uncritical and, at worst, revisionist falsehoods. For decades, film
westerns presented intrepid white settlers as righteously taming the Wild
West by vanquishing bands of hostile Indians, instead of presenting the push
westward as a violent imposition upon the indigenous population. The western reimagined domestic imperialism as the establishment of civilization
for the greater good. Such cinematic narratives affirmed the myth of American frontierism and served to smooth over the cultural chauvinisms of westward expansionism. Although the western has declined in production and
popularity, many features of the genre are signified in SF film. The gunsling-
ers of the Old West who passed through town after town have become the
space cowboys of the future who journey from planet to planet, the bound-
lessness of outer space has replaced the panoramic vistas of the open range,
and space aliens that zap humans into ashes have substituted for the image
of hostile Indians attacking white settlers. The high-noon showdowns, the
solitary sheriffs, and the patriotic jingoism common in the American western are found in SF films like *Westworld* (1973), *Outland* (1981), *Independence Day* (1996), and *Armageddon* (1998). Despite the similarity between
westerns and SF films, however, the latter genre is not limited to reimagin-

ing the American western within a SF motif. On the contrary, SF cinema articulates a broad range of meanings, frequently expresses multiple messages, and fulfills various gratifications that bear only the slightest resemblance to the one intended.

Planet of the Apes is an excellent example of an SF film that articulates multiple political and cultural subtexts beyond its intended message. The narrative presents an American astronaut far into the future who lands on an Earth-like planet populated with talking apes. Although *Planet of the Apes* makes a clear anti–nuclear war statement, signaled by the film's surprise twist at the end, the film is a favorite of white supremacist organizations as an allegory for the future of American race relations if whites fail to band together to protect their interests.[1] Of course the writers and directors of the *Planet of the Apes* film franchise did not intend for their films to resonate with such extreme hate groups. But as the seminal media theorist Stuart Hall has argued, intentionality does not restrict the meaning of a film nor is the message of a film passively consumed by the audience. Instead a film's meaning is open for interpretation along three axes: a preferred reading, a negotiated reading, and an oppositional reading.[2] Some viewers accept the dominant message(s) of a film, others accept some and reject some aspects of the preferred meaning promoted in a film, and still others may totally reject the preferred meaning, even going so far as to "read against the grain" of the film. Consequently, from an audience-centered perspective, the racial meaning of any SF film is up for grabs.

Take, for example, Francois Truffaut's SF film interpretation of Ray Bradbury's novel *Fahrenheit 451* (1966). The film is a well-established social critique of oppressive governments, but its ending has ideological implications that resonate with significant elements of the African American experience. The central character, Guy Montag (Oskar Werner), lives in a future where books are illegal and "firemen" start fires in order to burn books. The film's focus on books as a forbidden possession invokes issues associated with American slavery and the struggle of enslaved and post-enslavement blacks to have access to education. The ending of *Fahrenheit 451* is particularly evocative of the homespun African American folk wisdom that stressed the importance of "book learning," or education, as the only possession, once acquired, that white racism could not take away from a black person. The importance of "book learning" as a tool of liberation is underscored when Guy Montag flees to the countryside and finds other escapees living on the outskirts of the city. They are a community in which each person adopts a book for complete memorization and later shares that book through oral recitation with another similarly committed person who will memorize it.

Guy Montag (Oskar Werner) looks at a newspaper next to his wife, Linda (Julie Christie), in *Fahrenheit 451* (1966).

The stress on memorization and the transfer of knowledge by oral recitation immediately calls to mind Henry Louis Gates's critical work surrounding the black oral tradition and literature, along with his discussion of the trope of the "Talking Book," the "paradox of representing, of containing somehow, the oral within the written."[3] The oppressed "book people" of *Fahrenheit 451* adopt and advocate orality as the appropriate cultural platform and politically subversive practice to challenge the established order. In one fell swoop *Fahrenheit 451* erases an artificial hierarchy that privileges the written word over the spoken. In doing so, the ending affirms, albeit indirectly and most likely unintentionally, a significant aspect of black culture—orality and the oral text—as equal in importance to the written text for the preservation and transmission of critical knowledge.

Although my allegorical reading of *Fahrenheit 451* may appear to interject race into an SF film utterly devoid of any racial politics, this is not the case. A scene in which Montag and his wife, Linda (Julie Christie), are sitting in bed while he looks at the newspaper clearly suggests that racial oppression is intermeshed into the Orwellian theme of the film. The newspaper is filled with comic book panels that contain drawings with no words.[4] Positioned in several panels are drawings of several Ku Klux Klan members gathered together and wearing white hoods. The virtually inconspicuous yet obviously intentional placement of such imagery, together with the structured absence of black people in the film, signals a normalization of white supremacy in the future world of *Fahrenheit 451*. As a result, virulent white racism is indicated as part and parcel of the high-tech alienation and systemic illiterate status of the citizenry depicted in the film.

In spite of the interpretive latitude I have expressed in my rereading of sf film and the active construction of meaning in which an audience potentially engages, that rereading does not negate the fact that sf cinema is also a hegemonic medium. In fact, the nature of the genre is hegemonic, given that a fundamental aesthetic property of sf films—the "suspension of disbelief," together with the use of special effects to create and maintain an appearance of seamlessness between the unreal and reality—is the genre's representational stock-in-trade. In this manner, the genre dovetails with cultural hegemony, in that socially created expressions of political power and control are made to appear as natural relationships. However, the circuit of cultural meaning in sf film is not a closed one. As an electrical current vacillates from one pole to another, there are fluctuations and gaps in the current of meaning that pulses throughout any film. Even though many, if not the majority of, American sf films may affirm the dominant hegemonic order of the day, their meaning can never be fully guaranteed, merely brokered. As a result, all sf films are open (although to what degree remains debatable) to disputed decodings, oppositional conclusions, and subversive pleasures. This makes sf film one of the most fertile sites for allegorical construction and contestation in the grand struggle over the meaning of race and how race is imagined in America.

POLARITIES OF RACE

Race relations in America have created a spectrum of adherents and detractors who have lent their sentiments, expertise, and even naked prejudice to explaining racial inequality and the solution to it. There is the radical race politics of Louis Farrakhan, who advocates a black nationalistic brand of religious conservatism for black folk to follow; the staunch indictment of white racism by Supreme Court justice Clarence Thomas, who claimed he was the victim of a "high-tech lynching" during his confirmation hearing; and the so-called liberal centrism of former president Bill Clinton, who shepherded in a welfare reform policy that conservatives could be proud of. Indeed, the Rubik's Cube–like matrix of ideological combinations that inform the cultural politics of race in America can make for strange political bedfellows. In spite of instances where divergent claims and approaches to race overlap, a critical divide remains. For the most part, black political leaders and their constituencies have posed the solution to racial inequality as one dictated by group rights. But white liberals and conservatives alike are at odds with such a collectivist approach to race because it violates the deeply embedded and mythic belief that capitalist individualism is the cornerstone of American culture and sociopolitical stature in the world.[5] Nevertheless, the black freedom movement of the 1960s was moderately successful in convincing whites that racial equality was not a function of eliminating individual acts of discrimination but depended on institutional remedies and policies that would mark America's sociopolitical transformation as a whole.[6] Regardless of the outcome, the basis of these reforms required individual blacks to be recognized as members of a disadvantaged racial minority group. It is against this political backdrop that *Planet of the Apes* (1968) works as American SF cinema's most powerful allegorical response to the conundrum of American race relations at the end of the turbulent 1960s. The film offers a taut critique of institutional racism and pokes a hole in the myth of triumphant individualism by placing a white male in the crosshairs of institutional discrimination.

Planet of the Apes is a dense racial allegory, and any analysis of merit is greatly indebted to Eric Greene's book, *"Planet of the Apes" as American Myth*. In it he gives a rigorous and comprehensive examination not only of the cultural politics of race woven into this film but also of the evolution of the franchise in its sequels: *Beneath the Planet of the Apes* (1970), *Escape from the Planet of the Apes* (1971), *Conquest of the Planet of the Apes* (1972), and *Battle for the Planet of the Apes* (1973). Greene renders the parallels between the intraspecies hierarchy in the ape civilization and the racial pecking order of American society in striking detail. Furthermore, the four sequels are all tied together in Greene's analysis by their allegorical anxiety over the aggressive political posture of the Black Power movement and its goal, the overthrow of the white power structure. All of these aspects are central themes of interest. I want to focus, however, not only on how interspecies prejudice and discrimination in *Planet of the Apes* make the central protagonist, a white male, a signifier of black victimization but also on the manner in which the film aggressively works to decenter whiteness, allowing whites to symbolically trade places with blacks and vicariously experience the stifling impact of American racism.

Planet of the Apes begins with four crew members leaving Earth in a spaceship bound for a distant planet. Because the object of their destination is so far away, they must make the bulk of the journey in a sleep-inducing life support chamber. Later, a crash landing into a lake on what they believe is another planet causes them to abandon ship. The three survivors—Colonel George Taylor (Charlton Heston), Landon (Robert Gunner), and Dodge (Jeff Burton)—head out to explore their new home and wind up captured by a species of talking apes. The three spacemen find themselves prisoners in ape civilization, in which fellow humans are animalistic in their behavior and conscious development and are treated as animals by the ape population. Moreover, except for grunting sounds, none of the humans in the film can speak. Taylor, having been wounded by a bullet through his throat, is unable to speak for a portion of his captivity and blends in with the rest of the primitive humans until he recovers enough to exclaim, "Take your stinking paws off me, you damned dirty ape!" From this point forward the film shifts into high gear as a powerful racial allegory for American race relations.

The treatment and discussion of Taylor's existence in ape society invokes many of the tropes of race, particularly elements associated with notions of black intellectual inferiority. *Planet of the Apes* draws on and recodes the racist justifications for why blacks occupy or should occupy the lowest socioeconomic levels in America and, at its most extreme, the supposed intellectual inferiority that makes blacks subhuman. In the film, white humans are considered intellectually inferior to their ape counterparts, which gives license to ape officials in varying capacities to treat the human population as vermin that must be destroyed or in some instances studied. The treatment that Taylor receives underscores how "scientific" racism and the belief in the natural inferiority of another race/species that it fosters can negate even the most impressive countervailing facts. For example, despite the shocking evidence that Taylor, supposedly an inferior human, is not only able to speak in a manner that rivals or in several instances surpasses that of his captors, he is still considered inferior by the apes' scientific, political, and military elites. By recoding whites as subhuman and having the ape elites reject Taylor's communicative and cognitive abilities, whiteness occupies a symbolic status in this SF film that blacks have historically been forced to fill in American society.

Taylor becomes a semiotic testament to the racial punishment blacks have endured in America. Just as black slaves were subjected to the various acts of physical subjugation, Taylor is hunted down, kidnapped, periodically whipped, and even burned in order to compel his compliance. All of these signifiers of punishment and discipline historically imposed on the black body come to a head when Taylor is repeatedly assaulted by an ape using a high-powered hose to spray water on him. This image most specifically signifies the grainy television footage of fire hoses being used against black protestors at the height of the civil rights movement. All of these acts against Taylor are charged with racial meaning and underscore the experience of blacks when confronting institutional racism and their vulnerability in the face of institutional power. Finally, the ape tribunal at which Taylor is to be tried is loaded with semiotic cues and dialogue that draws much of its emotional and satirical punch from the ongoing debate over race relations raging at the time of the film's release.

Taylor (Charlton Heston) as a captive defendant in *Planet of the Apes* (1968).

Taylor, who in the beginning of the film symbolizes narcissistic American white masculinity, is poised to receive his racial comeuppance with a leash tied around his neck, stripped naked and paraded before an ape council as he attempts to defend his humanity. Yet the tribunal scene is not merely about white humiliation or turning the racial tables by symbolically victimizing whites in ways similar to those imposed on blacks. The scene is more sophisticated than such surface analysis would suggest. Instead it signifies how the American judicial system has been used to condone racial injustice. The tribunal scene alludes to institutional racism similar to that defined in the 1857 Dred Scott case, which articulated that a black man, as a subordinate and inferior being, had no standing as a citizen and therefore no standing before the court.[7] Taylor's predicament clearly resonates with the historical struggle of blacks in the American legal system when he is brought before the court and an ape representative states that "a man . . . has no rights under ape law" because of his inferior status as a human. The scene demonstrates how species discrimination between apes and humans is similar to the racial prejudice present in American society and is not constrained to personal beliefs but operates at the institutional level to severely invalidate the humanity of blacks and contribute to the denial of racial justice. In this sense, *Planet of the Apes* as racial allegory is addressing the crisis of political legitimacy hovering over America's institutions and their inability to deliver racial justice despite the *Brown v. Board of Education* verdict in the 1950s, which overturned the "separate but equal" justification for segregation.

Planet of the Apes was set in the distant future, but because the film was released during a period of black protests, demonstrations, race riots, and growing black militancy, the temporal disavowal only ratcheted up the allegorical power and significance of the narrative. As a black racial allegory, the film is easily read as criticizing the collusion of government institutions and officials in protecting and maintaining the rights and privileges of the

The symbolic fear of black militancy against whites is strikingly rendered in *Conquest of the Planet of the Apes* (1972).

status quo. The temporal disavowal of racial strife in *Planet of the Apes* also registers an extreme anxiety with the political push of blacks to acquire the rights and privileges of first-class citizenship during the racial upheaval of the 1960s. Most notably, the racial fear hinted at in *Planet of the Apes* is fully expressed as black racial revenge in the film's sequels (and repeated ad nauseam in the blaxploitation films that soon followed).

Conquest of the Planet of the Apes (1972) and *Battle for the Planet of the Apes* (1973) mark a dramatic shift away from the white protagonist as a symbol of black racial struggle to overt racial polemics and paranoia. The sequels present a racial apocalypse ushered in by an enslaved ape population, oppressed primarily by whites who liberated themselves and, in an act of violent militancy, overthrew the dominant political order. In these later sequels Taylor, the cynic-turned-antiwar-humanist at the end of *Planet of the Apes*, is replaced with Caesar, the revolutionary talking ape who frees his ape peers from human tyranny. *Conquest* is loaded with racially charged imagery that invokes African American oppression: an enslaved ape population in shackles, apes whipped, apes made to serve a predominantly white population, and humans-only segregation.[8] As a result, the mise-en-scène of an assortment of gorillas storming the citadels of white authority and privilege as an unstoppable violent mob that burns everything along the way all too easily referenced the images of militant blacks protesting and burning various neighborhoods during the race riots of the late 1960s. Even the cinematography of the ape population's violent attack against the police played to the worst racial fears that could be mustered concerning militant blacks. With the apes' bright red and green jumpsuits shown alongside the black police uniforms, the visual motif is evocative of the black nationalist flag, whose colors are red, black, and green. Despite such semiotic touches, *Conquest of the Planet of the Apes* and, to a lesser extent, *Battle for the Planet of the Apes*—with its narrative of apes squaring off against humans for control of the world—are clear examples of SF films that pandered to white political paranoia and possibly black political fantasy. Both films evoked some of the most strident fears associated with black militancy by imagining politically conscious and organized apes initiating the type of racial revolt that the rhetoric of black militancy advocated.

Finally, while the original *Planet of the Apes* succeeded in signaling the absurdity and unfairness of racial oppression and the later sequels expressed an acute fear of radical transformation of the prevailing racial order, Tim Burton's baffling remake of *Planet of the Apes* (2001) is virtually emptied of any allegorical significance on the subject of American racial politics. Unlike the finely crafted satirical edge of the original, the remake consists of heavy-handed symbolism and a confusing narrative. Like the original, however, the remake has an intrepid astronaut, Leo (Mark Wahlberg), crash-landing on a strange planet where talking apes rule and humans are social outcasts. Moreover, the remake attempts to present a surprise ending, as the original film did, by having Leo "escape" the planet in a spacecraft that time-warps him back to "Earth," where he crash-lands in front of what appears to be the Lincoln Memorial in Washington, D.C. Upon closer inspection, however, the monument is that of an ape villain, General Thade (Tim Roth), from the planet Leo supposedly just left. The inscription on the monument honors General Thade for saving ape civilization from extinction.

Even though the bulk of the remake sidesteps the cultural politics of race woven into the original *Planet of the Apes,* the twist at the end appears as a half-baked attempt to recapture or possibly pay homage to the social satire and political sting present in the original. Despite the utterly bewildering conclusion of the film, the image of Abraham Lincoln as an ape significantly underscores how the *Planet of the Apes* franchise is inextricably tied to American race relations even thirty years after the release of the original film. The allegorical power of *Planet of the Apes* is signaled by the ape image of an American president who is synonymous with the Civil War and the elimination of black enslavement. In this case, the semiotic coding of General Thade, the most villainous talking ape of the film, as Abraham Lincoln, the racial liberator, introduces an overdetermined signifier of American racial politics. Furthermore, by coding Lincoln as an ape liberator, a great ape citizen, and an advocate of ape freedom, race is referenced in a manner that equates the ape planet with a black planet. This image signified an association between blacks, black freedom, and primates. Although the remake, for the most part, skirted the issue of race, the twist ending made race a central reference point and reaffirmed the worst expressions of white racial anxieties, a world in which U.S. whites are an oppressed racial group. Ultimately, the "shock" ending of Burton's remake owed more to D. W. Griffith's crude rhetoric of race in the epic film *The Birth of a Nation* than to the racial morality tale of Arthur Jacobs's sf film classic, *Planet of the Apes*.

REIMAGINING AMERICAN IMMIGRATION

Alien Nation (1988) is an sf film similar in allegorical ambition, if not execution, to the *Planet of the Apes* franchise. The issue of species discrimination that was so central to the *Planet of the Apes* films is also a centerpiece of *Alien Nation*, making racial conflict a prominent allegorical presence in the film. The tenet of America as a land of immigrants and, in the wake of the civil rights movement, a model of racial tolerance is stretched to its metaphorical limits by a narrative in which a quarter of a million humanoid aliens, slaves on another planet, are given asylum in the United States. The Newcomers—or Slags, as they are pejoratively called—are highly adaptive and are genetically engineered to labor in any environment. After a quarantine period, the Newcomers make their new home in Los Angeles and begin assimilating into its multicultural maze. The film follows two police detectives—Matthew Sykes (James Caan), a self-professed bigot, and Sam "George" Francisco (Mandy Patinkin), a recently promoted Newcomer—in their efforts to track down the violent murderers of Sykes's longtime friend and partner by a group of Newcomers.

Alien Nation is dialoguing with the multiple racial anxieties of American race relations in a post–civil rights era. Although the coding of the aliens as slaves references blacks, and the resistance by whites to accept them unmistakably invokes the black struggle for social integration into American society, the film also suggests an acute anxiety with the growing numbers of Latin American immigrants and their offspring in the United States. This anxiety is signaled in the opening of the film with a series of man-on-the-street interviews in which whites complain about a loss of job opportunities and educational slots in light of the influx of Newcomer immigrants. Moreover, the association of the aliens with Mexican immigration is established early in the film when a white detective, Fedorchuk (Peter Jason), briefs Sykes and a Latino detective, Alterez (Tony Perez), about the leads concerning the murder of Sykes's partner. Fedorchuk notes how difficult it is to gather information from the Newcomer community:

> FEDORCHUK: You ever try to make a case down in Slagtown? The list of Newcomer informants is about as long as a list of Mexican war heroes.

ALTEREZ: Hey! Hey! Come on!

FEDORCHUK: Nobody talks to nobody down there. And half of them don't even speak English, and the other half only when it suits them.

The rhetoric of the camera further underscores the association between Mexican immigrants and unlawful aliens. Alterez is shown sitting on Sykes's desk, and a poster next to his head has the word "Illegal" written across the top in large red letters. Under the poster's title are lines of small print that are not distinguishable. Consequently, the only legible word is "Illegal." Furthermore, the camera angle makes it seem that the word is intended to describe Detective Alterez. This type of visual signification, along with other narrative elements, makes *Alien Nation* a film that views Los Angeles as the literal and symbolic front line of a multicultural transformation creeping across America. Hence the title *"Alien Nation."*

Not only do the camera rhetoric and the title of the film signify an acute anxiety with Latino immigration, but the aliens of the film also signify a growing anxiety with the possible economic impact that Latino immigration could have on America. This point is illustrated when Sam informs Sykes that many of his people work at the refinery because they were genetically engineered to work in any environment and thus are unaffected by the refinery's noxious gas. The status of the alien Newcomers as a source of inexpensive, highly exploitable, low-skilled labor that meets needs of a particular sector of the American economy is a minor element of the story, but it has major allegorical ramifications. The economic subtext concerning the Newcomers is not unlike the use of undocumented Mexican and Central American laborers who are used to fulfill America's demand for cheap and exploitable labor. Indeed, the Newcomers' overwhelming presence at the refinery suggests a similar type of economic relationship. Interestingly, the burgeoning presence of Newcomers as working professionals rather than refinery laborers is a source of vocalized resentment. The promotion of Sam, a Newcomer, to the rank of detective, as part of an early advancement government program, spurs several detectives to complain about the unfairness of his professional advancement. Sam's response to the expressed overt hostility to his promotion is where the allegorical significance of *Alien Nation* fully surfaces.

The film clearly communicates that government policies that seek to level the racial playing field are undemocratic and foster resentment. Ironically, Sam, the beneficiary of this affirmative action for aliens, validates this premise by demonstrating that the fight for racial equality is most effective at the level of personal interaction rather than through government interfer-

The camera rhetoric of race is used to visually underscore immigrant anxieties in *Alien Nation* (1988).

ence. This point is illustrated by the change in Sykes, who rails against the Newcomers as geeks and creeps in the opening of the film but by the end accepts the alien Sam as his partner and friend because he has proven himself worthy. No longer the immigrant Sykes abhorred in the beginning of the film, Sam is shown attending the marriage ceremony of Sykes's daughter as his personal guest. This degree of acceptance is possible only because the narrative has conveniently created Sam Francisco to embody, in excess, all the attributes of a model minority. He is nauseatingly self-sacrificing (he accepts Sykes's renaming of him as "George"), a solidly middle-class family man, and gravely concerned that the image of Newcomers not be sullied by other, less wholesome aliens. In this sense, Sam/George is a cipher for the re-articulation of melting-pot racial/ethnic ideology, along with a generous dose of Anglo conformity to round out the message. This hyper-assimilationist image is the ideological centerpiece of the film, which becomes even more apparent when Sam is contrasted with the William Harcourt (Terence Stamp) character, an alien social climber and potential Newcomer politician of the future.

Harcourt, while publicly championing the values of American civic responsibility and tolerance, privately promotes drug use and the distribution of an alien drug that is effective only on Newcomers. Certainly Harcourt's duplicitous manner signifies the type of cynical, self-serving, and hidden-agenda politics that racial minority leadership is often criticized for exhibiting. But it also works as a metaphor for the hyphenated identity of racial/ethnic minorities who self-consciously choose to have two civic identities rather than just define themselves as American. In contrast, the Sam/George figure privileges the wholesale adoption of a single identity by trading in his intergalactic alien identity for one informed by the expectations of Anglo conformity. Indeed, in order both to fit in and to promote his interests, he and his family fully embrace the American mainstream and demonstrate that alien/racial/ethnic identity is a pliable subjectivity that should be shed and replaced with an all-American one. Sam/George aggressively makes use of Anglo conformity as the surest and most direct approach to gain accep tance not only from the dominant society but also from Sykes, one of its most prejudiced members. The predicaments and interests of the group that is discriminated against in *Alien Nation* are not resolved by revolution or a substantive critique of the institutions that discriminate, as in *Planet of the Apes*. Instead, racial justice is dictated according to individual accomplish ment and personal patience in the face of racial prejudice. Although *Alien Nation* does openly display white racial prejudice against the Newcomers, the onus of responsibility for its elimination is squarely placed on the shoulders of the recipients of prejudice, rather than on the source of it.

Ultimately, the message of *Alien Nation* fits hand in glove with the crescendo of claims by conservatives and liberals alike that racism was no longer the virulent institutional problem it once was. For many Americans the turbulent sixties had brought racial inequality to the foreground and eliminated segregation. The implementation of affirmative action during the 1970s, however, had by the 1980s created the perception that the racial social equation had tilted too much to the left and too far away from mainstream whites. As white America approached the 1990s, the temporal setting of *Alien Nation*, racism was considered effectively eliminated, and all that was left were bigoted holdovers from the prior generation. The decade would witness the legitimacy of racial rhetoricians like Dinesh D'Souza, an intellectual pundit who advocated "rational discrimination" and proposed that, rather than racism, blacks' inability to adapt to the sociopolitical mi-

Matthew Sykes (James Caan) and his new partner, Sam "George" Francisco (Mandy Patinkin), in *Alien Nation*.

lieu explained their inability to succeed in present-day America.⁹ Likewise, Sam/George, the model Newcomer of *Alien Nation* whose adaptability and Anglo conformity underscored his acceptance, suggests that blacks and other minorities need to culturally adapt, shorten their hyphenated identity, and become "American." In just over twenty years from the release of *Planet of the Apes*, the allegorical critique of racial inequality in sf film had dramatically changed, and *Alien Nation* was proof of just how much.

THE POLITICS OF RACIAL ABANDONMENT

Alien Nation was a film of its time in the way it reflected the increasing cultural and political conservatism of the 1980s. In particular, *Alien Nation* expressed multiple anxieties around the real-world specter of white displacement and so-called racial set-asides. Yet the film was not emblematic of the type of neoconservative racial paranoia that became increasingly evident at the beginning of the Reagan era. Admittedly, hostility toward government intervention or regulation to address racial disparities was mounting and was signaled in popular films like Michael Winner's *Death Wish* (1974) and Martin Scorsese's *Taxi Driver* (1976), which privileged vigilante justice as a social solution, along with Walter Hill's *The Warriors* (1979), which imagined New York City as infested with youth street gangs roaming the city and tapped into the well of fear concerning the urban decay that had begun to define major inner-city areas across America. As severe as these films were in expressing the rejection of social liberalism as an ideological compass for guiding Americans out of the domestic quagmire of black demands, white guilt, and scarce resources, John Carpenter's *Escape from New York* (1981) consolidated all the anxieties of race, place, and urban dystopia with its depiction of New York City as a maximum security prison where hard-core criminals were sent to serve life sentences.

In the American public imagination, New York City—a dense polyglot of ethnic groupings—at one time represented a beacon of ethnic diversity and was the centerpiece of the mythologized American melting-pot society. In the wake of rampant crime, the threat of bankruptcy, and a major power blackout in 1977 that led to unprecedented looting and violence, the city came to be seen as a violent and dangerous place for white professionals and working-class stiffs. Although *Escape from New York* draws on this latter image of a city on the edge of disaster, also encoded into the film's grand fantasyscape of urban dystopia is a racial subtext that has allegorical ramifications. *Escape from New York* underscored the crisis of American inner cities, with their faltering infrastructure and decreasing quality of life, and

The Duke of New York (Isaac Hayes) holding court in *Escape from New York* (1981).

in the rhetoric of race associated with this decline, spatial location had become another stigmatizing element of racial identity. The terms "urban" and "inner city" became political shorthand for discussing a myriad of social ills that disproportionately affected blacks—such as poverty, crime, drug abuse, high unemployment, and welfare abuse—without focusing on race as the specific source of the problem. Instead, geography or spatial location defined the scope of the problem.

The narrative setup of *Escape from New York* has Snake Plissken (Kurt Russell), a new prisoner, being offered his freedom in exchange for rescuing the president of the United States (Donald Pleasence), whose escape pod was ejected from his hijacked plane and landed inside the prison-city. Snake accepts the mission. Inside the prison-city a population of criminals roams the city and scavenges for survival, they include the Turks, Skulls, and Crazies, as well as an assortment of motley ne'er-do-wells. The overwhelming use of whites as the criminals of New York disavows the commonly perceived racial association of blacks with the inner city and extreme urban blight—until the Duke of New York (Isaac Hayes) appears. The title given to the black crime lord clearly indicates that location and race have been bundled together to signify blackness. Furthermore, the Duke drives a garishly decorated limousine decked out with matching chandeliers affixed to the front hood, an image meant to denote the transgressive black street style of the urban ghetto. His title and style define the prison-city as a black space, despite the overwhelming depiction of hard-core white criminals who populate it. This point is made more obvious when the Duke is shown pursuing several white protagonists through the city as they try to escape.

Unmistakably, the film projects New York as a failed city of the future. But even more allegorically telling is the way in which the inhabitants of the walled prison-city have been abandoned by the outside society. Not even electricity or food rations are provided to those inside. In this sense, the film embodies the most strident example of a policy of "benign neglect," an approach associated with Daniel Patrick Moynihan's prescription for addressing America's most socioeconomically depressed living spaces.[10] *Escape from New York* is easily read as an allegorical endorsement of a policy of abandonment for black ghettoes and other poor communities of color that experience a high degree of crime and gang violence, deeming them as hopelessly beyond help and requiring stringent containment.[11] Whites throughout the 1970s had already begun "escaping" the black inner city for the suburbs, leaving behind a depleted tax base, an underdeveloped political constituency, and increasing crime. Thus the image of the Duke, a violently crazed black man, chasing several whites through an urban wasteland symbolically confirmed that poor urban communities of color are unsafe areas for whites, and "escape" or "white flight" from the inner city was the smartest decision whites could make.

Predator 2 (1990), like *Escape from New York*, reflected anxiety over urban blight and violence associated with the inner city. In *Predator 2*, Los Angeles—a sprawling metropolis crammed with crisscrossing ethnic enclaves—is the staging ground for urban violence and the symbolic affirmation of vigilantism. Rival drug gangs wage brazen street shoot-outs in the middle of the afternoon in populated sections of the city. Moreover, the police are outarmed and depicted more as third-party spectators than a preventative force. For a significant portion of the film, however, the Predator alien preys on the violent criminals who populate the urban jungle of Los Angeles. Even though the alien kills a couple of police officers, his primary victims are black and brown criminals who, after he kills them, are shown as mutilated corpses, hanging upside down. The unseen alien in *Predator 2* clearly symbolizes an urban vigilante who is more effective than the police force at combating the gang forces that terrorize the city. Indeed, after the Predator kills several members of a Latino drug gang, an officer quips, "Maybe we should give him a job. Put him on the payroll." The sporting violence of the alien is eventually turned against the police department, including Detective Mike Harrigan (Danny Glover) and members of his team, but by the time this transition point occurs, the privileging of urban vigilantism against brown and black criminals is firmly in place. In this case, street justice is signified as more effective in addressing gang violence than conventional rules of law enforcement and due process.

The crisis of urban decay and racial violence in Los Angeles is further expressed in the SF films *Strange Days* (1995) and *Escape from L.A.* (1996). A fear of a racial revolt is woven into the ideological fabric of both films with narratives that respectively have blacks and Latinos mounting a violent campaign to overthrow the established political order. On one hand, *Strange Days* plays to the recent memory of the 1992 Los Angeles riots, even invoking the image of a black male dying at the hands of white police, reminiscent of the beating of Rodney King by several white officers. On the other hand, *Escape from L.A.* is an allegorical text that speaks to white anxieties about Latino immigrants and American border politics. In 2013, Los Angeles has been expelled from the United States in *Escape from L.A.* and serves as a destination of deportation and relocation of people who are deemed undesirable, unfit, and immoral. Inside the cordoned-off city, a Peruvian terrorist, Cuervo Jones (Georges Corraface), plots to take over the world at the same time the U.S. government plans to attack Cuba and Mexico. In a film ostensibly about the rise of an ultraright religious theocracy in America, the ethnic coding is rather simple to read. The depiction of Latinos as members of a militant movement emerging out of Los Angeles is a blatant illustration of acute racial paranoia that imagines Latinos as a threat to American society.[12] Despite this paranoia, the representation of Los Angeles as a dangerous urban space full of drugs, gangs, and senseless violence is not purely a function of the white imagination. A score of black melodramatic ghettocentric films released throughout the 1990s made escape from urban America, colloquially referred to as the "hood," a central theme.[13] Black filmmakers such as John Singleton (*Boyz N the Hood*, 1991), Matty Rich (*Straight Out of Brooklyn*, 1991), the Hughes brothers (*Menace II Society*, 1993), and Spike Lee (*Clockers*, 1995) echoed the same apocalyptic social sentiments portrayed in SF films like *Escape from New York*, *Strange Days*, *Escape from L.A.*, and to a lesser extent the cult classic *Repo Man* (1984). Unfortunately, whether black melodrama, SF spectacle, or even sociological statistic, all expressed a common conclusion—that escaping the ghetto environment of America's inner cities was the only way to avoid the poverty, limited opportunity, and likelihood of a violent death that lay in store for those who chose to stay or were unable to leave.

POST-9/11 ALLEGORIES OF RACE

In many instances, racial representation in American SF films of the post–civil rights era no longer draws allegorical inspiration from the binary configuration of black and white race relations present in *Planet of the Apes*. Instead, the border politics of Latino immigration stands out as the central anxiety in several SF films released in the 1980s and 1990s. Similarly, American SF cinema in a post-9/11 era presents a broader canvas for allegories concerning race, many of which are fraught with fear of terrorism from the "Arab world." Certainly, Steven Spielberg's manic remake, *War of the Worlds* (2005), is a blatant example of how the most disturbing imagery and fears generated from the events of September 11 are recoded and recast in a SF film. Even the tagline from the billboard advertising campaign—"They're already here"—taps into a collective well of paranoia and dread circulating in an American society reeling from real news blurbs that "sleeper" terrorist cells are suspected of operating inside U.S. borders. *War of the Worlds* is beset with semiotic references to 9/11, as well as the global turmoil and war that followed: the vivid soundscape of a commercial airliner crashing into the ground; images of a panicked populace covered in ash and fleeing for their lives; and the display of killing machines buried deep beneath the earth and emerging to destroy an American suburb, a thinly veiled reference to the threat of "weapons of mass destruction" that was so prominent in instigating the invasion of Iraq in the Second Gulf War. The visual histrionics of *War of the Worlds* symbolically marshals the collective fear of capricious acts of violence against civilians by having virtually unseen enemies from another world—allegorically speaking, the Islamic/Arab world—attack America and obliterate its citizens.

In contrast to the very visceral rendering of fear and uncertainty in the *War of the Worlds* remake, the SF film *Code 46* (2003) depicts a subdued picture of the border politics of the future that nevertheless has chilling implications for today. In *Code 46* the citizens who live in highly modernized cities are monitored, and their personal information, including their genetic makeup, is contained in an institution called the Sphinx. Against this backdrop of hypersurveillance, a twenty-four-hour, genetically illegal love affair takes place between William (Tim Robbins), a married insurance investigator, and Maria (Samantha Morton), a corporate worker who makes fake "papelles," special insurance permits. In the indeterminate future of *Code 46*, travel is possible only if one possesses a papelle. The film is an allegorical treatise on the power and pitfalls of government surveillance. Yet what is more compelling as an allegorical point of analysis is the contextual backdrop for the illicit affair, rather than the affair itself.

The insides of cities are corporate hubs of economic activity in *Code 46*. Outside, desolate tracts of desert land are occupied primarily by people of color. The juxtaposition is a visual reminder of the gap between the abundance of modernized industrial society and the Third World poverty of today. Moreover, the outside area is the site where William and Maria have intercourse, despite their awareness of the genetically incestuous quality of their relationship. In the desert towns of the outside, normalcy is transgressed without reprisal, and the rules of civilization do not apply. Lastly, the visual and aural elements of the film help code the outside areas as Islamic. Indeed, at the film's conclusion, Maria, the main female character, is a social outcast banished from the city and, marking her fallen state, is no longer dressed in Western clothes. Instead, she wears a tunic and is enveloped in fabric, similar to the way in which Muslim women in strict Islamic societies cover themselves in public. Despite the ambient look and feel of *Code 46*, the film is a powerful post-9/11 allegory concerning surveillance, compromised domestic borders, and the perceived threat associated with Islamic culture and the Arab world.

Minority Report (2002) is another SF film that resonates with post-9/11 fears. The narrative is set in the year 2054. John Anderton (Tom Cruise) is the chief officer in the Precrime Division in Washington, D.C., where the dreams of three young adults known as precogs are recorded because they contain the name of the perpetrator and the victim of a murder that will occur in the future. With the use of advanced computer technology and video imagery, Precrime Division police officers are dispatched to prevent the murder before it occurs. The dilemma at the center of this film concerns the issue of punishment. Should a person seen committing a crime in the future be arrested for that crime, even though it has not been committed? John is a zealous advocate of the system until the precogs predict that he will kill a man he does not know in several hours. The precognitive ability of three psychics is problematic, however, because in some instances they disagree on the outcome of events. When a disagreement occurs among them, a "minority report" is secretly generated to document the event and is stored in the female precog, Agatha (Samantha Morton). In order to prove he is not intent on murdering the stranger he supposedly is fated to kill, John must find his minority report.

Certainly, *Minority Report* invokes an SF film version of the George W. Bush administration's geopolitical foreign policy of preemptive war. The image of John Anderton and his special agents at work—ensconced in a high-level security room in the nation's capital, they use a digital holographic "chalkboard" with addresses, mug shots, and grainy surveillance-like photos to construct scenarios that prevent heinous acts of violence—is an example of the type of fantasy wish fulfillment fermented in a post-9/11 America. *Minority Report* speaks to a deep desire in American society for proof that the policies its leaders have chosen are imbued with some sense of foreknowledge and intelligence. The film also evokes many of the questions and the anxiety concerning American intelligence that arose after the attacks on September 11. Will the intelligence agencies be able to prevent the mass murder of thousands in the future? What information, if any, can be gathered beforehand to prevent another attack? Clearly, the idea of a special law enforcement unit designed to stop murder before it happens taps into the collective American desire for a sense of security and protection.

Admittedly, on a grand scale, *Minority Report* is a morality tale that flirts with existential issues of free will, fate, and criminal intent. Yet, allegorically, it is also a part of a specific discourse surrounding race. The title of the film signifies a racial reading of the meaning of *Minority Report* that is radically different from the one intended. Even the narrative of the film is open for a subversive allegorical interpretation, given that the central topic of the film concerns an American criminal justice system guilty of sentencing people for crimes they have not committed. The criminal intent element of the story easily overlaps with the real-world controversy surrounding black racial profiling, such as the experience and perception of black drivers who believe they have been pulled over for no justifiable reason except that they were viewed as suspicious, particularly if their car was a luxury vehicle or the neighborhood they were driving in was predominantly white. In this sense, *Minority Report* lends itself to a subversive racial interpretation of the Precrime sentencing system. Statistical disparities of black incarceration and subjective experiences have led many blacks to believe that local and national law enforcement has an informal policy of detaining or arresting black folk before even witnessing a criminal act, as a form of crime prevention. Consequently, *Minority Report* underscores the cynicism and mistrust that many African Americans have for the American criminal justice system, because they perceive the process of law enforcement as one in which blacks, like the victims of the film's Precrime unit, are judged as guilty before they have broken the law.

Minority Report lends itself in another way to a subversive racial interpretation. The narrative backstory of the precogs sounds strikingly similar to the popular media descriptions of the impact of the crack cocaine epidemic on black America. The precogs, on whom the Precrime unit depends for information about future crimes, are all children of drug-addicted mothers who were part of a "neuroin" drug epidemic that swept over the country, creating thousands of physically and psychologically scarred children. Crack cocaine, whose use was epidemic in the 1980s, has been described in much the same way—a highly addictive drug that created scores of addicted black mothers whose "crack babies" cropped up in inner-city maternity wards across the country.[14] The backstory in *Minority Report* of how the Precrime unit was created appears lifted from the racial hysteria surrounding the "crack epidemic." At the time, written and televised exposés on the social conditions of various communities of color that were facing the crack cocaine epidemic served as "minority reports" by often collapsing drugs, crime, and black or brown racial identity into a single pathological entity for white America to fear.[15] This point became particularly prominent among critics of the disproportionate impact that the "war on drugs" has had on inner-city communities of color.[16]

COUNTERNARRATIVES OF RACE

While *Minority Report* and the other sf films discussed thus far in this chapter evoke different allegories of race that read against the films' preferred or intended messages, they are all similar in their draconian racial politics. Most of these films are conservative racial critiques of the post–civil rights state of black America or alarmist allegories about Latinos spearheading the transformation of America's racial demographics. The Wachowski brothers' *The Matrix* (1999), however, invites a radical reading that challenges both the racial conventions of sf film and the popular conservative racial orthodoxy of the day, which views racism as no longer a systemic problem in American society.

Much like Stanley Kubrick's *2001: A Space Odyssey* and George Lucas's *Star Wars*, *The Matrix* is a film that redefines its genre. The stylish, sleek look of the computer world of the Matrix, the stop-motion and slow-motion camera tricks, and the metaphysical mumbo jumbo peppered throughout the film combined not only to make the film popular but also to give it a rich and layered text that has even compelled philosophical analysis.[17] Ostensibly, *The Matrix* is about how a white computer hacker, Neo (Keanu Reeves), discovers that the present time is not 1999 but centuries later and that the world he thinks is real is in fact a computer simulation called the Matrix. The real world is a barren and dark planet in which machines rule and humans are kept alive only so that their electrical energy can be siphoned to power the numerous artificial intelligence machines that now exist. After meeting Morpheus (Laurence Fishburne)—a rebel leader of a crew of humans who have rejected the Matrix program—Neo joins the group to overthrow the machines. Because race in general, and blackness in particular, is such a significant visual element of the series, this film—as well as the *Matrix* trilogy as a whole—courts being defined as the first black sf film epic.

The racial contours of the virtual reality of the Matrix stand in sharp contrast to the real world outside. On one hand, inside the Matrix the symbols of social authority are overwhelmingly white and male—the police force, the military soldiers, and the "Agents" the rebels face. On the other hand,

The Oracle (Gloria Foster) shares her insights with Neo (Keanu Reeves) in *The Matrix* (1999).

outside the virtual reality of the Matrix the figures associated with human liberation are represented in a more multiracial manner. The crew of the *Nebuchadnezzar* has several black members and a South Asian member, the Oracle (Gloria Foster/Mary Alice) is a black woman who oversees a multiracial group of children in her apartment, and, in the sequels, the rebel home base, Zion, is significantly populated by black people. The high degree of visibility allotted to blackness in *The Matrix* is not the only pillar that supports the radically alternative racial reading I propose. The wooden, if not blank, performance of Reeves displaces the emotional weight of the film from him to Morpheus, the Oracle, and, to a lesser extent, the other significant black characters introduced in the second and third installments. As a result, the ultracool black characters—including Morpheus, the Oracle, and Niobe (Jada Pinkett Smith)—thoroughly upstage Neo, the main protagonist. Although Morpheus, the Oracle, and Niobe are not the lead characters, they nevertheless carry the emotional weight of the film as revolutionary humanists.

On the whole, the quest to liberate millions of humans who are unwittingly being exploited and oppressed appears to be more a mission led by a black man and black woman than one led by a white savior.[18] Indeed, after one gets beyond the convoluted plot twists and the overwrought special effects, the black characters are easily read as symbolic cultural touchstones and respective reminders of the civil rights and Black Power movements. The Oracle, with her nonthreatening southern hospitality and discussions of dreams and destiny, signifies the civil rights movement and Martin Luther King Jr., while Morpheus, with his black leather jacket and dark sunglasses, invokes the political swagger and radical chic machismo of the Black Panther Party. *The Matrix* is thus steeped in the signifiers of the Black Freedom movement of the past and brings many of the issues of American race relations to bear in a narrative that uses virtual reality as the site to imagine a grand struggle for human justice. With even more black characters included in the sequels—*The Matrix Reloaded* (2003) and *The Matrix Revolutions* (2003)—the series openly courts racial difference as a source of oppression and a platform of committed social struggle against systemic forces.

The sequels, like the original, present the power elite of the Matrix as white males. Zion, the rebel base in the real world, however, is populated by people of color. In a tribal rave dance scene in *The Matrix Reloaded*, black men and women make up the bulk of the population, and in subsequent planning scenes blacks appear as leading officers. The racial politics of Zion appears to be based on a multicultural model of racial equality and participation. In the Zion setting, a racial utopia is presented where blacks, whites, and other people of color live and work together, and in many cases whites are subordinate but not subservient to blacks. Whites in the Zion society of *The Matrix Reloaded* and *The Matrix Revolutions* are represented in positions that blacks have occupied in primarily all-white sf film extravaganzas. For example, the second in command or generic helper has historically been roles that blacks and other people of color have usually occupied in American sf cinema. The *Matrix* franchise, however, inverts many of those poles of power and privilege, making it the most radical American big-budget sf film series when it comes to the cultural politics of imagining race in the future.

The film imagines the liberation of enslaved humans from a computerized virtual reality of the future in a way that narratively and semiotically evokes the struggle of blacks to reclaim their humanity and acquire the full rights of citizenship in America. The fight against the reality-defining power of the Matrix finds its allegorical equivalent in the idea of being freed from mental slavery as a necessary step in the complete eradication of racism as

Morpheus (Laurence Fishburne) leading the way in *The Matrix Reloaded* (2003).

a system of oppression. Additionally, the practice of rescuing enslaved humans and delivering them to freedom in the film evokes allegorical connections to the Underground Railroad, a committed network of abolitionists who helped fugitive black slaves escape bondage. In terms of semiotics, the cameo-like inclusion of Cornel West—the highly public African American theologian and academic who is best known for his book *Race Matters*—in the sequels works to place race in the center of the debate over the meaning of the *Matrix* trilogy. West's career of vigorous advocacy for racial justice outside of the narrative of the films becomes intermeshed with the meaning or message. In this case, the struggle for human liberation from the Matrix is similar to the struggle for racial justice in America by blacks, other people of color, and progressive whites. In order to break the constraints of both forms of oppression, a change in how one thinks and defines the world is required.

The last installment of the film, however, settles for a more pragmatic vision of what type of freedom is achievable in the world. Homeostasis between both warring factions is privileged over any type of permanent victory for the Zion rebels and the multicultural Left they symbolize. In this sense *Revolutions* taps into the political stalemate that has come to define American race relations in the post–civil rights era. On one hand, liberals of all colors have suffered eroding support for racial justice to such an extent that they no longer vigorously debate or advocate racial justice, for fear that it will further alienate them from an increasingly conservative white constituency. On the other hand, conservative race baiting appears nearly exhausted, and the race card is often played in the opposite direction, with conservatives claiming they want and need to include more minorities in their overwhelmingly white political parties. The cumulative impact is a racial stalemate, as in the case of affirmative action, which was "mended but not ended." Like the warring factions of the *Matrix* trilogy, the left and right constituencies of the American political order have tentatively agreed to live beside one another in a fragile truce—mapped out as blue zones beside red zones that checker the American cultural landscape—that will last only until one side can gain the political upper hand.

At its best, SF cinema is an allegorical site that invites the audience to safely examine and reflect on long-standing social issues in an unfamiliar setting, providing the possibility of viewing them in a new light. At its worst, the process of allegorical displacement invites audiences to affirm racist ideas, confirm racial fears, and reinforce dubious generalizations about race and the place of African Americans in U.S. society without employing overt racial language or explicit imagery. The outcome of the latter process is a silencing of the discussion of racial inequality in real words while promoting ideas and preconceived notions that support racial inequality. Thus, the established hegemonic order gets to have its cake and eat it too, by allegorically expressing racially biased representations of blacks and other people of color yet avoiding criticism for promoting a particular racial politics.

All that said, even though American SF cinema often presents narratives encoded with conservative or less-than-flattering racial beliefs concerning African Americans and other people of color, many SF films do not merely buttress the ideological constructs of America's racial hierarchy but instead breach it in multiple ways. Not only is the "preferred" allegorical implication of various SF films contested, but in some cases pleasure might even be derived from constructing an alternative to the suggested meaning. This makes many SF films, in various ways, open to racial readings that are not only on the margins of the "preferred" meaning but malleable to radically altered claims as to what these films, in the end and on the whole, communicate about race.

Like the social construction of race in U.S. society, American SF cinema is not static. Both have the capacity to express richly layered and critical portrayals of the human experience. It is a taken-for-granted premise that nearly all American popular films, regardless of genre, affirm and seek to engender a desire in the viewer to accept the predominant social and political ideologies of the day. Certainly, race in American SF cinema does not exist outside the commonsense beliefs, ideas, and perceptions circulating in society, no matter how far in the future or distant a world is presented. But in some instances, like the original *Planet of the Apes*, *Fahrenheit 451*, and the *Matrix* trilogy, SF films can provide some of the most stimulating models of possibility and critiques of American race relations. Taking up this point, the next chapter focuses exclusively on the subversive racial meanings and pleasures that are routinely poached from SF films and expressed in other media alongside the genre.

CHAPTER 6

SUBVERTING THE GENRE

The Mothership Connection

Swing down sweet chariot. Stop, and let me ride.

GEORGE CLINTON, Mothership Connection

Music is the weapon of the future.   FELA KUTI

Not only has the presence of black characters increased in science fiction film—a trend witnessed in *The Core* (2003), *The Chronicles of Riddick* (2004), and *Aeon Flux* (2005), for example—but black actors have also become central characters in the genre, as demonstrated by films like *Supernova* (2000), *Alien vs. Predator* (2004), *Serenity* (2005), *The Hitchhiker's Guide to the Galaxy* (2005), and *Children of Men* (2006). Although the increase of black representation in SF film has been dramatic, this does not mean that these characters convey or are even meant to communicate any impression concerning black cultural identity, history, subjectivity, or political sensibilities, much less draw on, expand, or self-consciously reconfigure historical, conventional, and/or alternative notions of blackness and project it into the future. Admittedly, such a specific representation appears, on the surface, unlikely since most of the iconography associated with the genre—spaceships, robots, ray guns, an odd assortment of aliens—has very little to do with race. Yet SF cinema has exhibited an impressive capacity for offering serious, thought-provoking images and ideas that address a myriad of social issues. By the late 1960s and early 1970s, no longer was SF cinema an escapist genre. Films such as *Charly* (1968), *Planet of the Apes* (1968), *The Illustrated Man* (1969), *A Clockwork Orange* (1971), *Slaughterhouse-Five* (1972), and *Soylent Green* (1973) offered more reflexive narratives rather than special effects–driven SF films. This was one of the most productive and innovative periods for the SF film genre. Moreover, the focus on social and cultural issues exhibited in the SF films of the time held immense potential for the inclusion of other critical concerns, such as American race relations, as a significant point of exploration. But with the mega-success of *Star Wars* (1977) and the subsequent success of films such as *Close Encounters of the Third Kind* (1977), *Star Trek: The Motion Picture* (1979), and *E.T. the Extra-Terrestrial* (1982), the era of the big-budget, special effects–driven SF blockbuster was born, marking a dramatic shift in the genre.[1] These films not only raised the visual stakes of depicting alternative worlds, futuristic technology, and strange aliens but also upped the financial ante for subsequent SF films to achieve widespread popular appeal and garner greater commercial success. Of course there was no set formula that could guarantee a hit. *The Black Hole* (1979), *Saturn 3* (1980), *Flash Gordon* (1980), *Outland* (1981), *Tron* (1982), *Dune* (1984), and *The Last Starfighter* (1984) are just a few of the SF films released on the heels of the *Star Wars* saga that failed to generate any mass popularity.

While numerous misfires resulted from trying to imitate the success of *Star Wars*, nevertheless the swashbuckling, action-adventure theme woven into the film became a staple of the genre. As a result, SF films that were self-consciously "serious," expressed a high concept, or presented slowly unfolding plots, like *2001: A Space Odyssey* (1968) and *Silent Running* (1972), were no longer popular. Instead, much of the SF cinema of the 1980s and beyond was just as much an action-adventure movie as science fiction film. A perfect example of this hybrid is *The Island* (2005), a cloning parable starkly divided into two parts. The first half is a sober, thoughtful examination of cloning ethics, and the second half is a spectacle of special effects and monotonous chase scenes. The emphasis on nonstop action and big-budget special effects has come to define much of contemporary American SF film. Typically, "serious," story-driven efforts like *The Handmaid's Tale* (1990), *Contact* (1997), the remake of *Solaris* (2002), and, to a lesser extent, *Signs* (2002)—none of which are action-oriented, fast-paced, or quick-cutting films—did not achieve blockbuster status. Accordingly, in today's SF film marketplace the absence of big-budget special effects leaves room for either raucous parodies of the genre like *Sleeper* (1973), *Spaceballs* (1987), *Galaxy Quest* (1999), *CQ* (2001), and the inanely half-baked *Adventures of Pluto Nash* (2002) or reflexive, thought-provoking narratives like *Code 46* (2003) and *Primer* (2004) that occupy the margins of the genre as independent art-house films.

Yet it is at the margins of American SF cinema that some of the most radical expressions of the cultural politics of blackness have emerged. Tim Burton's parody of 1950s American SF film in *Mars Attacks!* (1996) is a noteworthy example. Virtually all of the genre's signature iconography is parodied. The overall look of *Mars Attacks!*—with its clunky special effects—constantly calls attention to the artifice of the genre. The alien spaceships resemble the type of retrograde flying hubcaps found in doctored UFO photos, while the Martian invaders are little more than cartoonish images pasted onto the screen. Then there is the comic cruelty of showing a woman's head transplanted onto the body of her small dog, a white American scientist continuing to pontificate after he has been decapitated, and the vaporization of a roomful of politicians. All of these special effects push the film into hyperbolic overdrive. Easily overlooked, however, in the ostentatious display of visual irreverence for the genre is how the way in which blackness is situated in the film sharpens the satiric edge of *Mars Attacks!* to a fine point.

In contrast to the discordant visual imagery used to parody the media and American military through their symbolic representatives, the film reserves a more serious tone for the socially marginalized heroes of the film. The most effective challenge to the big-brained alien invaders of *Mars Attacks!* is mounted not from shrill generals but from the most socially powerless persons in the film and, by extension, in American society: Richie (Lukas Haas), a nebbish Midwestern male adolescent; Grandma (Sylvia Sidney), his semi-lucid, semi-senile grandmother; and Byron (Jim Brown), a retired black boxer who works as an underpaid greeter in a Las Vegas casino. The core of the subversive racial representation in *Mars Attacks!* is the working-class black characters: Byron; his wife, Louise (Pam Grier), who is a bus driver; and their two teenage sons. By foregrounding these characters in *Mars Attacks!* the film satirizes a signature feature of the genre—the structured absence of black representation. Most significant for my analysis is that Byron and his family are not figures of parody in the film; rather, they are played extremely straight, in stark contrast to most everyone else. Consequently, their privileged position of gravitas in an otherwise slapstick comic narrative self-consciously foregrounds blackness as a symbol of social significance, in this case black working-class agency.

The working-class status of Byron is first indicated by his position as a casino greeter. A former heavyweight boxing champion, he has been reduced to working as a hotel mascot clad in an Egyptian guard costume, including a gaudy headdress. In addition, economic disenfranchisement is a constant refrain when Byron is onscreen. He intimates in a conversation with another character that others profited off him when he was a fighter, the issue crops up when his wife admonishes him to cut a long-distance call short because of how much it costs, and a lack of money appears as the cause for his divorce from her. Although these elements may easily be defined as the backstory of a superfluous character, a working-class black racial identity is symbolized by Byron's economic disenfranchisement, particularly when contrasted against the only other black character of consequence, General Casey (Paul Winfield).

The General Casey character is a member of the inner circle of the president's cabinet and is given the honored and important assignment of being the human representative who will first greet the Martian landing party. On his way to his assignment, the general reflects on the secret to his success during a phone conversation with his wife: "Didn't I always tell you, honey, if I stayed in place and never spoke up, good things were bound to happen?" Casey stands in stark contrast to Byron. Early on, Byron is shown complaining to his supervisor about the low pay he receives and is subsequently informed that he is highly expendable because his status as a down-on-his-luck former fighter makes him interchangeable with a host of other former fighters. On one hand, Casey has accrued status and power because of purposefully silencing his voice. Byron, on the other hand, has vocalized his discontent to his supervisor about his salary and appears confined to his menial position. In Tim Burton's comically twisted sf parody, General Casey is the first human to be vaporized by the Martians. But the violent demise of Casey, more than signaling how expendable a character he was, functions as an overt criticism of the politics of race that he symbolized: black tokenism. Casey signifies the cynical use of a black face in a highly visible context to connote racial progress and the purported elimination of racial discrimination. Such criticism has been hurled at the Republican Party for its most recognized black members—Supreme Court justice Clarence Thomas, General Colin Powell, and Secretary of State Condoleezza Rice. Accordingly, the General Casey character in *Mars Attacks!* may easily be read as a send-up of General Colin Powell and the conservative politics he symbolizes, while the killing of Casey by the Martians represents a form of ideological character assassination.

Yet *Mars Attacks!* is more complex in its appraisal of the cultural politics of race in America than the derision directed at the General Casey character and what he symbolizes. *Mars Attacks!* speaks to the limited social role of blackness in the American labor market and possibly even society as one of superficiality, appearance, and tokenism. Byron's dinky PR position as a greeter in the casino is similar to that of General Casey, who is assigned the job of greeting the Martians. Clearly, the parallel between the two black characters as public relations representatives, despite their polar-

General Casey (Paul Winfield) greets the Martians in *Mars Attacks!* (1996).

opposite social and professional statuses, suggests that the most acceptable and expected social role for blacks in America is as symbols of inclusion and participation in mainstream America while simultaneously occupying the margins of economic power and political influence. Byron is a doorman literally laboring on the periphery of a multibillion-dollar gambling industry. General Casey, although a member of the inner circle of governmental power and a military figure, has little to no input regarding the use of the armed forces as a first response to the alien presence. Even though both men symbolize the marginalization of blackness in American society, Byron is nevertheless a central player in the film for his participation in the fight against the overwhelming alien forces.

Byron takes on a horde of aliens in a bare-knuckle brawl in order to distract the Martians from a group of people trying to escape on a nearby airplane. He is able to knock out a few but is soon overwhelmed, and an aerial point of view shows him drowning in a tide of alien attackers. In Hollywood films of the past, the death or self-sacrifice of a black character was used to signal the virtuous qualities of all blacks, evoke white sympathy, and ultimately suggest that the black race—or certain members who were a credit to it—deserved at least racial tolerance and at most acceptance. Films such as *The Defiant Ones* (1958), *Glory* (1989), *The Green Mile* (1999), *The Legend of Bagger Vance* (2000), and the SF film *Star Trek: The Wrath of Khan* (1982) have black characters demonstrate some form of personal sacrifice to affirm the lives, loves, or ideas that the white protagonists hold dear. When Byron decides to distract a throng of aliens long enough for a few acquaintances to flee in a plane and baits them into a bare-knuckle brawl, *Mars Attacks!* is poised to repeat a well-worn Hollywood cliché of marginal black characters sacrificing their lives to protect or save whites. Byron, however, is able to avoid dying, and like Odysseus, the adroit hero of Homer's *Odyssey*, he returns home alive and well from his battle against the aliens, ready to fix his fractured family. When Byron shows up on foot after traveling nearly 2,500 miles from Las Vegas to Washington, D.C., his journey, even though it occurs offscreen, takes on epic proportions, and his homecoming appropriately closes out the film. By having the return of a black man to his home provide the film's resolution, *Mars Attacks!* is more than a satire of the sci-fi B movies of the 1950s and contemporary SF films like it. The film uses race to assail the privileged place that white heterosexual male authority holds in SF film, frequently cloaked in the iconography of American militarism and scientific intellectualism. All of the typical symbols of white authority and institutional power—scientists, military generals, army heroes, and even the president—are thoroughly lampooned as incompetents full of hubris, in stark contrast to the down-to-earth Byron, who single-handedly defeats scores of big-brained aliens.

Although Burton's parody of the SF film genre was a major studio production, for me it resonates as an independent film, at least in feel and sensibility, if not look. Like the independent film idiom, which is often a refuge for the experimental, the avant-garde, and the socially taboo subject that appeals to a narrow audience,[2] *Mars Attacks!* exhibits similar subversive qualities when compared with the usual staid morality plays seen in mainstream big-budget SF films like *The Island*. Tim Burton's maverick impulse is clearly discernible and fully expressed in *Mars Attacks!* As a result, the subversive spirit and, to a lesser degree, the stylistic flourishes typically found in the independent genre make their way into Burton's biting parody of American SF film and, most evocatively, of the American racial order. Admittedly, Burton's success at subversively foregrounding race in an SF film produced by a major studio is the exception to the rule that the independent film idiom is a more fertile site for black representation across all film genres. Black

The triumphant return home of Byron (Jim Brown) in *Mars Attacks!*

filmmakers such as Oscar Micheaux, Melvin Van Peebles, Haile Gerima, Charles Burnett, Julie Dash, and Larry Clark, as well as Spike Lee, have used the independent film idiom as an outlet to present racial themes on the big screen.

Because the independent film idiom has historically operated outside the mainstream Hollywood film industry, many of the conventional pressures, market trends, and financial expectations and the broad audience appeal associated with the latter are perceived as not significantly affecting the content and style of most independent films. Indeed, independent black filmmakers—who for the most part were forced to operate outside the purview of the mainstream Hollywood film industry—have an established history of working apart from the apparatus of mainstream cinematic production. Yet their films stand as some of the most daring and cutting-edge expressions of black love, sexuality, history, and violence, as well as the cultural politics of black racial identity. Ironically, however, two of the most self-consciously black sf films in American cinema, Space Is the Place (1974) and The Brother from Another Planet (1984), were directed and for the most part produced by white men. Nevertheless, both sf films are ideologically robust in directly confronting white supremacy and the politics of racial inequality in its historical and contemporary guises by exploring the interior social dynamics of the black community and the politics of resistance that resides there.

In Space Is the Place (1974), time travel, interdimensional travel, and black aliens are woven into a narrative focused on addressing black racial unity, and separation from the dominant white society is advocated as the most viable solution for racial justice. The film has a benevolent black alien gather black people onto his spaceship before Earth explodes. The Brother from Another Planet locates its narrative in the black community of Harlem, New York, where a black man as a fugitive alien traverses and negotiates the inner-city ghetto to escape his white intergalactic captors. Both films exemplify how signature elements of mainstream Hollywood science fiction films are appropriated and racially recoded to communicate images and messages that speak to historical, contemporary, and potential black political agency. Ed Guerrero's faultless reading of The Brother from Another Planet discusses the importance of the film as a nearly pitch-perfect allegory for the travails of the historical runaway slave, along with the black migration from southern racism to northern economic opportunity. Although The Brother from Another Planet is an excellent allegory addressing the pitfalls of the postindustrial black urban experience, Space Is the Place is particularly noteworthy because of the broader cultural currents and contradictions of black racial subjectivity it presents alongside the foreshadowing of several

significant cultural shifts in the black community. Despite the extreme racial fantasy that *Space Is the Place* represents, the film accurately touches on
the somber and conflicted state of black America in the immediate wake of
the decline of the civil rights and Black Power movements.

IMAGINING BLACK FREEDOM

As the decade of the seventies approached the halfway mark, the focus on
the War on Poverty began to give way to the war in Vietnam and the promise
of a "great society" remained unfulfilled for scores of black residents living
the inner-city blues of the American ghetto. The pledges of white politicians
advocating economic development for poor blacks and the threats of revolution by black nationalists grew increasingly brittle as the 1970s wore on.
In response, black individuals with newly acquired educational credentials
scrambled to take advantage of individual social and economic opportunities to enter the middle class, while a less educationally fortunate stratum of
black folk tried to eke out an existence on the societal margins. The idea of a
black revolution, championed by black political militants and radical black
artists in the late 1960s, was quickly losing steam in the 1970s to career
advancement as defining black progress rather than collective struggle
and political victories.[3] The tides of social protest were turning away from
mass demonstrations and collective acts of civil unrest that addressed race
relations to more global problems looming on the horizon of public consciousness. Overpopulation, pollution, and hunger seemed to present bigger
challenges and a grander threat to all of humanity, regardless of race (even
though Third World countries of color bore the brunt of these global issues
considerably more than America). The waning racial justice movement no
longer appeared viable as an energizing social response or a solution to a
myriad of issues blacks still faced. With the decline in organized black political mass movement, the loss of galvanizing leadership and direction in
the civil rights movement, the virtual demise of black radical groups like the
Black Panther Party, the Republic of New Africa, and the Us Organization,
together with the unprecedented popularity of blaxploitation cinema, the
real struggle for racial justice was increasingly being replaced with imaginary revolution and escapist fantasies on the movie screen. While films like
Superfly (1972), *Cleopatra Jones* (1973), *Gordon's War* (1973), and *The Spook
Who Sat by the Door* (1973) signaled that urban and political fantasy had
begun to define the cultural politics of race for black America, *Space Is the
Place* explicitly confirmed it.

Admittedly, given the campy aesthetic of the film and the inclusion of

gratuitous nudity, it is quite easy to categorize *Space Is the Place* as a derivative expression of white SF films like *Dark Star* (1974), *Attack of the Killer
Tomatoes* (1978), *Flash Gordon* (1980), or possibly even *Flesh Gordon* (1974).
Although the look and feel of the film are similar to those of these other
"cheesy" parodies, *Space Is the Place* is undeniably a serious black SF film.
Below the surface of the clumsy special effects, amateur acting, and dis-
jointed narrative rests a robust racial discourse on the power of black nationalism, the failed promises of white liberal integrationism, and the vacuous
nature of American materialism as a reward for blacks who do not challenge the status quo and the social consequences for blacks who do. In this
sense, *Space Is the Place* is not self-consciously poking fun at itself, nor is it
an imitative expression of Hollywood SF films of the past. To the contrary,
the film is markedly original when compared with the blaxploitation horror movies of the period that drew many of their narrative cues from past
mainstream white Hollywood films. The intersection of blaxploitation and
the American horror genre clearly expresses this imitative impulse. Films
such as *Blacula* (1972), *Blackenstein* (1973), and *Dr. Black, Mr. Hyde* (1976)
convincingly demonstrate that white gothic horror was merely repackaged
as black versions of the same narratives with only two principal differences:
placing black actors in the lead and situating the narrative in a ghetto context. These films functioned more as plagiarized texts than anything innovative and demonstrated a racial imagination that could conceive of blacks,
in the realm of fantasy and horror, as occupying only the previously mapped-
out figures drawn from the white imagination of Bram Stoker, Mary Shelley,
and Robert Louis Stevenson. Unlike the crudely derivative representation of
blackness in the blaxploitation horror films of the period—envision a film
titled *The Werewolf from Watts*—*Space Is the Place* breaks from such extremely imitative and hackneyed renderings of blackness. Arguably, just by
having Sonny Blount as the lead character, the film asserts its aesthetic orig-
inality. Like Sun Ra's cryptic persona and improvisational music, the film
plays out in a series of strange interrelated but nonlinear scenes.

Sonny Blount, the avant-garde free jazz musician commonly known as
Sun Ra, is the fitting star of this film, given that he adamantly professed to
be from the planet Saturn.[4] His role as a black space alien visiting Earth to
save the black inhabitants of America from white racism is virtually a cameo
performance. Sun Ra is shown piloting his canary-yellow oblong spaceship
down to Earth, materializing in and out of different temporal and spatial settings, and providing clever non sequitur racial wisdom to nearly everyone
he encounters. Sun Ra is cast as an intergalactic guardian angel sent to battle
the Overseer (Raymond Johnson)—a time-traveling metaphysical pimp—for

Sun Ra, the interdimensional time traveler sent to save black people in *Space Is the Place* (1974).

the future of black people living in America. The two are periodically shown confronting each other in the middle of a desert wasteland, where they wager in a cosmic card game to determine whether or not black people should be spared from America's "death sentence." The competition between Sun Ra and the Overseer in this quirky and, at times, outright kooky film symbolizes competing currents of black racial political identity and thought vying for the hearts and minds of black people.

The Overseer character signifies black economic success as vulgar integration into the American materialistic mainstream. He drives a luxury Cadillac convertible, dresses in expensive-looking white suits, and has a white woman companion, all of which he flamboyantly displays. Luxury cars, expensive clothes, and desirable sex partners are the visual accoutrements of the materialistic spoils of the type of economic success and racial progress the Overseer character represents. In contrast, Sun Ra rides around the streets of Oakland, California, in an old convertible, and his appearance is ridiculed by several black youth. The diminished material trappings of black nationalism are further underscored when Sun Ra visits a black youth center. Pictures of black nationalist leaders are posted throughout the youth center. Against this semiotic backdrop, black teenagers are shown singing, playing pool, talking, and gambling.

The juxtaposition of the overtly political posters against the vice of gambling and the wholesale embrace of leisure activities by black ghetto youth signifies a disjuncture between the ideas and political agency espoused by various figures of the Black Power movement and the real economic conditions of unemployment that black youth face and accept in their ghetto environment along with their desire to quickly change their economic standing. Sun Ra steps into the middle of this overtly symbolic debate about the status of black nationalist politics among black youth when he materializes in the youth center. Creating a spectacle with his strange clothes and flanked by even stranger companions, he spurs one of the youths to ask, "Is he for real?" Sun Ra responds with oxymoronic splendor and drops the ultimate mind bomb on his youthful audience, stating he is not real, in the same way that they, as black people, are not real. He goes on to share the logic of his retort by explaining that if black people were real, they would not need to petition and protest for rights to validate their existence. Consequently, Sun Ra asserts that black people are "living myths" because white America treats them in ways that deny their full human existence. The exchange between Sun Ra and the teenagers speaks to black peoples' sociopolitical invisibility and foregrounds a form of black existentialist angst on par with the themes of Ralph Ellison's tome, *Invisible Man*. Moreover, despite the organic people who populate the film and the raw-footage appearance of the cinematography, scenes such as this exemplify how *Space Is the Place* contains, and explicitly expresses, sophisticated and provocative ideas concerning the cultural politics of race and the sociopolitical consequences of American racism.

Sun Ra and his small group orchestra represent a science fiction response to the racial injustice experienced by black folk in America—that is, Sun Ra will ferry a small number of black people on a "space ark" to another inhabitable planet so that they can escape the culmination of racial injustice, the self-destruction of Earth. The film envisions black liberation as intergalactic travel and the fulfillment of black peoples' desires as achievable only on another planet that is absent of whites. At its core, *Space Is the Place* is symbolically dialoguing with the limited black integration into the economic mainstream along with the problematic aspects of black political cooptation once mainstream access is achieved, a point underscored when Sun Ra is accused of being a sellout because his album is advertised on the radio for purchase. Unfortunately, the film ends up retreating from the complicated debate and tensions between black economic inclusion and racial justice. Instead, it settles for an imaginary solution to the quagmire of American race relations in the form of black people leaving Earth to relocate on a planet where white people are not present.

The simple resolution offered to the complex issue of racial justice in *Space Is the Place* is noteworthy because it suggests that despite a phenomenal increase in black elected officials during the 1970s and a burgeoning black middle class, symbolic escapism from America was a representa-

Sun Ra battles the Overseer (Raymond Johnson) in a cosmic card game to determine the fate of black people in *Space Is the Place*.

tional outlet. In *Space Is the Place* the appropriation of Egyptian iconography to create a science fiction aura and signify the alien status of Sun Ra and his band members is significant in this way. Arguably, the loose combination of black nationalism and Egyptian iconography present in *Space Is the Place* is an aesthetic forerunner of what would later become theoretically formalized as Afrocentricity, a black nationalist philosophy that includes the assertion that ancient Egypt was a black civilization.[5] Regardless of the debate concerning the historical validity of ancient Egypt as a black civilization, the use of Egyptian iconography alongside strident expressions of black nationalism in *Space Is the Place* offers a cinematic referent for imagining African Americans as direct descendants of a highly advanced race of people. It also functions as a form of symbolic escapism that allows African Americans, still stranded in ghetto poverty on Earth, to take symbolic refuge in a glorious past, possibly to avoid a troublesome present and an unsure future. Without a doubt, by combining ancient Egyptian imagery with an ending in which black people escape Earth's destruction on a spaceship, *Space Is the Place* revels in escapist racial fantasy, similar to that of SF films like *When Worlds Collide*, *The Time Machine*, and *Logan's Run*.

Yet the racial fantasy of *Space Is the Place* is not fueled by an uncomplicated notion of "reverse racism." The film is a caveat to whites of the consequence of political disengagement with issues of racial inequality in America and signals that advocates of radical black politics have become resigned to the view that alliances and points of common ground with whites appear impossible. In this sense, *Space Is the Place* is a reworked version of

the SF film classic *The Day the Earth Stood Still* (1951), in which an alien visits Earth to warn the population to administer their nuclear weapons pru-
dently or risk being destroyed. Unlike the ending in *The Day the Earth Stood
Still*, Earth is destroyed in *Space Is the Place*, but its forewarning theme is
still a significant part of the film. As Sun Ra periodically cautions, destruction of the planet is avoidable if racism is no longer practiced.

The racial politics of *Space Is the Place* begins with a strident expression
of black nationalism, goes on to give a tentative symbolic acknowledgment
to Third World solidarity with the inclusion of a Latina aboard Sun Ra's ship,
and in the end descends into an uninspired display of political fatalism in
which the total population of the planet, except for a handful of blacks, is
doomed as the planet explodes into pieces. Consequently, the end of *Space
Is the Place* indicates a profound disillusionment with the political struggle
for racial equality and a desire for escape, even if only to an imaginary destination beyond the stars. But *Space Is the Place* was not the only black SF
expression that prodded blacks to look to the sky for deliverance. The image
and message of the music of George Clinton became increasingly important
during the 1970s as an alternative visual site for the representation of black
science fiction. The appropriation of SF imagery in Clinton's early funk-
music career was just as independent and bizarrely esoteric as *Space Is the
Place* but more accessible in its exhortation to "put a glide in your stride and
a dip in your hip and get on board the Mothership."

COSMIC BLACKNESS

Because filmmaking tends to be cost-prohibitive, art, independent black
comic books, black music, and even hip-hop videos have functioned as alternative sites where futuristic fantasyscapes populated by black people can
find expression. This form of science fiction blackness is broadly captured
under the term "Afrofuturism," a word used to describe the variegated expressions of a black futurist imagination in relation to black cultural production, technology, cyberculture, speculative fiction, the digital divide, and
science fiction.[6] In this sense, the intersection of black racial formation and
SF film is an area of analysis that is multidimensional in scope, wildly imaginative, politically provocative, and, most importantly, not confined to just
the cinematic idiom. A case in point is the SF graphic art, images, and liner
notes on the outside and inside of the album covers of the various incarnations of George Clinton's funk music groups. These alternative expressions
of science fiction blackness epitomize how the black imagination has cir-
cumvented cost-prohibitive SF filmmaking and created intergalactic visions

of blackness that are more accessible than art-house films like the virtually unknown *Space Is the Place* or the critically recognized *Brother from Another Planet*. Instead, funk music was the more accessible medium, and the message was inflected throughout with science fiction iconography and black imagery that often stood outside mainstream cultural conventions.

Ricky Vincent accurately maps out the significance of George Clinton to the emergence of an sf film black imagination in the graphic art displayed and associated with the music:

> P-Funk's fantastic science fiction created a series of spectacular "other worlds" that Africans could inhabit freely, in which one could be loving, caring, sensual, psychedelic, and nasty without fear of cosmic retribution, and whites simply did not exist. The symbolic connections of P-Funk concepts to one's earthly struggles for freedom were felt by many listeners, particularly black teenagers. Furthermore, the assertion of a black worldview that incorporates modern technology, the demographics of the seventies, and a black aesthetic was a profound theoretical breakthrough, despite the silliness. *Such grand visions of black people were not found in black film, black literature, or black politics* in the late 1970s. (Emphasis added)[7]

The serial format of the albums' sf art and the cryptic black narratives that were part of the album package proxied for both the absence of black representation and the exclusion of racism and racial agency as a topic of concern and narrative exposition in American sf cinema. The album art and liner notes of George Clinton's Funkadelic and Parliament groups offered a sci-fi version of black self-determination, similar to the blaxploitation film movement. Ironically, an aural medium became the most viable visual source of black sf ideas, imagery, and narratives, mainly for two reasons. First, black representation in film and television became increasingly obsessed with addressing issues of black authenticity that primarily focused on black urban and underclass representations, which, almost by default, ruled out imaginary and speculative constructions of blackness associated with the type of futurescapes found in sf film. Second, with the decline of blaxploitation cinema by the late 1970s, the genre never had the opportunity to mature and begin to explore other creative possibilities such as science fiction. Against this backdrop, George Clinton's music, comic book liner notes, and graphics became virtually the only medium for the presentation of black sf imagery. To this point, Clinton and his various band members presented themselves as extraterrestrial jesters who simultaneously appropriated and subverted elements of the sf genre along with destabilizing the obsession with black authenticity and realism that came to define black representation during and after the popular success of blaxploitation cinema. In the end, their appropriation of sf functioned as a source of satirical visual pleasure and racial subterfuge that culminated in a multitude of alternative and sf images of blackness.

The sf image of blackness offered by Clinton is clearly observable with the Parliament albums *Mothership Connection* (1975) and *Motor Booty Affair* (1978). The *Mothership Connection* album cover has a picture of Clinton, decked out in a spacesuit made of metallic shorts and silver platform boots and sitting in the entrance of a saucer-shaped vessel flying in space. The *Motor Booty Affair* album art has a rendering of the lost city of Atlantis that opens to reveal a pop-up illustration of the underwater Atlantis cityscape with a saucerlike rocket ship in the foreground. Although both albums are visual examples of how sf film imagery is poached and reconfigured to embellish the idea of blackness as an intergalactic identity, the creation of such images is more than a visual homage or satirical appropriation of sf film conventions. The bold Afrofuturist blending of blackness and science fiction that is presented in George Clinton's albums, art, and even live concerts—which included a metal spaceship that was lowered onto the stage—represent an attempt to destabilize fixed concepts of black identity and historical origin and reframe both as transcendent. On one hand, Clinton's funk music promised the possibility of sonic deliverance of the black nation from America's racial constrictions. On the other hand, like the space ark in *Space Is the Place*, the various space vessels depicted in Clinton's artwork and live stage shows also invoke the idea of a black exodus in his appropriation of a signature element of science fiction film—a *mothership*. In doing so, Clinton created a funkified version of the classic sf film iconography of a large space vessel, similar to that depicted in films like *2001: A Space Odyssey, Close Encounters of the Third Kind*, and *Independence Day*. But George Clinton's Mothership symbolized cosmic salvation in the form of a superspaceship arriving in urban ghettoes across America to pluck black youth up so they could join the ranks of his funky Afronauts.

Of course the worlds of black popular music and American sf film are not the only sites that express some version of sf blackness. For example, buried in the cosmological mythology of the black separatist religious organization the Nation of Islam is a doomsday scenario that reads like a science fiction film. Michael Gomez, in *Black Crescent: The Experience and Legacy of African Muslims in the Americas*, lays out the sf film–like scenario for the near destruction of the planet in the future:

. . . the Mother Plane, a machine built in Japan by Allah. Envisioned in the prophesies of Ezekiel and John (Ezekiel 10:2–11; Revelations 19:20), it is made "like a wheel" and is a "human-built planet," its dimensions "a half-mile by a half-mile square." The vehicle contains 1,500 "small bombing planes," which altogether will unleash weapons of mass destruction in the form of bombs, poison gas, and fire. . . . The atmosphere over that portion of the earth will explode into a gigantic fireball; "America" will burn for 390 years, a veritable lake of fire, and will require another 610 years to cool. After this millennium, a population of slightly more than 144,000 will restore the area, obliterating the memory of old America after a mere twenty years.[8]

It is quite evident that the Mother Plane is a central feature of this fantastic narrative, and even more importantly, this scenario demonstrates how the intersection of SF and black racial subjectivity has operated alongside and possibly prefigured well-established themes and iconic imagery popularly associated with American SF cinema. As a case in point, the image of an enormous mothership hovering above America and raining down death and destruction in the Nation of Islam's doomsday prediction dramatically foreshadows the movie poster for *Independence Day*, in which a humongous circular spaceship hovers above the White House before blowing it up. Clearly there is a vast difference in tone and consequence in the imaginative use of a mothership in the Nation of Islam's narrative of destruction and George Clinton's playful appropriation. Yet both expressions demonstrate how the intersection of the black imagination with the SF medium often results in imagery and ideas that work to destabilize fixed notions of black subjectivity and create a powerful, albeit marginal, space for the articulation of a racialized SF aesthetic.[9]

Another example of this impulse is found inside George Clinton's Parliament album *Motor Booty Affair*. The inside cover art articulates an antiracist poetics vis-à-vis the idea and image of Atlantis as a lost city inhabited by black people. Written below the Atlantis pop-up picture are the words, "We got ta raise Atlantis to the top." The mythology of Atlantis as a lost city located below the surface of public visibility is an appropriate and ingenious metaphor for characterizing the state of the urban black ghetto in America. Moreover, given that the nation's urban ghettoes are often defined as populated by a black underclass, a group buried below the poverty line, the statement "We got ta raise Atlantis to the top" signifies a desire for black upward social mobility on a grand scale and the need for black people to "uplift the race." Consequently, both the imagery and the slogan suggest a critique of the politics of "benign neglect" in which the black ghetto is constructed as socially and politically invisible, making it an urban space that is "lost" to the American public consciousness until periods of acute social crisis erupt.

Then there are the SF illustrations found inside George Clinton's Funkadelic album *Standing on the Verge of Getting It On* (1974), which work to destabilize fixed notions of black subjectivity by blending human sexuality and mechanical technology. For example, the inside cover art displays a large picture of a bare-breasted black woman with a skeleton face and oversized black oval eyes, a common visual trope used to signify an alien being. Her head is encased in a metallic contraption, and a tube is attached to the nipple of her left breast that leads to a drawing of a space portal, a window to the universe filled with stars, a planet, a medieval knight, and a nude green, oblong-headed alien woman. These images are underscored by a narrative that places the protagonist, Sir Lleb, at the center of a series of sexual misadventures and conquests. The next panel of images displays drawings of the various members of the group. One in particular shows a band member, Calvin Simon, with his face framed between a woman's labia, and another has a representation of George Clinton's face covered with several orifices. A subsequent album, *One Nation under a Groove* (1978), repeats the techno-erotic motif with an image of a nude black woman connected to tubes going into her ears.

At a distance the sexually charged imagery and objectification of black women and their bodies on and inside the album covers reflect the burgeoning public articulation of black sexuality in the 1970s, epitomized by the crass nudity of Pam Grier in blaxploitation films like *Black Mama, White Mama* (1972) and *Coffy* (1973), the sexually provocative cooing of Donna Summer on *Love to Love You Baby* (1976), and the raucous comedy albums of Richard Pryor such as *That Nigger's Crazy* (1974) and *Bicentennial Nigger* (1976). Upon closer inspection, however, the interface between sexuality, technology, and the future found in many of the early George Clinton albums is noteworthy because of its similarity to sci-fi films like *Demon Seed* (1977), *Star Trek: The Motion Picture* (1979), and *Alien* (1979), where the fusion of human sexuality with technology is also vividly imagined. Accordingly, although much of the art of George Clinton's albums appears to draw a good deal of its style from the psychedelic counterculture of the late 1960s and early 1970s, as well as the alternative underground comic book movement epitomized by the overtly sexual, controversial, and periodically racist work of Robert Crumb, Clinton's mélange of sexually charged graphic art and science fiction imagery is linked to contemporary American sf cinema but also is politically provocative because of its broader racial implications.

First, the album artwork symbolically reclaims the black libido from a long history of racist distortions, and it functions as a subversive significa-tion that suggests black sexual freedom is interchangeable with black politi-cal freedom. Admittedly, this is a problematic equation, previously grappled with by both critics and supporters of the controversial black film *Sweet Sweetback's Baadasssss Song* (1971).[10] Nevertheless, and most importantly, the depiction of technology interfacing with the black female body inside the Funkadelic albums *Standing on the Verge of Getting It On* and *One Na-tion under a Groove* are the first glimpses of a black articulation of a bio-mechanical future. Second, the overt fusion of sexual imagery with the ico-nography of science fiction inside the Funkadelic album covers is similar to the biomechanical artistic renderings found in H. R. Giger's work. Giger's striking, but darkly disturbing, images have in various incarnations funda-mentally shaped the contemporary vision of the alien other and future tech-nology in science fiction cinema.[11] Admittedly, the surreal drawings on the outside and inside of the album covers of Clinton's funk groups are much more crude and literal than Giger's version of techno-erotica. Nonetheless, the combination of overt sexuality and technology is suggestive of H. R. Giger's own trademark version of techno-erotica and fetishization of female sexual orifices, a visual hallmark of the surreal vision of the first *Alien* film. Certainly, Clinton's Afrofuturist art served as an imaginary springboard for African Americans to grapple with dramatic shifts in the political and sexual landscape occurring during the 1970s. But for me, George Clinton's sf techno-erotica also has as much in common with the techno-sexuality of H. R. Giger's work and, by extension, Ridley Scott's sf film masterpiece, *Alien* (1979), as it does with the articulation of repressed black sexuality through sf imagery. Yet, for as much as Clinton's Afrofuturist aesthetic was groundbreaking, it was a relatively obscure phase in comparison with sub-sequent Afrofuturist expressions. The next wave of Afrofuturist representa-tion became the catalyst for one of the most sweeping popular culture phe-nomena to emerge in America—hip-hop.

B-BOYS IN OUTER SPACE

A myriad of scholars, cultural critics, and music pundits have picked vari-ous "starting" points to chart the evolutionary arc of hip-hop. The popular black radio DJs of the 1950s, the imported sound system of Kool Herc, the Black Power compositions of the Last Poets, and even the underground gay disco clubs of 1970s New York nightlife have been, at one time or another, deemed a focal catalyst in the emergence of hip-hop.[12] Although not exhaustive, these examples provide a sense of the range of foundational "moments" that jockey for center stage. But as Jeff Chang wonderfully details in his hip-hop tome, *Can't Stop Won't Stop*, the cultural currents that contributed to the origin of hip-hop are not reducible to one seminal event.[13] Instead, a series of sequential developments, serendipitous discoveries, chance meetings, determined individuals, raw opportunism, economic setbacks, and successes all combined to create the popular culture phenomenon called hip-hop. But most importantly, an Afrofuturist aesthetic is central in the early development of hip-hop and is later expressed in contemporary hip-hop music videos.

Afrika Bambaataa, a pioneering force in hip-hop, established a science fiction perspective as part of hip-hop by ushering in the creation of electrofunk in the hit song "Planet Rock." In its unadulterated state, the eerie sound effects and discordant computer-created notes played by Kraftwerk, an experimental music group out of Germany that Bambaataa sampled for "Planet Rock," sounds like the perfect score for a futuristic science fiction film. Remixed and accelerated by Bambaataa, however, Kraftwerk became the source of material for one of hip-hop's biggest dance hits. Along with the space-age music, Bambaataa offered up an urban SF aesthetic on the cover of his album.[14] Bambaataa is flanked by three black males, the Soulsonic Force, and all are dressed in an amalgamation of gothic and Western styles complete with capes, standing in outer space hovering above Earth. The science fiction impulse embedded in hip-hop is important because it contributes to unmooring black subjectivity from strictly southern or urban expressions of the "black experience" that often overdetermine the visual and sonic discourse of blackness in general and black masculinity across all idioms of black cultural production. In this sense, the Afrofuturism of hip-hop is not merely escapism but an extension of the politics of black racial transformation, minted in the crucible of America's institutionalized disenfranchisement of African Americans.[15]

Of course the predominant mode of black racial representation in hip-hop is not of some intergalactic or futuristic black figure.[16] Instead, hip-hop appears most concerned with securing an aura of ghetto authenticity. The near-neurotic obsession with ghetto authenticity in hip-hop is witnessed in the imagery and performative display of "thug life" found in scores of hip-hop magazines and rap videos. In the post–civil rights era of today, hip-hop is most responsible for the depiction of the black urban street gangster as the epitome of the contemporary black antihero. This shift is even registered

Desolation Williams (Ice Cube) in *Ghosts of Mars* (2001).

in John Carpenter's science fiction–horror film *Ghosts of Mars* (2001). Although Carpenter's film was poorly received and is considered a retrograde B movie[17] and possibly the creative last gasps of the science fiction and horror film auteur, for me it is significant for its seminal racial representation. The film marks the first appearance of the hip-hop aesthetic in American SF cinema.

The setting of *Ghosts of Mars* is some two hundred years into the future. Rapper and actor Ice Cube plays the character James "Desolation" Williams, a wanted criminal who is reported to have been captured in a remote mining outpost on the planet Mars. A police team is dispatched to the distant settlement to transport Williams back to a Martian court to stand trial for an assortment of misdeeds. Unfortunately, when the team arrives in the secluded town, they find it deserted and discover that the former inhabitants of the planet have the ability to possess the humans they come in contact with. Despite the setting of *Ghosts of Mars* in the future and on Mars, the Desolation Williams character is more reminiscent of the actor's rapper alter ego than of any futuristic black outlaw. Ice Cube's past membership in the controversial gangster rap group Niggas with Attitudes (NWA) and his breakout performance as a Los Angeles gang tough named Doughboy in the coming-of-age melodrama *Boyz n the Hood* (1991) inform the gangster swagger he parades throughout *Ghosts of Mars*. His trademark scowl, which legions of hip-hop fans know him by, is unmistakable in this film and contributes to making his performance an intertextual tour de force. It is almost as if Ice Cube's Doughboy survived his death in *Boyz n the Hood* and somehow found himself alive centuries later on the planet Mars, sans the Jheri-curl hairstyle but still angry and willing to make his anger felt by anyone foolish enough to cross his path.

For many, *Ghosts of Mars* is most likely considered a quite unremarkable film. But for me nothing could be further from the mark. The film imagines the first hip-hop, albeit gangsta, B-boy in space. Arguably, Laurence Fishburne's Morpheus character in *The Matrix* is a front-runner for the title, but Morpheus signifies more the detached cool of Miles Davis or the menacing machismo of Richard Roundtree in *Shaft* (1971). In this sense, Morpheus does not possess, nor is he able to display, the aggressive gangster bravado that is now a signature convention in hip-hop and magnificently marshaled by Ice Cube in *Ghosts of Mars.* Undoubtedly, James "Desolation" Williams's signification of hip-hop's gangster aesthetic via the black antihero in *Ghosts of Mars* does little to counter criticisms that black representation is still overdetermined by socioeconomic location or in this case popular culture referents such as hip-hop. There are, however, instances where the intersection of hip-hop and science fiction do not invite such an obvious example of racial overdetermination in form if not content. Andre Benjamin, the unconventional half of the rap group Outkast, offers a notable example of how science fiction and hip-hop can intersect in ways that are less determined and more suggestive of an expansive vision of blackness in general and black masculinity in particular. Although not a feature film, the music video "Prototype" is a dense semiotic representation of the popular tradition of characterizing blackness as an extraterrestrial orientation. The video suggests that black racial subjectivity is not a category defined by minority status but a cosmic alien majority, and it poetically links blackness with imagined cosmic communities as a symbolic way to transcend the limiting constructions of black racial identity in America.

The video begins with a white geodesic dome (the spaceship) set in the middle of a lush meadow, and it occupants emerge, a family composed of multiracial beings: an Asian child, two black older "parents," a white female, a black female, and a black male. All of the extraterrestrial visitors have platinum-white hair, except for the bald father figure, whose pointed, *Star Trek*–inspired, Vulcan-like ears are a significant marker of his alien physiognomy. Narration underscores these images with the statement that a small family "visits Earth from the planet Proto, three thousand light-years away," and upon landing, they experience "the rarest of all human emotions—love." As the alien family tentatively explores the green countryside, an attractive black female hiding behind a nearby tree surreptitiously takes pictures of the group until she is spotted. She subsequently becomes their cultural guide and the love interest of the Protonian black male. In a series of montages they are shown conversing and sharing cultural practices with each other. The black male alien visitor receives the blessing of the eldest extraterrestrial to stay with the black Earth female and start a family on

Earth. Before the Protonian family departs, the elder male alien transforms the black male Protonian, clad in an all-white space uniform, into a clean-cut, collegiate-looking African American male.

On one hand, the racial semiotics of the video suggests that, outside of Earth, racial distinction and discrimination are not recognized, a point signified by the multiracial quality of the extraterrestrial family. The family unit is a model of color-blind race relations outside of Earth and represents the possibility for the same type of racial egalitarianism on Earth. On the other hand, the transformation of the black male Protonian, at the end of the video signals that blackness, although cosmic in orientation and possibly in origin, requires a localized particular appearance, at the very least, for negotiating America's racial landscape. Of course, this hip-hop science fiction music video is not the only example of an SF black cultural production that weighs in on black people's response to the sociopolitical forces of race by adopting the appearance of surface assimilation. A similar idea is illustrated in *The Brother from Another Planet.*

Possibly the most cogent cinematic expression of alien identity as a sociopolitical metaphor for black alienation in America is found in *The Brother from Another Planet* (1984). Near the conclusion of the film, the nameless and mute black alien protagonist, "the Brother" (Joe Morton), succeeds in escaping from his intergalactic white slave masters because other fugitive black aliens who have already assimilated into the primarily black community of Harlem join him in warding them off.[18] More than indicating the latent political quality of black racial identity, which expresses its collective orientation when confronting white racism, the scene underscores the dual character of black subjectivity as separate from and connected to real and imagined communities of racial nationhood. The assimilated black aliens of *The Brother from Another Planet* who are living the inner-city blues of black urban America alongside poor and working-class blacks on Earth symbolize the diasporic (read: alien) foundation of the black experience and the intertwined histories of shared struggle and solidarity for all black folk across broad-reaching political mappings and cultural geographies of black resistance. Consequently, the film registers a sublimated Pan-African perspective and becomes a powerful metaphor for the articulation of a transcendent black diasporic consciousness that reaches across national borders—that is, the intergalactic blackness that the black aliens symbolize—to imagine new geographies of black identity and larger points of racial contestation in a global context.

In the end, the attempts to construct a black science-fictionalized racial identity in the "Prototype" music video and in *Brother from Another Planet* reflect a nascent but growing attempt by African Americans to renegotiate the complex historical and contemporary sociopolitical cultural currents of real physical displacement exemplified by the Middle Passage, the Great Migration, and the looming transition from geographically bounded communities of color to the infinite realm of virtual communities on the Internet. A legacy of racial discrimination in American society has fueled a desire, if not the need, for black folk to periodically reimagine an identity beyond the prison house of language, the slaughterhouse of history, and the chopping block of popular culture. In forging these science fiction or Afrofuturist forms of black identity, the discourse around what Paul Gilroy calls the Black Atlantic is challenged and possibly reconfigured—even if only tentatively or fleetingly—in creative ways that are beyond media stereotypes, vulgar nationalism, reductive Marxism, and any garden-variety conservative or liberal responses to the crisis of the color line in this country.[19] The intersection of blackness and the SF film aesthetic marks the struggle to imagine a new form of black cultural production that creates new reference points for race, identity, and space in the immediate and far-off future.

FUTURE SHOCK

The best of SF film seeks to challenge our conventional ideas about space, society, sexuality, power, politics, and even race. Too often, when it comes to race, SF cinema does not acknowledge it, or if it does, the viewer is invited to experience race only as a deeply repressed subtext. But when race is present in the form of nonwhite characters, the picture offered in many of these films is a future explicitly painted as color-blind. Black people just exist. Asian people just exist. Latinos just exist. The historical struggles of these groups as racialized others rarely if ever are overtly acknowledged, and certainly the subject matter is not mined as a major narrative theme in virtually any SF film. If the genre ever becomes consciously committed to combining a science fiction aesthetic with blackness, it must at some point engage and imagine the effects of racism in the far future or explore extraterrestrial phenomena through the interior dynamics of the black community. Moreover, in my judgment, the quality and complexity of SF film as a genre, when it comes to race, will have to be evaluated by the genre's openness not only to including black characters and other people of color but also to adapting the SF literature of Octavia Butler, Samuel Delaney, Walter Mosley, and even Derrick Bell for the big screen. These black SF authors are as mind-bending, speculative, imaginative, provocative, and darkly bizarre as Philip K. Dick, Arthur C. Clarke, or Isaac Asimov. Yet their works, which often directly tackle race, have not found a cinematic outlet, although they are critically received, deconstructed in insular academic circles, and possess a cult following of fans.

On one hand, such striking omissions speak to the persistent constraints on the American SF film genre to remain wedded to the more coded and metaphoric engagement with race and issues of racial inequality as a subject for exploration. On the other hand, the fact that no black director or actor of substance has, up to this point, been successful in bringing an adaptation of Butler's or Delaney's work to the big screen seems to suggest that nagging issues around the articulation of a black aesthetic tied to realism and questions of racial authenticity circumscribe the range of feasible projects that are conceived and brought to completion. The closest example of what a black-written, -directed, and -acted SF film would entail is found in Reginald and Warrington Hudlin's HBO cable television film, *Cosmic Slop* (1994), in which an SF vignette titled *Space Traders* is the standout feature. The segment is adapted from Derrick Bell's book *Faces at the Bottom of the Well: The Permanence of Racism*, in which Bell adopts a science fiction format to examine contemporary racial politics in America. The film, like the story, begins with several spaceships arriving in the United States and an extraterrestrial representative announcing that they are here to offer virtually unlimited wealth, energy, and the ecological renewal of America in exchange for all of America's black population, for an unknown purpose. The film follows Gleason Golightly (Robert Guillaume), a black political adviser to a conservative presidential administration, as he attempts to marshal opposition to a national referendum in which whites will vote on whether to accept or reject the aliens' offer. Various political contingents are shown debating the issue prior to the big vote, which results in the majority of whites agreeing to exchange the black populace for alien wealth. Although the vignette is hampered by tacky special effects, a low-budget look, severely one-dimensional white characters, and misfires in developing the right tone for the film, nevertheless the content of the segment is riveting. Despite its shortcomings, *Space Traders* is a notable black SF film because it provides a glimpse of how racial issues, reimagined in SF film, can bring preconceived and sometimes uncomfortable notions about race into the open in innovative and thought-provoking ways, as well as expand the public space for confronting the cultural and political history of American race relations.

In the final analysis, any black representation in a science fiction film evokes America's struggle to confront and, too often, repress the nagging problem of race. Obviously, how SF film addresses race is not a panacea for real racial issues that are present in American society. Nevertheless, SF film is a bellwether genre for how we imagine ourselves, who we think we want to become, and possibly what we will become if we continue on our present course. In this sense, SF film is an important symbol of the social progress of a society still struggling to come to terms with the legacy of American racism. If we cannot look toward the future to imagine new possibilities and solutions for a history of race relations marred with fear, violence, institutional discrimination, and deep-seated ambivalence, then where else?

NOTES

INTRODUCTION

1. The following works cover a wide range of material and approaches: Annette Kuhn, ed., *Alien Zone: Cultural Theory and Contemporary Science Fiction Cinema* (London: Verso, 1990); J. P. Telotte, *Science Fiction Film* (London: Cambridge University Press, 2001); Richard Hodgens, "A Brief, Tragical History of the Science Fiction Film," *Film Quarterly* 13 (1959): 30–39; Vivian Sobchack, *Screening Space: The American Science Fiction Film* (New York: Rutgers University Press, 2004); Susan Sontag, "The Imagination of Disaster," in *Liquid Metal: The Science Fiction Film Reader*, ed. Sean Redmond (London: Wallflower Press, 2004), 40–47; Thomas C. Sutton and Marilyn Sutton, "Science Fiction as Mythology," *Western Folklore* 28 (1969). 230–237.

2. For examples of examinations of race in SF film that are nearly as imaginative as the films they discuss, see articles such as Bryan Carr's "At the Thresholds of the 'Human': Race, Psychoanalysis, and Replication of Imperial Memory," *Cultural Critique* 39 (1998). 119–150; David Columbia's "Black and White. Race, Ideology, and Utopia in 'Triton' and 'Star Trek,'" *Cultural Critique* 32 (1995): 75–95; and Susan Bridget McHugh's "Horses in Blackface: Visualizing Race as Species Difference in *Planet of the Apes*," *South Atlantic Review* 65 (2000): 40–72.

CHAPTER I

1. Daniel Bernardi, ed., *Birth of Whiteness: Race and the Emergence of U.S. Cinema* (New Brunswick, NJ: Rutgers University Press, 1996).

2. James Snead, *White Screens/Black Images: Hollywood from the Dark Side* (New York: Routledge, 1994), 6.

3. Vivian Sobchack, in *Screening Space*, 89–110, applies the speculative element of SF cinema primarily to the creation of alien imagery and geography. Yet, futuristic times and even the extreme past are the temporal terrain in which such imagery takes

place. Thus, in my judgment, temporal speculation is the overarching category in SF cinema. Also see Hodgens, "Brief, Tragical History."

4. Edward Said, *Orientalism* (New York: Pantheon, 1978).

5. The association of blacks with monkeys and apes is a common representational motif. See Snead, *White Screens/Black Images*, 20; John Fiske, *Media Matters: Race and Gender in U.S. Politics* (Minneapolis: University of Minnesota Press, 1996); and Greene, *"Planet of the Apes."*

6. See Harry M. Benshoff, "Blaxploitation Horror Films: Generic Reappropriation or Reinscription?" *Cinema Journal* 39, no. 2 (Winter 2000): 31–50, which describes the representational tendency to animalize blacks in the horror genre.

7. Spencer R. Weart, *Nuclear Fear: A History of Images* (Cambridge, MA: Harvard University Press, 1988); Sontag, "Imagination of Disaster;" and Robert Torry, "Apocalypse Then: Benefits of the Bomb in Fifties Science Fiction Films," *Cinema Journal* 31 (1991): 7–21.

8. See Jonathan Bignell's article "Another Time, Another Space: Modernity, Subjectivity, and *The Time Machine*," in *Alien Identities*, ed. Deborah Cartmell, I. Q. Hunter, Heidi Kaye, and Imelda Whelehan (London: Pluto Press, 1999), 87–103; and Krin Gabbard's *Black Magic: White Hollywood and African American Culture* (Piscataway, NJ: Rutgers University Press, 2004), 117.

9. Guerrero, *Framing Blackness*, 70; David James, *Allegories of Cinema: American Film in the Sixties* (Princeton, NJ: Princeton University Press, 1989), 189–191; and Donald Bogle, *Toms, Coons, Mulattoes, Mammies, and Bucks: An Interpretive History of Blacks in American Film*, 3rd ed. (New York: Continuum, 1998).

10. Todd Gitlin, *The Whole World Is Watching: Mass Media in the Making and Unmaking of the New Left* (Berkeley: University of California Press, 1980), 152–154, 163–164.

11. Michael Omi and Howard Winant, *Racial Formation in the United States from the 1960s to the 1990s*, 2nd ed. (New York: Routledge, 1994), 102–107.

12. Vladimir Propp, *Morphology of the Folktale* (Austin: University of Texas Press, 1968).

13. Guerrero, *Framing Blackness*, 117.

14. Ibid., 118.

15. See Karla Rae Fuller's essay "Creatures of Good and Evil: Caucasian Portrayals of the Chinese and Japanese during World War II," 281–300, in Daniel Bernardi, ed., *Classic Hollywood Classic Whiteness* (Minneapolis: Minnesota Press, 2001).

16. Doug Williams's "Not So Long Ago and Far Away: *Star Wars*, Republics and Empires of Tomorrow," in *The Science Fiction Film Reader*, ed. Gregg Rickman (New York: Limelight Editions, 2004), and Guerrero's *Framing Blackness*, 117–119, amplify these points in a broader scope that links *Star Wars* to a slew of war films that emerged post-Vietnam, in effect to win on film the war that had been lost on the ground.

17. Daniel Bernardi, *Star Trek and History: Race-ing toward a White Future* (New Brunswick, NJ: Rutgers University Press, 1998), 80; Bogle, *Toms, Coons, Mulattoes*, 275; Guerrero, *Framing Blackness*, 117.

18. Omi and Winant, *Racial Formation*, 113–115.

19. Ellis Cose, *Rage of a Privileged Class* (New York: Harper Collins, 1993).

20. Geoff King and Tanya Krzywinska, *Science Fiction Cinema: From Outerspace to Cyberspace* (London: Wallflower Press, 2000), 95–113.

21. See Bernardi, *Star Trek and History*.

22. See Stephen Steinberg's *Turning Back: The Retreat from Racial Justice in American Thought and Policy* (Boston: Beacon Press, 1995). Another reading of the "Re-elect Goldie" segment is that it is a veiled send-up of Jesse Jackson's second presidential bid. Nevertheless, the broader ideological point remains the same.

CHAPTER 2

1. Weart, *Nuclear Fear*, 191–194.

2. Omi and Winant, *Racial Formation*, 63–64.

3. See Haney Lopez, *White by Law* (New York: New York University Press, 1996), 27, for an analysis of the social construction of whiteness through a process of negation in which bloodlines become a significant element in determining racial descent.

4. Susan Courtney's reading of the ending of the film amplifies the homoerotic aspect of the triad. For her, Sarah is merely the conduit for the two men to forge an intimate interracial relationship. See Courtney, *Hollywood Fantasies of Miscegenation: Spectacular Narratives of Gender and Race, 1903–1967* (Princeton, NJ: Princeton University Press, 2005), 235–246.

5. Ryan Baker makes a similar observation about the Family as a representation of black America, as well as the film's expression of deep-seated racial anxieties. His analysis has a decidedly psychological focus, while the topic of black and white race relations is collapsed into Jungian archetypes that, in my opinion, conceal the particular racial discourse of the narrative with psychological extrapolation. See Baker, "'Conclusion of All Our Yesterdays': The Jungian Text of *The Omega Man*," in *Science Fiction America: Essays on SF Cinema*, ed. David J. Hogan (Jefferson, NC: McFarland, 2005), 196–205.

6. See Michael Gomez, *Black Crescent: The Experience and Legacy of African Muslims in the Americas* (New York: Cambridge University Press, 2005).

7. Edwin Black, *War against the Weak: Eugenics and America's Campaign to Create a Master Race* (New York: Four Walls, 2003), 79.

8. Ibid.

9. In *The COINTELPRO Papers: Documents from the FBI's Secret Wars against Dissent in the United States* (Cambridge, MA: South End Press, 2002), Ward Churchill and Jim Vander Wall document how J. Edger Hoover's covert program COINTELPRO worked to discredit and destroy black militant organizations.

10. Mike Davis, *Ecology of Fear: Los Angeles and the Imagination of Disaster* (New York: Metropolitan Books, 1998), 330–339.

11. Black, *War against the Weak*, 79.

12. Ibid., 30, 159–182.

13. The ending of this film has been and continues to be a source of vociferous debate and deconstruction, particularly among the large cult-film fan base the movie has acquired over the past twenty years. A host of Internet blogs and Web sites debate the merits of evidence used to support who is a Thing. For me, the importance of the last scene is not in discovering who is and who is not a Thing but in the symbolism of a white male and a black male confronting one another about the authenticity of their humanity, a topic ripe with racial implications.

14. Omi and Winant, *Racial Formation*, 113–115.

15. Arguably, Jean-Luc Godard's *Alphaville* (1965) is the forerunner to *Blade Runner* as an example of SF film noir.

16. Bart Landry, *The New Black Middle Class* (Berkeley: University of California Press, 1987).

17. See Thomas B. Byer, "Commodity Futures," in *Alien Zone: Cultural Theory and Contemporary Science Fiction Cinema*, ed. Annette Kuhn, 39–50 (New York: Verso, 1990), 49. He comes to a similar conclusion about the link between "skin-job" and the "N-word."

18. See Giuliana Bruno, "Ramble City: Postmodernism and *Blade Runner*," in *Alien Zone*, ed. Kuhn, 183–195; and Telotte, *Science Fiction Film*, 57, 58.

19. For a discussion on the politics of constructing Asian people as homogeneous, see Lisa Lowe, *Immigrant Acts: On Asian American Cultural Politics* (Durham, NC: Duke University Press, 1998), 68. Lowe views *Blade Runner* as a cinematic diatribe against the Third World and multiculturalism through the use of orientalist typographies (84–95).

20. Daniel Bell, *The Cultural Contradictions of Capitalism* (New York: Basic Books, 1996), 322; and William Julius Wilson's analysis in *The Truly Disadvantaged: The Inner City, the Underclass, and Public Policy* (Chicago: University of Chicago Press, 1987), 132.

21. Omi and Winant, *Racial Formation*.

22. See Office of Policy Planning and Research, U.S. Department of Labor, *The Negro Family: The Case For National Action*, reprint (Westport, CT: Greenwood Press, 1981), in which Daniel Patrick Moynihan weighs in on the crisis of the black family and its broader sociopolitical implications for the state of American race relations. Also see Orlando Patterson's *Rituals of Blood: Consequences of Slavery in Two American Centuries* (New York: Civitas Books, 1999) for a further historical contextualization of the "crisis" of the black family as it relates to American slavery.

23. The countryside is often imagined in SF film as a sanctuary for taboo relationships. For instance, in *Nineteen Eighty-Four* (1984), the countryside is an imaginative site for forbidden lovers, while in *Blade Runner* the relationship between Deckard, a human, and Rachael, a Replicant, has forbidden qualities in that it parallels an interracial one. An alternative reading, however, to the sexual pairing of Deckard and Rachael rests on the idea that Deckard himself is a Replicant. Thus, his possible status as a Replicant resolves the disturbing tension of human and cyborg intercourse, along with its racially coded representation of white and "black" sexual intimacy.

24. James Jones, *Bad Blood: The Tuskegee Syphilis Experiment* (New York: Free Press, 1981).

25. Andrew Hacker, *Two Nations: Black and White, Separate, Hostile, and Unequal* (New York: Ballantine Books, 1992).

26. Nathan Glazer's *We Are All Multiculturalists Now* (Cambridge, MA: Harvard University Press, 1997), Greg Tate's *Everything but the Burden: What White People Are Taking from Black Culture* (New York: Broadway Books, 2003), and Leon E. Wynter's *American Skin: Pop Culture, Big Business, and the End of White America* (New York: Crown Publishers, 2002) are examples of the diverse spectrum of cultural criticism around the synergy of black and white race relations in America, yet they share similar premises about the impact of each group on the other.

27. Guerrero, *Framing Blackness*, 59.

28. See George Lipsitz, *The Possessive Investment in Whiteness: How White People Profit from Identity Politics* (Philadelphia: Temple University Press, 1998), 37.

CHAPTER 3

1. Bogle, *Toms, Coons, Mulattoes.*

2. See Christian Metz, *The Imaginary Signifier: Psychoanalysis and the Cinema* (Bloomington: Indiana University Press, 1982).

3. Margaret Tarratt, "Monsters from the Id," *Films and Filming* (December 1970–January 1971): 38–42.

4. For a racial deconstruction of both films, see Guerrero, *Framing Blackness.*

5. An interesting attempt at addressing this dynamic in SF cinema is found in *Aliens R Us,* ed. Sardar and Cubitt.

6. See my discussion of this dynamic in "More Symbol Than Substance: African American Representation in Network Television Dramas," *Race and Society* 6, no. 1 (2003): 21–38. The issue of "positive" and "negative" black stereotypes is historicized and critiqued.

7. Adam Roberts makes a similar observation when deconstructing the racial meaning of the alien in *Science Fiction: The New Critical Idiom* (New York: Routledge Press, 2000), 119–120.

8. Frantz Fanon, in *Black Skin, White Masks* (New York: Grove Press, 1959), 170, declared that the black man had been turned into a penis—his humanity had been reduced to his sexuality and virtually all things sexual. Fanon offered a compelling psychoanalytic construction of race and sexuality in which he articulated the reductive quality of black racial identity circulating in the Western popular imagination.

9. See Arthur Asa Berger's *Signs in Contemporary Culture: An Introduction to Semiotics,* 2nd ed. (Salem, WI: Sheffield, 1998), for a straightforward discussion of the symbolic meaning of guns from a psychoanalytical perspective.

10. See Patrica Hill-Collins, *Black Sexual Politics: African Americans, Gender, and the New Racism* (New York: Routledge, 2004), 219; and Patterson, *Rituals of Blood,* 169–232.

11. Jonathan Markovitz, in *Legacies of Lynching: Racial Violence and Memory* (Minneapolis: University of Minnesota Press: 2004), 98–100, raises this connection in his deconstruction of the Tawana Brawley case, in which the teenager was found with feces spread on her, supposedly by her alleged rapists. He proposes that mainstream media paid little attention to this fact—regardless of whether she smeared it on herself or not—because the association with dirt and black racial identity is "taken for granted" and thus not a point of critical analysis, shock, or investigation.

12. Eric Lott, *Love and Theft: Blackface Minstrelsy and the American Working Class* (New York: Oxford University Press, 1995).

13. See Thomas E. Wartenberg, "Humanizing the Beast: King Kong and the Representation of Black Male Sexuality," in *Classic Hollywood, Classic Whiteness*, ed. Daniel Bernardi (Minneapolis: University of Minnesota Press, 2001), 157–177.

14. See Kobena Mercer's *Welcome to the Jungle: New Positions in Black Cultural Studies* (New York: Routledge, 1994). At times Mercer engages in a tortured debate over the fetishization of the black penis in the nude photography of Robert Mapplethorpe.

15. See Vivian Sobchack's article "The Virginity of Astronauts: Sex and Science Fiction Film," in *Alien Zone: Cultural Theory and Contemporary Science Fiction Cinema* (London: Verso, 1990), 103–115.

16. The issue would finally find considerable political traction in California's university system. See Lydia Chavez's thorough discussion of this conflict in *The Color Bind: California's Battle to End Affirmative Action* (Berkeley: University of California Press, 1998).

17. See Mike Davis, *City of Quartz: Excavating the Future in Los Angeles* (London: Verso, 1992).

18. For historical mapping of the various racial fault lines that are Los Angeles, see Raphael J. Sonenshein's *Politics in Black and White: Race and Power in Los Angeles* (Princeton, NJ: Princeton University Press, 1993), 68.

19. See Eric Avila's "Dark City: White Flight and the Urban Science Fiction Film in Postwar America," in *Classic Hollywood, Classic Whiteness*, ed. Bernardi, 53–71.

20. See Hill-Collins, *Black Sexual Politics*.

CHAPTER 4

1. See William Julius Wilson's analysis of the racial and social cost of deindustrialism in his books *The Declining Significance of Race* (Chicago: University of Chicago, 1978) and *The Truly Disadvantaged*.

2. See Stephen Vaughn's discussion of the ratings board and the films, including *Rollerball*, that were part of the debate in *Freedom and Entertainment: Rating the Movies in an Age of New Media* (New York: Cambridge University Press, 2006), 54–57.

3. See Guerrero, *Framing Blackness*.

4. See "Feminism, Humanism, and Science in *Alien*," 73–81, by James H. Kava-

nagh, and "Feminism and Anxiety in *Alien*, 82–87, by Judith Newton, in *Alien Zone: Cultural Theory and Contemporary Science Fiction Cinema*, ed. Annette Kuhn (London: Verso, 1990).

5. Kavanagh, "Feminism, Humanism, and Science in *Alien*," and Newton, "Feminism and Anxiety in *Alien*." Parker's relationships with Brett and with the white female protagonist, Ripley (Sigourney Weaver), are rightfully deconstructed for their racial meaning.

6. See Dick Hebdige, *Elements of Style* (London: Routledge, 1979), and Paul Willis, *Learning to Labor* (New York: Columbia University Press, 1977), for analyses of how racial and class subordinates strike back at elites through subversive expressions of style and language.

7. See Stanley Aronowitz and William DiFazio, *The Jobless Future: Sci-Tech and the Dogma of Work* (Minneapolis: University of Minnesota Press, 1994).

8. Renato Rosaldo, "Cultural Citizenship, Inequality, and Multiculturalism," in *Race, Identity and Citizenship*, ed. Rodolfo D. Torres, Louis F. Miron, and Jonathan Xavier Inda (Massachusetts: Blackwell Publishers, 1999), 257.

9. For a critical reading of *Men in Black*'s implicit attack on American immigration, see Adam Roberts, *Science Fiction*.

10. The criticism that government programs create dependency in economically disadvantaged blacks is contextualized by Norman Fainstein in "Black Ghettoization and Social Mobility," in *The Bubbling Cauldron: Race, Ethnicity, and The Urban Crisis*, ed. Michael Peter Smith and Joe Feagin (Minneapolis: University of Minnesota Press, 1995), 123–141.

11. See Adolph Reed Jr.'s concise analysis of the arguments and counterarguments surrounding changing race relations over the last thirty years in "Demobilization in the New Black Political Regime," in *The Bubbling Cauldron*, ed. Smith and Feagin, 182–208.

12. See Telotte, *Science Fiction Film*, 161–178, for an in-depth deconstruction of what *RoboCop* signals about fears of technology and dehumanization in the postmodern moment.

13. See the discussion of suburban segregation in Farley Reynolds, Sheldon Danziger, and Harry J. Holzer, *Detroit Divided* (New York: Russell Sage Foundation, 2000).

14. Ibid.

15. For an analysis of how racial subjectivity informs the perception of media events, see Darnell Hunt's *Screening the Los Angeles "Riots": Race, Seeing, and Resistance* (Cambridge: Cambridge University Press, 1997).

16. Steinberg, *Turning Back*, 195–204.

17. Tommie Shelby, *We Who Are Dark: The Philosophical Foundations of Black Solidarity* (Cambridge, MA: Harvard University Press, 2005), 85.

CHAPTER 5

1. Greene, *"Planet of the Apes" as American Myth*, 176.

2. Stuart Hall, "Encoding/Decoding," in *The Cultural Studies Reader*, 2nd ed., ed. Simon During (New York: Routledge, 1999), 507–517.

3. Henry Louis Gates, *The Signifying Monkey: A Theory of African-American Literary Criticism* (Oxford: Oxford University Press, 1988), 131.

4. Interestingly, a similar trend might currently be afoot, as the visual format of the comic book becomes an accepted medium for communicating information. In "Comic-Book Duo Re-create Unlikely Story: 9/11," *Los Angeles Times*, calendar section, September 8, 2006, Alex Chun details how the original 567-page report of the 9/11 Commission is reworked as 131 comic book–style pages.

5. See Daniel Bell's treatise on the contours of these fault lines in *The Cultural Contradictions of Capitalism*.

6. For a thought-provoking analysis of the future of American race relations, see David A. Hollinger's *Postethnic America: Beyond Multiculturalism* (New York: Basic Books, 1995), 148.

7. Lopez, *White by Law*, 40–41.

8. Greene, *"Planet of the Apes" as American Myth*, 91.

9. See Dinesh D'Souza, *The End of Racism: Principles for a Multiracial Society* (New York: Free Press, 1995).

10. Steinberg, *Turning Back*, 100.

11. *The Bubbling Cauldron: Race, Ethnicity, and the Urban Crisis*, ed. Michael Peter Smith and Joe Feagin, examines the statistical reality as well as cultural mythology of the inner city.

12. See Robert Shail, "Masculinity, Kurt Russell, and the *Escape* Films," in *The Cinema of John Carpenter: The Technique of Terror*, ed. Ian Conrich and David Woods (London: Wallflower Press, 2004), 107–117.

13. See Kenneth Chan, "The Construction of Black Male Identity in Black Action Films of the Nineties," *Cinema Journal* 37, no. 2 (Winter 1998): 35–48. Also see Glazer, *We Are All Multiculturalists Now*, 134.

14. William Julius Wilson, *When Work Disappears* (New York: Vintage Books, 1996), 60–61; Hill-Collins, *Black Sexual Politics*, 131–133; and Dorothy E. Roberts, "Punishing Drug Addicts Who Have Babies: Women of Color, Equality, and the Right of Privacy," in *Critical Race Theory: The Key Writings That Formed the Movement*, ed. Kimberle Crenshaw, Neil Gotanda, Gary Peller, and Kendall Thomas (New York: New Press, 1995), 384–426.

15. See *Crack in America: Demon Drugs and Social Justice*, ed. Craig Reinarman and Harry G. Levine (Berkeley: University of California Press, 1997), 19–22.

16. Ibid.

17. Matt Lawrence, *Like a Splinter in Your Mind: The Philosophy behind the "Matrix" Trilogy* (Maiden, MA: Blackwell Publishing, 2004).

18. For a rather negative appraisal of the racial politics in *Matrix* as white hege-

monic representation, see Herman Vera and Andrew M. Gordon, *Screen Saviors: Hollywood Fictions of Whiteness* (Lanham, MD: Rowman and Littlefield, 2003), 48–49.

CHAPTER 6

1. See Telotte, *Science Fiction Film*, 105, and Vivian Sobchack, "Postfuturism," in *Liquid Metal*, ed. Sontag, 221.

2. See James, *Allegories of Cinema*.

3 See Landry, *The New Black Middle Class*.

4. See John Szwed, *Space Is the Place: The Lives and Times of Sun Ra* (New York: Da Capo Press, 1998).

5. During the 1980s and early 1990s, Afrocentricity would become a heated point of debate in academia and a radical form of cultural expression in segments of the black community. See Molefi Kete Asante, *Kemet, Afrocentricity, and Knowledge* (Trenton, NJ: Africa World Press, 1990).

6. See the journal *Social Text*, no. 71 (Summer 2002), published by Duke University Press in Durham, NC. The entire journal is devoted to the Afrofuturist rubric.

7. See Ricky Vincent, *Funk: The Music, the People, and the Rhythm of the One* (New York: St. Martin's Griffin, 1996), 244.

8. See Gomez, *Black Crescent*, 329, for a rigorous and thoughtful analysis of the historical foundations of African American Islamic traditions as well as an in-depth consideration of the metaphoric meaning of the language and fantastic imagery found in black Muslim groups that have been central in establishing Islam in America yet remain extremely obscure in mainstream histories and academic historiographies.

9. Adam Roberts, in *Science Fiction*, 127, makes a similar observation about the significance of George Clinton.

10. See James, *Allegories of Cinema*, 191–195.

11. Telotte, *Science Fiction Film*, 75.

12. For overlapping and competing characterizations of the respective roots of hip-hop, see Tricia Rose, *Black Noise: Rap Music and Black Culture in Contemporary America* (New York: Wesleyan University Press, 1994); Nelson George, *Hip-Hop America* (New York: Penguin Press, 1998); and Paul Gilroy, *The Black Atlantic: Modernity and Double Consciousness* (Cambridge, MA: Harvard University Press, 1993); as well as Ulf Poschardt, *DJ Culture*, trans. Shaun Whiteside (London: Quartet Books, 1995).

13. Jeff Chang, *Can't Stop Won't Stop: A History of the Hip-Hop Generation* (New York: St. Martin's Press, 2005).

14. Robin Kelley, in *Freedom Dreams: The Black Radical Imagination* (Boston: Beacon Press, 2002), 30–35, connects Afrika Bambaataa's space-age representation to Sun Ra and George Clinton as precursors to Afrofuturism and the articulation of a chronic African American collective desire to escape the stifling constraints of American racism.

15. Ibid., 16–35.

16. See Ursula Rucker's video *Supa Sista* (?uestlove Remix, 2001) for a woman-centered expression of the Afrofuturist expression of blackness in hip-hop as an intergalactic journey to discover one's black male counterpart.

17. See Ian Conrich and David Woods, *The Cinema of John Carpenter: The Technique of Terror* (London: Wallflower Press, 2004), 4, for a wide-ranging analysis of the body of John Carpenter's work.

18. See Guerrero, *Framing Blackness*, 44–50, for his sketch of a Pan-Africanist discourse as well as a less sanguine analysis of the meaning of the film's conclusion as a form of ideological containment.

19. Gilroy, *The Black Atlantic*.

BIBLIOGRAPHY

Adare, Sierra S. *"Indian" Stereotypes in TV Science Fiction: First Nations' Voices Speak Out*. Austin: University Texas Press, 2005.

Aronowitz, Stanley, and William DiFazio. *The Jobless Future: Sci-Tech and the Dogma of Work*. Minneapolis: University of Minnesota Press, 1994.

Asante, Molefi Kete. *Kemet, Afrocentricity, and Knowledge*. Trenton, NJ: Africa World Press, 1990.

Avila, Eric. "Dark City: White Flight and the Urban Science Fiction Film in Postwar America." In *Classic Hollywood, Classic Whiteness*, edited by Daniel Bernardi, 53–71. Minneapolis: University of Minnesota Press, 2001.

Baker, Ryan. "'Conclusion of All Our Yesterdays': The Jungian Text of *The Omega Man*." In *Science Fiction America: Essays on SF Cinema*, edited by David J. Hogan, 196–205. Jefferson, NC: McFarland, 2005.

Bell, Daniel. *The Cultural Contradictions of Capitalism*. New York: Basic Books, 1996.

Benshoff, Harry M. "Blaxploitation Horror Films: Generic Reappropriation or Reinscription?" In *Cinema Journal* 39, no. 2 (Winter 2000): 31–50.

Berg, Charles Ramirez. *Latino Images in Film: Stereotypes, Subversions, and Resistance*. Austin: University of Texas Press, 2002.

Berger, Arthur Asa. *Signs in Contemporary Culture: An Introduction to Semiotics*. 2nd ed. Salem, WI: Sheffield, 1998.

Bernardi, Daniel, ed. *Birth of Whiteness: Race and the Emergence of U.S. Cinema*. New Brunswick, NJ: Rutgers University Press, 1996.

———. *Star Trek and History: Race-ing toward a White Future*. New Brunswick, NJ: Rutgers University Press, 1998.

Bignell, Jonathan. "Another Time, Another Space: Modernity, Subjectivity, and *The Time Machine*." In *Alien Identities*, edited by Deborah Cartmell, I. Q. Hunter, Heidi Kaye, and Imelda Whelehan, 87–103. London: Pluto Press, 1999.

Black, Edwin. *War against the Weak: Eugenics and America's Campaign to Create a Master Race.* New York: Four Walls, 2003.

Bogle, Donald. *Toms, Coons, Mulattoes, Mammies, and Bucks: An Interpretive History of Blacks in American Film.* 3rd ed. New York: Continuum, 1998.

Bruno, Giuliana. "Ramble City: Postmodernism and *Blade Runner.*" In *Alien Zone: Cultural Theory and Contemporary Science Fiction Cinema,* edited by Annette Kuhn, 183–195. New York: Verso, 1990.

Byer, Thomas B. "Commodity Futures." In *Alien Zone: Cultural Theory and Contemporary Science Fiction Cinema,* edited by Annette Kuhn, 39–50. New York: Verso, 1990.

Carr, Brian. "At the Thresholds of the 'Human': Race, Psychoanalysis, and Replication of Imperial Memory." *Cultural Critique* 39 (1998): 119–150.

Chan, Kenneth. "The Construction of Black Male Identity in Black Action Films of the Nineties." *Cinema Journal* 37, no. 2 (Winter 1998): 35–48.

Chang, Jeff. *Can't Stop Won't Stop: A History of the Hip-Hop Generation.* New York: St. Martin's Press, 2005.

Chavez, Lydia. *The Color Bind: California's Battle to End Affirmative Action.* Berkeley: University of California Press, 1998.

Chun, Alex. "Comic-Book Duo Re-create Unlikely Story: 9/11." *Los Angeles Times,* Calendar, September 8, 2006.

Churchill, Ward, and Jim Vander Wall. *The COINTELPRO Papers: Documents from the FBI's Secret Wars against Dissent in the United States.* Cambridge, MA: South End Press, 2002.

Conrich, Ian, and David Woods. *The Cinema of John Carpenter: The Technique of Terror.* London: Wallflower Press, 2004.

Cose, Ellis. *Rage of a Privileged Class.* New York: HarperCollins, 1993.

Courtney, Susan. *Hollywood Fantasies of Miscegenation: Spectacular Narratives of Gender and Race, 1903–1967.* Princeton, NJ: Princeton University Press, 2005.

Davis, Mike. *City of Quartz: Excavating the Future in Los Angeles.* London: Verso, 1992.

———. *Ecology of Fear: Los Angeles and the Imagination of Disaster.* New York: Metropolitan Books, 1998.

D'Souza, Dinesh. *The End of Racism: Principles for a Multiracial Society.* New York: Free Press, 1995.

Fainstein, Norman. "Black Ghettoization and Social Mobility." In *The Bubbling Cauldron: Race, Ethnicity, and the Urban Crisis,* edited by Michael Peter Smith and Joe Feagin, 123–141. Minneapolis: University of Minnesota Press, 1995.

Fanon, Frantz. *Black Skin, White Masks.* New York: Grove Press, 1959.

Fiske, John. *Media Matters: Race and Gender in U.S. Politics.* Minneapolis: University of Minnesota Press, 1996.

Fuller, Karla Rae. "Creatures of Good and Evil: Caucasian Portrayals of the Chinese and Japanese during World War II." In *Classic Hollywood, Classic Whiteness,* edited by Daniel Bernardi, 281–300. Minneapolis: University of Minnesota Press, 2001.

Gabbard, Krin. *Black Magic: White Hollywood and African American Culture.* Piscataway, NJ: Rutgers University Press, 2004.

Gates, Henry Louis. *The Signifying Monkey: A Theory of African-American Literary Criticism.* Oxford: Oxford University Press, 1988.

George, Nelson. *Hip-Hop America.* New York: Penguin Press, 1998.

Gilroy, Paul. *The Black Atlantic: Modernity and Double Consciousness.* Cambridge, MA: Harvard University Press, 1993.

Gitlin, Todd. *The Whole World Is Watching: Mass Media in the Making and Unmaking of the New Left.* Berkeley: University of California Press, 1980.

Glazer, Nathan. *We Are All Multiculturalists Now.* Cambridge, MA: Harvard University Press, 1997.

Golumbia, David. "Black and White: Race, Ideology, and Utopia in 'Triton' and 'Star Trek.'" *Cultural Critique* 32 (1995): 75–95.

Gomez, Michael. *Black Crescent: The Experience and Legacy of African Muslims in the Americas.* New York: Cambridge University Press, 2005.

Greene, Eric. *"Planet of the Apes" as American Myth: Race, Politics, and Popular Culture.* Hanover, NH: Wesleyan University Press, 1996.

Guerrero, Ed. *Framing Blackness: The African American Image in Film.* Philadelphia: Temple University Press, 1993.

Hacker, Andrew. *Two Nations: Black and White, Separate, Hostile, and Unequal.* New York: Ballantine Books, 1992.

Hall, Stuart. "Encoding/Decoding." In *The Cultural Studies Reader,* 2nd ed., edited by Simon During, 507–517. New York: Routledge, 1999.

Hebdige, Dick. *Elements of Style.* London: Routledge, 1979.

Hill-Collins, Patrica. *Black Sexual Politics: African Americans, Gender, and the New Racism.* New York: Routledge, 2004.

Hodgens, Richard. "A Brief, Tragical History of the Science Fiction Film." *Film Quarterly* 13 (1959): 30–39.

Hollinger, David A. *Postethnic America: Beyond Multiculturalism.* New York: Basic Books, 1995.

Hunt, Darnell. *Screening the Los Angeles "Riots": Race, Seeing, and Resistance.* Cambridge: Cambridge University Press, 1997.

James, David. *Allegories of Cinema: American Film in the Sixties.* Princeton, NJ: Princeton University Press, 1989.

Jones, James. *Bad Blood: The Tuskegee Syphilis Experiment.* New York: Free Press, 1981.

Kavanagh, James H. "Feminism, Humanism, and Science in *Alien.*" In *Alien Zone: Cultural Theory and Contemporary Science Fiction Cinema,* edited by Annette Kuhn, 73–81. London: Verso, 1990.

Kelley, Robin. *Freedom Dreams: The Black Radical Imagination.* Boston: Beacon Press, 2002.

King, Geoff, and Tanya Krzywinska. *Science Fiction Cinema: From Outerspace to Cyberspace.* London: Wallflower Press, 2000.

Kuhn, Annette, ed. *Alien Zone: Cultural Theory and Contemporary Science Fiction Cinema.* London: Verso, 1990.

Landry, Bart. *The New Black Middle Class.* Berkeley: University of California Press, 1987.

Lawrence, Matt. *Like a Splinter in Your Mind: The Philosophy behind the "Matrix" Trilogy.* Maiden, MA: Blackwell Publishing, 2004.

Lipsitz, George. *The Possessive Investment in Whiteness: How White People Profit from Identity Politics.* Philadelphia: Temple University Press, 1998.

Lopez, Haney. *White by Law.* New York: New York University Press, 1996.

Lott, Eric. *Love and Theft: Blackface Minstrelsy and the American Working Class.* New York: Oxford University Press, 1995.

Lowe, Lisa. *Immigrant Acts: On Asian American Cultural Politics.* Durham, NC: Duke University Press, 1998.

Markovitz, Jonathan. *Legacies of Lynching: Racial Violence and Memory.* Minneapolis: University of Minnesota Press: 2004.

McHugh, Susan Bridget. "Horses in Blackface: Visualizing Race as Species Difference in *Planet of the Apes.*" *South Atlantic Review* 65 (2000): 40–72.

Mercer, Kobena. *Welcome to the Jungle: New Positions in Black Cultural Studies.* New York: Routledge, 1994.

Metz, Christian. *The Imaginary Signifier: Psychoanalysis and the Cinema.* Bloomington: Indiana University Press, 1982.

Nama, Adilifu. "More Symbol Than Substance: African American Representation in Network Television Dramas." *Race and Society* 6, no. 1 (2003): 21–38.

Newton, Judith. "Feminism and Anxiety in *Alien.*" In *Alien Zone: Cultural Theory and Contemporary Science Fiction Cinema,* edited by Annette Kuhn, 82–87. London: Verso, 1990.

Office of Policy Planning and Research, U.S. Department of Labor. *The Negro Family: The Case for National Action.* Reprint. Westport, CT: Greenwood Press, 1981.

Omi, Michael, and Howard Winant. *Racial Formation in the United States from the 1960s to the 1990s.* 2nd ed. New York: Routledge, 1994.

Patterson, Orlando. *Rituals of Blood: Consequences of Slavery in Two American Centuries.* New York: Civitas Books, 1999.

Poschardt, Ulf. *DJ Culture.* Translated by Shaun Whiteside. London: Quartet Books, 1995.

Pounds, Micheal. *Race in Space: The Representation of Ethnicity in "Star Trek" and "Star Trek: The Next Generation."* Lanham, MD: Scarecrow Press, 1999.

Propp, Vladimir. *Morphology of the Folktale.* Austin: University of Texas Press, 1968.

Reed, Adolph, Jr. "Demobilization in the New Black Political Regime." In *The Bubbling Cauldron: Race, Ethnicity, and the Urban Crisis,* edited by Michael Peter Smith and Joe Feagin, 182–208. Minneapolis: University of Minnesota Press, 1995.

Reinarman, Craig, and Harry G. Levine, eds. *Crack in America: Demon Drugs and Social Justice.* Berkeley: University of California Press, 1997.

Reynolds, Farley, Sheldon Danziger, and Harry J. Holzer. *Detroit Divided.* New York: Russell Sage Foundation, 2000.

Roberts, Adam. *Science Fiction: The New Critical Idiom*. New York: Routledge Press, 2000.

Roberts, Dorothy E. "Punishing Drug Addicts Who Have Babies: Women of Color, Equality, and the Right of Privacy." In *Critical Race Theory: The Key Writings That Formed the Movement*, edited by Kimberle Crenshaw, Neil Gotanda, Gary Peller, and Kendall Thomas, 384–426. New York: New Press, 1995.

Rosaldo, Renato. "Cultural Citizenship, Inequality, and Multiculturalism." In *Race, Identity, and Citizenship*, edited by Rodolfo D. Torres, Louis F. Miron, and Jonathan Xavier Inda, 253–261. Maiden, MA: Blackwell Publishers, 1999.

Rose, Tricia. *Black Noise: Rap Music and Black Culture in Contemporary America*. New York: Wesleyan University Press, 1994.

Said, Edward. *Orientalism*. New York: Pantheon, 1978.

Sardar, Ziauddin, and Sean Cubitt, eds. *Aliens R Us: The Other in Science Fiction Cinema*. London: Pluto Press, 2002.

Shail, Robert. "Masculinity, Kurt Russell, and the *Escape* Films." In *The Cinema of John Carpenter: The Technique of Terror*, edited by Ian Conrich and David Woods, 107–117. London: Wallflower Press, 2004.

Shelby, Tommie. *We Who Are Dark: The Philosophical Foundations of Black Solidarity*. Cambridge, MA: Harvard University Press, 2005.

Smith, Michael Peter, and Joe Feagin, eds. *The Bubbling Cauldron: Race, Ethnicity, and the Urban Crisis*. Minneapolis: University of Minnesota Press, 1995.

Snead, James. *White Screens/Black Images: Hollywood from the Dark Side*. New York: Routledge, 1994.

Sobchack, Vivian. *Screening Space: The American Science Fiction Film*. New York: Rutgers University Press, 2004.

———. "Postfuturism." In *Liquid Metal: The Science Fiction Film Reader*, edited by Sean Redmond, 220–227. London: Wallflower Press, 2004.

——— . "The Virginity of Astronauts: Sex and Science Fiction Film." In *Alien Zone: Cultural Theory and Contemporary Science Fiction Cinema*, 103–115. London: Verso, 1990.

Social Text No. 71 (Summer 2002). Durham, NC: Duke University Press.

Sonenshein, Raphael J. *Politics in Black and White: Race and Power in Los Angeles*. Princeton, NJ: Princeton University Press, 1993.

Sontag, Susan. "The Imagination of Disaster." In *Liquid Metal: The Science Fiction Film Reader*, edited by Sean Redmond, 40–47. London: Wallflower Press, 2004.

Steinberg, Stephen. *Turning Back: The Retreat from Racial Justice in American Thought and Policy*. Boston: Beacon Press, 1995.

Sutton, Thomas C., and Marilyn Sutton. "Science Fiction as Mythology." *Western Folklore* 28 (1969): 230–237.

Szwed, John. *Space Is the Place: The Lives and Times of Sun Ra*. New York: Da Capo Press, 1998.

Tarratt, Margaret. "Monsters from the Id." *Films and Filming* (December 1970–January 1971): 38–42.

Tate, Greg. *Everything but the Burden: What White People Are Taking from Black Culture.* New York: Broadway Books, 2003.

Telotte, J. P. *Science Fiction Film.* London: Cambridge University Press, 2001.

Torry, Robert. "Apocalypse Then: Benefits of the Bomb in Fifties Science Fiction Films." *Cinema Journal* 31 (1991): 7–21.

Vaughn, Stephen. *Freedom and Entertainment: Rating the Movies in an Age of New Media.* New York: Cambridge University Press, 2006.

Vera, Hernan, and Andrew M. Gordon. *Screen Saviors: Hollywood Fictions of Whiteness.* Lanham, MD: Rowman and Littlefield, 2003.

Vincent, Ricky. *Funk: The Music, the People, and the Rhythm of the One.* New York: St. Martin's Griffin, 1996.

Wartenberg, Thomas E. "Humanizing the Beast: King Kong and the Representation of Black Male Sexuality." In *Classic Hollywood, Classic Whiteness,* edited by Daniel Bernardi, 157–177. Minneapolis: University of Minnesota Press, 2001.

Weart, Spencer R. *Nuclear Fear: A History of Images.* Cambridge, MA: Harvard University Press, 1988.

Williams, Doug. "Not So Long Ago and Far Away: *Star Wars,* Republics and Empires of Tomorrow." In *The Science Fiction Film Reader,* edited by Gregg Rickman, 229–252. New York: Limelight Editions, 2004.

Willis, Paul. *Learning to Labor.* New York: Columbia University Press, 1977.

Wilson, William Julius. *The Declining Significance of Race.* Chicago: University of Chicago, 1978.

———. *The Truly Disadvantaged: The Inner City, the Underclass, and Public Policy.* Chicago: University of Chicago Press, 1987.

———. *When Work Disappears.* New York: Vintage Books, 1996.

Wynter, Leon E. *American Skin: Pop Culture, Big Business, and the End of White America.* New York: Crown Publishers, 2002.

INDEX

Page numbers in *italics* indicate photographs.